The Art of Food Processor Cooking

Jane Salzfass Freiman

Contemporary Books, Inc.
Chicago

Illustrations by
Bill and Judie Anderson

Published by Contemporary Books, Inc.
180 North Michigan Avenue, Chicago, Illinois 60601
Library of Congress Catalog Card Number: 80-65936
International Standard Book Number: 0-8092-7005-6 (cloth)
0-8092-7004-8 (paper)

Published simultaneously in Canada by
Beaverbooks
953 Dillingham Road
Pickering, Ontario L1W 1Z7
Canada

Grateful acknowledgment is made for permission to reprint the
following:

Excerpts from *The Ascent of Man,* Copyright © 1973 by J.
Bronowski. By permission of Little, Brown and Company.

"Panzanella" reprinted by permission of *Woman's Day*
magazine. Copyright © 1980 by CBS Publications, Inc.

"Richard Olney's Roast, Split Chicken" adapted from "Split,
Stuffed, Baked Chicken" (pp. 382–386), in *Simple French Food* by
Richard Olney. Copyright © 1974 by Richard Olney. Used with
permission.

Other material in this book has appeared in altered form in
Cuisine, Cooking and *House & Garden* magazines.

Library of Congress Cataloging in Publication Data

Freiman, Jane Salzfass.
    The art of food processor cooking.

    Includes index.
    1. Food processor cookery.   I. Title.
TX840.F6F73   641.5'89   80-65936
ISBN 0-8092-7005-6
ISBN 0-8092-7004-8 (pbk.)

For my best friend Allan Freiman,
up up and away, and for my Grandmother

Contents

Acknowledgments

I wish to thank the following persons, sisters all, whose help, support, and contributions were invaluable: Dianna Meyers who assisted me and helped to develop and test recipes for the first draft; Thayer Wine who indefatigably tested recipes and provided a valuable sounding board; Brenda Newman and Suzan Kehoe for testing recipes and offering suggestions; Leslee Reis for sharing her knowledge as well as her sense of humor; Elaine Sherman for her good judgment; Nao Hauser for her generous and sensitive editor's eye; Jane Shay Lynch for being a good friend and a lawyer as well; Helen Jonsson for her lovely cookies; Lucille Davis for calmly keeping my life together; Helen Fadim for her sharp red pencil; my mother, Harriet Publicker, for her encouragement. Special thanks go to Sharon Hart, Patsy Perlman, and Barbara Mathes for listening so patiently to all my complaints.

Foreword

Fertile turf: James Beard's teaching kitchen. How harmonious that we should meet there, mastering the art of fine cooking. I remember carrot quiche. Potatoes Anna. A gigot boned, rolled, poached in a peppery broth. Tart cassis sorbet. And our eyes meeting over floury fingers. How prim she looked in her cotton shirtwaist and serious envelope of apron. Aristocratic even. Hardly a budding sensualist. But there was something in the way she phrased a question. A certain aggressiveness as she rolled that dough. The impatience of an arched eyebrow. A sure judgment in the smack of lips. Yes, I knew . . . even then. Here was the making of a Very Serious Food Person, Jane Salzfass Freiman.

She was quite frankly, a neophyte, young editor of graphic arts, exploring the culinary arts. I was already an established restaurant critic, polishing technique. But once bitten by the passion, how quickly she developed, an instant fountain of authority, pointedly opinionated, endlessly inquisitive and hungry for gastronomic adventure. Till she grew into what she is today: a gifted cook, an inspiring teacher, an innovative technician, an unquenchable critic . . . a hopelessly obsessed celebrant of cuisinary joy.

As a student of fine arts, earning a living in the graphic arts, Jane instinctively fashioned food to delight the eye. And it was clear she was gifted with splendid taste. For a time food was just another element of a beautiful life. But very quickly, an innocent interest bloomed into a serious fixation. It was not enough simply to find a source for the best butter in town. She was soon making her own. Pasta, brioche, sausage . . . no project was too ambitious to tackle. Transplanted to Chicago by the demands of her husband's career, the time seemed ripe to make food her metier. That was the beginning of her cooking classes and inevitably, the inspiration for her writing. Her food world profiles and features in the *Chicago Tribune, Cuisine* and *Wine and Food* are full of delicious notions, explicit instructions, pickles and burrs. No one can ever accuse Jane of apple polishing or lacking courage. No sacred cow is too holy. As the mythic Paul Bocuse, don of France's Three-Star chef Mafia, can testify as the target of her criticism for his weighty cookbook. She is thorough, opinionated, a perfectionist . . . and demanding as she is . . . most demanding of herself.

So I guess I shouldn't be surprised to discover that her first cookbook is both a primer and a post-graduate course in fine cooking and baking. If you just flew in from Mars and landed in an American kitchen, you could probably find your way around with this book, its instructions are so thoughtful and explicit. Larding the text is a treasury of information on shopping, wrapping and storage of food, theories on equipment, when to salt and how to clarify butter . . . even a warning to keep your fingers away from your eyes after seeding hot peppers. With this book a beginner can start to cook. And even Very Serious Food People are likely to discover unimagined gifts in that superhuman machine, the food processor. For some time now frankly, I have regarded the chunky little wonder as my permanent sous-chef. In it I blend my tenderest pie crusts. It has taken the strain out of my fettucine confrontations. And in summer it does magic with beefsteak tomatoes, sour cream, dill, basil and pine nuts—grinding, creaming, whirling forth great cold soups, sauces and herb butters. Now, reading this book, I realize I've scarcely begun to plumb the talents of the mighty machine. In her creative zeal, Jane has come up with brilliant new techniques for handling yeast and dough and for making child's play of the trickiest sauces. Watching her one evening recently take a batch of food processor Hollandaise from the freezer and heat it to silken perfection was to me, a happy astonishment. And her emphasis on timing has to make machine processing a cinch for anyone.

Knowing Jane well, I must admit I'm surprised this book actually got to the bookstore shelves. I would have bet she'd be testing and tasting and re-testing right up to the moment a man came from the bindery to sew the book's pages together. But here it is? Do you need a food processor cookbook? I do. Keep it in your plastic cookbook-stand, you're going to want it around forever. Between the lines you will hear the bossy, loving, perfectionist voice of Jane Salzfass Freiman. And believe me, it's a lark and a promise of culinary splendor to cook with Jane at your side.

Gael Greene, 1980

Introduction

"Even in prehistory man already made tools that have an edge finer than they need have. The finer edge in its turn gave the tool a finer use, a practical refinement and extension to processes for which the tool had not been designed. . . . The tool that extends the human hand is also an instrument of vision. It reveals the structure of things and makes it possible to put them together in new, imaginative combinations . . ."

—Jacob Bronowski, *The Ascent of Man*

It all began with zucchini purée. I shall never forget my astonishment at seeing those lovely chunks whirled with a few dabs of mustard and a dollop of cream into an utterly smooth silky mixture, in just seconds.

It was an auspicious beginning, for the cooking class was taught by Simone Beck in James Beard's New York kitchen and the food processor she used was a restaurant-size fuchsia and white model that Beard had just brought back from France.

When I learned there was a smaller version available for home use, I immediately put in my order. By Christmas of 1972 my Magimix (the French name still used in Europe) was installed on the kitchen counter of my New York apartment, and my food processor adventure was underway.

The following October my cooking career was officially launched when Gael Greene included me in a New York magazine article. At the time I was on a food processor butter-making spree and Gael mentioned this in the article, calling the processor a "superhuman machine." How right she was.

After moving to Chicago and opening my cooking school in 1974, I began to teach my students how to use the food processor as a supplement to conventional cooking techniques to make pâtés, breads, pastries, and scores of other foods. By that time the Magimix was beginning to be marketed under another, and now more famous, name.

The roots of this book go back to those early years before the food processor became a national, and international, phenomenon. My early food processor recipes were adapted to, rather than created especially for, the food processor, and now they seem hopelessly outdated.

Throughout my years of teaching cooking, I presented techniques for using the food processor along with "conventional" cooking instruction. I never wanted to expand to food processor classes because I felt it was more important to teach students how to cook than how to use an expensive piece of cooking equipment.

As the number of machine owners grew, however, the problems of cooking with food processors multiplied. I began to see beyond the fad and status appeal and realized that this machine was having a profound psychological impact on many people who wanted to cook but lacked confidence in their abilities. Not only did the processor build confidence and boost cooking skills, it opened the door to many delicious but previously time-consuming recipes that were also popular in French restaurants at the time. Then the tidal wave of the new French cooking (nouvelle cuisine) hit America full force and the food processor made French cooking more approachable than ever before. I began converting my recipes, whenever possible, to dual methods.

The turning point came when one of my very good students called to complain that despite all her reading and all her cooking classes, she still could not control her processor. I gave her a few pointers. "You should write a book," she said, as people do, and at that moment the idea was born.

For a long time, many good cooks did not consider books written for food processors to be necessary. Many still do not. Yet the fact remains that the food processor has inexorably changed the way we cook. We can never go back. Nor should we.

Benjamin Franklin called man a "tool-making" animal. Bronowski embroidered on that, describing "the hand when it uses a tool as the instrument of discovery." The food processor was, and will remain, a serious instrument of discovery for cooks because it challenges us to rethink and restructure cooking to create, adjust, and improve the food we are preparing more quickly than ever before in history.

An analogy could be drawn between the food processor and the computer: two technological marvels with broad application, each requiring a language of its own. Yet the food processor is the more democratic of the two—the language is simpler—and therefore it, and the recipes and techniques created for it, must inevitably play an important role in the life of anyone who cares about what he eats.

But there is more to good food than following a recipe or using a machine. Cooking, tasting, and eating are all arts to be cultivated. As the world grows smaller and good cooks travel, tastes broaden and become more eclectic.

This book travels too. While French cooking forms its base, my love of Northern Italian food and interest in the cuisines of Greece, China, Spain, Mexico, and, yes, America belong here.

Yet the heart of this book lies in its techniques and methodology. My general approach is new and unique. I believe that the technique of controlled timing is critical to the successful use of single-speed food processors by most cooks, especially those who have not had the advantage of attending cooking classes.

These controlled timing techniques are included in every recipe. I have also offered general guidelines for applying them to recipes not included in this book. Further, there is a chart that equips the reader to use the machine to process foods even without recipes.

In addition to controlled timing, I have developed other new methods which I consider to be "breakthroughs."

There are two new methods for preparing three French sauces—hollandaise, béarnaise, and beurre blanc (white wine and butter sauce)—that permit the sauces to be made in advance and reheated. The "modified sabayon method" for hollandaise and béarnaise and the "hot butter method" for beurre blanc also permit these relatively inexpensive and delicious sauces to be made with confidence in about 15 minutes of working time.

The "pulse and bead" method for making pasta yields tender, nutritious high-protein dough in six seconds or less. These pasta doughs, many enriched with vegetables or whole wheat, are the basis of inexpensive, elegant, and sensationally delicious meals.

The warm- and cool-foaming techniques are unique to food processor baking and a particularly exciting discovery. Foaming eggs with butter or oil and sugar gives the best results for quick breads, coffee cakes, and other batter-based foods. These methods are faster than others and produce fresh, wholesome baked goods that are preservative- and junk-free.

The "pulse and clump" method for making pastry produces doughs and crusts that are especially tender since the technique promotes even mixing and prevents dough from becoming overworked.

Yeast breads, all made with an old-fashioned starter or sponge that eliminates unnecessary sugar from bread dough, are kneaded in 30 seconds when the yeast mixture is added last while the machine is running. I call this the "running start" method, since in effect the machine has a running start. As a result, bread doughs are kneaded quickly and thoroughly with no hand kneading required.

These are just a few of the methods I have developed in an effort to expand the use of the food processor and elevate the state of the art, while still keeping the processes simple enough to be used by cooks who range from beginning to accomplished. Each of the techniques is explained in detail in chapter introductions; many are illustrated. For novices there are eight special recipes which may be used as "mini-lessons" and for the initiated, challenging recipes.

"Civilization," wrote Bronowski, "is not a collection of finished artefacts, it is the elaboration of processes. In the end, the march of man is the refinement of the hand in action." A hand that cooks.

1

How the Food Processor Works

Food processors seem to work by magic, spinning so fast that the human eye perceives only a blur. Actually about 3,000 slicing, chopping, shredding, or mixing strokes occur each minute of continual use—space age speed that many people find awesome.

The key to using the machine easily and efficiently is to understand how it works.

The base of the processor houses the motor that drives the center shaft or post at a constant rate. Starting and stopping the motor, whether by twisting the lid or pressing the "pulse" button, controls the processing action on most machines.

Processing takes place in the plastic container or work bowl that locks into place on the base. The blades and disks for the various processing functions fit in the bowl over the shaft.

On many machines the lid has a dual function. It is a cover for the container and doubles as the on/off switch although a separate button, commonly called a "pulse," is also a standard feature. Lids have a food chute or feed tube, an elevated funnel that permits food to be assembled for processing or added to the container while the motor is running. The food chute also may be used as a handle for the lid.

The pusher fits into the food chute, function-

ing as a cork when the machine is running and as a pusher for food assembled in the chute for slicing, shredding, or cutting. Some pushers also are calibrated as measuring cups.

Most food processors have three or four basic attachments: the two-arm metal knife blade, the medium shredding disk, the medium slicing disk, and the french-fry disk. Some machines include a plastic knife blade for mixing or beating or a stubby plastic blade for kneading yeast doughs.

The blades work in the bottom of the container, causing food to spatter up and onto the side which must be frequently scraped down with a rubber spatula.

The disks turn in the top of the container just under the lid. Depending upon the disk inserted, food may be sliced, shredded, or cut into french-fry shapes. As food passes through the disk, it falls into the container which must be emptied before food touches the underside of the disk or if desired, before a new food is introduced.

Unlike fine knives, food processor blades and disks are designed to last through years of processing without sharpening. However, the metal knife blade may need to be replaced when it bruises, rather than cleanly chops, towel-dried parsley leaves.

2

Machine Care, Safety, and Performance

CARING FOR YOUR MACHINE

For detailed instructions on the care of your machine, consult the manufacturer's booklet enclosed in the box at the time of purchase. In addition, you may wish to study this general list of common sense dos and don'ts for all machines.

- Wash parts of a new machine before using.

- Use vegetable oil to coat rim of lid and container if the lid of a new machine does not twist easily.

- Learn which parts of machine are dishwasher safe.

- Keep machine on a convenient kitchen counter so that you will use it often.

- Do not store machine with container and lid in locked position.

- Do not store machine with pusher inserted in lid as air will not circulate and container may retain odors.

- Store machine with lid upside down in container and pusher inserted in food chute from underneath.

- Store blades and disks in the same way as sharp knives—out of the reach of children.

- Unplug food processor when it is not in use.

- Do not operate the processor if the cord or plug is damaged.

- Do not operate the processor after base has been dropped or damaged in any manner.

- Do not use the machine on a wet surface or counter.

- Wipe base clean after every use.

- Clean hollow core of blades with a toothpick, pipe cleaner, or dull end of a small knife after each use.

- Do not use abrasive material, such as scouring pads, to clean container or base.

USING YOUR FOOD PROCESSOR SAFELY

Operate the machine only after you have read the manufacturer's instruction booklet thoroughly. If you are in doubt about how to use your machine, always check the instruction booklet—never proceed on guesswork. Remember that the blades and disks of these machines have extra-sharp edges and handle them accordingly.

- If a blade or disk accidentally falls from any counter or cabinet, do not attempt to catch it. Step back and out of its path.

- Handle the metal knife blade only by the handle, never by the metal part.

- Wait for blades and disks to come to a complete stop before removing processor lid. *Never* attempt to stop a blade or disk with your hands!

- Keep kitchen utensils away from moving blades and disks. Never insert spatulas, knives, spoons, or fingers into food chute while machine is running. Always use pusher provided by manufacturer or specially designed implement, such as a slicing guide or spear.

- If food sticks on a blade or disk, never attempt to dislodge it with your fingers. Use a spatula or a spoon.

- Do not place blades or disks in soapy water where you cannot see them. While reaching in to find them, you run the risk of cutting yourself.

- Never force the pusher when shredding or slicing.

- If hard ingredients become trapped between lid and disk causing the machine to vibrate, turn it off immediately and remove the trapped food.

- Do not allow container to become overloaded while shredding or slicing. Processed foods may lift the disk upward and cause it to cut into the plastic lid.

- If machine is operated with an extension cord, check the electrical rating of the cord and be sure it matches the electrical rating of the processor.

- Do not immerse the base in liquid.

- Do not use attachments from other machines to process foods in your machine.

NOTES ON PERFORMANCE

Food processors vary greatly in quality and power. Not every machine on the market is guaranteed to perform each task in this book. Check the instruction booklet to see which tasks your processor will or will not perform. Many machines do not knead yeast breads. Others do not have blades sharp enough to grind citrus rind or chocolate.

Most food processor manufacturers *do not* recommend the following tasks:

- Grinding coffee beans
- Chopping ice
- Slicing hard-boiled eggs
- Slicing or chopping firmly frozen meat or fish
- Slicing unchilled raw or cooked meat
- Slicing or shredding unchilled cheese
- Grinding meat bones
- Grinding grain
- Whipping egg whites to full volume
- Grinding hard spices, such as whole peppercorns, nutmeg, or allspice
- Processing nonedible substances such as makeup
- Shredding paper

Most food processors do not whip egg whites to the full volume necessary for use in cakes and soufflés, when the leavening power of egg whites is required. Egg whites may be processed for use in clarifying broth or stock. See page 57.

Cooked potatoes do not mash well in the processor since the action of the blade brings out the starch. See page 90 for an adjusted method.

Note: In double-testing the recipes in this book, we used some 20 different food processors. All but 3 or 4 brands proved satisfactory for the difficult tasks such as kneading yeast dough, slicing *pain de mie,* and grinding hard cheeses, chocolate, and citrus rinds.

In the development and initial stages of recipe testing, a standard size Cuisinart food processor and the Cousances food processor were used. This does not imply an endorsement of either of these machines over any others.

3

Some Notes on Ingredients and Kitchen Equipment

The following information on ingredients and equipment may prove helpful and informative.

INGREDIENTS

Butter

Recipes have been tested with unsalted (sweet) butter with a low moisture content. Using such a fine quality butter is especially important for pastries and cakes. It is essential to use unsalted butter in recipes that specify it in the ingredient list. If unsalted butter is not used, adjust all salt to taste.

Clarified butter. Butter is clarified by melting it and removing the foamy white milk solids. The remaining clear yellow liquid is used for high heat cooking, because it does not burn easily, and for sauces such as hollandaise and béarnaise. Clarified butter can be made in any one of three ways; each uses ½ pound (225 g) unsalted butter and yields about ¾ cup (1¾ dL) clarified butter, which may be refrigerated in an airtight container for several weeks.

Method 1: Melt butter in a medium saucepan without stirring. Heat until it begins to pop gently (about 160° F/71° C). Watch carefully and continue heating until the first bubbles break the surface (about 180° F/82° C); remove saucepan from heat. Set aside 3 minutes; skim white foam (milk solids) carefully off top using a large spoon.

Method 2: Preheat oven to 450° F (230° C). Place butter in an oven-proof saucepan or deep baking dish. Place in oven 8 minutes or until butter separates and milk solids rise. Remove and cool 3 minutes; skim.

Method 3: Place butter in a 1-quart (1-L) glass measuring cup and cover with plastic wrap. Microwave on medium power 2 minutes or until foam rises and butter separates; skim.

Clams

Both littleneck and cherrystone clams have hard shells and are gathered along the Atlantic Coast. Littlenecks range in size from about 1½ to 2 inches (4 to 5 cm) in diameter. Cherrystones are larger and chewier when cooked. Surf clams are generally canned and have a slightly different flavor. Canned clams are precooked and will toughen if overheated.

Semisweet Chocolate

Semisweet chocolate may be melted in the food processor container if first ground to small irregular beads. The higher the quality of the chocolate, the faster and more evenly it will become beadlike. Lesser quality chocolates have a tendency to grind into a powder and fly around the container because they are lower in chocolate liquor, the substance derived from grinding roasted hulled cocoa beans.

There are several fine brands of semisweet chocolate. Semisweet chocolate chips also may be used providing they are real, not imitation, chocolate. Do *not* substitute unsweetened chocolate as it will be too hard to grind in the processor. See page 133 about "quick-melting" semisweet chocolate.

Whipping Cream

On the basis of testing, I have found that the processor whips cream 30 to 40 percent more densely than a conventional beater or whisk; therefore processor-whipped cream is good for fillings, frostings, and piping.

Before whipping cream, dry and chill the food processor container and blade. Normally 1 cup (¼ L) of non-ultra pasteurized cream will reach soft peaks in 20 to 30 seconds of processing. Because processors and creams vary, it is best to rely on the look and feel of the cream as follows:

- Test for soft peaks by lifting gently with a spatula. If peaks form but lean over, cream is at soft-peak stage. Sugar may be added after this point.

- Test for firm peaks in the same way as for soft peaks. If peaks stand firmly and cream adheres to an inverted spatula for several seconds, cream is at firm-peak stage. Beware of overprocessing: Once cream has reached soft-peaks, process at five-second intervals and check frequently or butter will result.

Eggs

Egg size is controlled by the government. The recipes in this book were tested with "large" eggs, each weighing approximately 2 ounces (60 g). It will take about 7 "large" egg whites to equal 1 cup (¼ L). Using the correct size eggs is especially important in baking and pastry recipes and for pasta doughs.

Egg glaze. Glaze used for pastries, pies, and some breads is made by mixing 1 egg yolk with 1 teaspoon milk in a cup or small jar. Keep refrigerated as long as 2 days.

Flour

Flour is a very complex subject. The U.S. government has no regulations concerning the amount of protein required in flour. As a result, the protein content, or strength, of white flours varies tremendously from region to region.

Because many of the recipes call for 2 types of flour, it is important to know what you are purchasing. All bags and boxes of flour contain nutritional information on the side of the package. The protein content is always listed. While this is considered to be "nutritional protein," it is the only general guide to flour we have. Protein is usually measured in grams per 4-ounce (about 1-cup/140-g) portion.

Recipes have been tested with flours containing the following protein contents. Your recipes will work best if you can match your flours to these protein counts.

Bread flour. Also called high-protein, high-gluten, or strong flour, it is unbleached, made from hard wheat and should contain 14 grams protein per 4 ounces (1 cup/140 g).

Unbleached all-purpose flour. Flour which has not undergone a chemical whitening process. The best is made from a blend of hard and soft wheats and contains 12 to 13 grams protein per 4 ounces (1 cup/140 g). *Some unbleached flours contain only 11 grams protein; in that case substitute bread flour in yeast doughs.*

Cake flour. Made from soft wheat and designed especially for cakes and pastries, cake flour should contain 8 grams protein per 4-ounce (1-cup/140-g) portion. Do *not* substitute self-rising cake flour.

Whole wheat flour. Made by grinding the entire wheat berry, this flour contains both the bran and wheat germ, the most nutritious and fibrous parts of the wheat. Do *not* use coarse or stone-ground whole wheat flour in recipes.

Miller's or unprocessed bran. The natural fibrous outer shell of the wheat berry is used for both fiber and flavor. Do not substitute processed bran cereal or flakes.

Mixed Herbs

Herbs are a yearly product of our small garden. We use them fresh during the summer months and dry them in bunches on the pasta rack for winter use. Use double the amount of fresh herbs if recipe calls for dried herbs. Store bunches of dried herbs in an airtight tin box and blend the leaves for use in cooking. As a general rule, I mix and use five herbs: basil, savory, marjoram (or oregano), thyme, and sage. I use equal amounts of the first three and half amounts of the last two. The quantity depends on your needs. The same mixture can be made with store-bought herbs.

After mixing herbs (do not process or grind—they will lose flavor), place in a separate well-marked bottle and store in a dark cool place. Crush between fingers before using. If crushed herbs emit faint rather than strong aromas, discard and purchase new ones for blending.

Mussels

These bluish-black bivalve mollusks, usually sold by the pound, range in length from 1 to 3 inches (2½ to 8 cm); avoid very large mussels which tend to have strong flavors and slightly tough meat.

Mussels must be thoroughly cleaned before cooking. First scrub with a brush or Teflon scrubber under cold running water to remove all grit and barnacles from outside of shells. Firmly grasp fiber protruding from straight edge of shell and pull it free. Then soak mussels in enough cold *salted* water to cover for several hours to allow them to disgorge sand. Drain in a colander after soaking; store in refrigerator covered with a damp towel.

Oils

Store oils in a dark cool place in tightly closed containers or refrigerate as label directs. If purchased in quantity, decant after opening into clean wine or screw-top liquor bottles; cork or cover tightly. Always taste oil before using to be sure it is fresh.

Olive oil. Fine-quality olive oil is excellent for cooking. Taste varies with quality, country of origin, and type of pressing. Best quality is pale green or golden and labeled "extra-virgin." This has a strong fruity flavor; use judiciously in salad dressings until a taste for this oil is acquired. It is expensive.

A milder oil comes from Lucca, Italy, and this type is best for salad dressings and mayonnaise. Lucca brands are widely available in supermarkets and specialty food stores. If not available, substitute vegetable oil. Do not use olive oil for deep frying.

Vegetable oil. Pressed from various seeds and fruits (see label for listing), this oil provides a neutral taste. Store as for olive oil. Especially good for deep frying.

Safflower oil. A light-bodied, low-cholesterol product but with the same calorie content as other oils, safflower oil is especially good for salad dressing and mayonnaise but generally is considered to be too light for sautéing or deep frying. May need refrigeration.

Sesame oil. A potent amber oil made from sesame seeds, sesame oil is available in Oriental food stores; use sparingly.

Use and care of oil used for stir frying or deep frying:

- Wait until hot oil cools to room temperature; do not stir.

- Slowly strain oil through cheesecloth or a towel-lined strainer. When cloudy residue appears, stop and discard remaining oil.

- Transfer clear oil into a jar or wine bottle; cover and label, noting type of oil and ingredients cooked in it.

- To cleanse oil used twice, add 1 peeled, cubed potato to oil as it heats. Remove and discard potato before adding ingredients to be fried.

- Oil may be reused several times if cleansed as described, unless it has been used to fry fish.

Oysters

Oysters are best when eaten in season (months with the letter "r"). May through August is spawning season and flavor tends to be less desirable. Three basic types are found, but Eastern oysters are most common. Check for tightly closed shells and a clean fresh smell. Oysters are usually sold by the piece. For information on handling and storing oysters, see page 54.

Parmesan Cheese

The type of cheese purchased for grating can make an enormous difference in the taste of food. Imported Parmesan cheese is best but most expensive. Look for the names *parmigiano reggiano* or *grana padano* stamped into the rind. Do not pay a high price for so-called imported cheese that is not so stamped.

Store Parmesan cheese in wedges, tightly wrapped in plastic and double-wrapped in aluminum foil—it will keep well for a month or two. If it hardens or becomes very white, wrap the cheese in a damp Handi-wipe and place in a plastic bag for 24 to 48 hours. Unwrap and store as before.

Before grinding to "grate" Parmesan cheese, always bring it to room temperature, remove rind, and break cheese into 1-inch (2½-cm) chunks. Save rind (removing wax) for flavoring soup.

Pepper

Use freshly ground pepper whenever possible. Fill a pepper mill with either white or black whole peppercorns or an even quantity of both. Red pepper flakes may be added to the mixture by pepper lovers.

Phyllo Pastry

Phyllo leaves are paper-thin and rectangular sheets of this pastry are used in Greek and Middle Eastern cuisines. Phyllo is available fresh or frozen in the delicatessen of many supermarkets, and it is easy to handle once you become accustomed to it. Use a scissors to trim phyllo to size needed.

Sausage Casings

The following companies mail order natural sausage casings and will send information upon request. Sausage Casings, 1964 Cottonwood, Coos Bay, Oregon 97420. The Standard Casing Company, Inc., 121 Spring Street, New York, New York 10012.

Scallops

Three types are commonly found: bay, sea, and calico scallops. Bay scallops are delicate in flavor and measure less than half an inch (about 1 cm) in diameter. Their peak supply is October and November. Calico scallops have mottled shells and are larger than bays with a slightly more pronounced flavor. Sea scallops are often several inches in diameter; most measure 1 to 2 inches (2½ to 5 cm). Sea scallops are widely available and are harvested year round. They are less firm than bays or calicos, and will throw off more liquid (called milk) during cooking. Check for a fresh smell. Scallops are sold by the pound.

Tomato Paste

Tomato paste can be made at home from the liquid leftover in canned Italian-style plum tomatoes. Strain liquid and place in a heavy nonaluminum saucepan. Reduce by slowly boiling until thick; take care bottom does not scorch. When reduced by two-thirds, transfer to a small nonaluminum saucepan and continue reducing over very low heat until thick and pasty and most of the liquid has evaporated; cool. Refrigerate as long as one week, or freeze in packets of two tablespoons each (a handy quantity) or in small jars. Good tomato paste should never be bitter; always taste before using. Imported brands, packed in convenient (tooth-paste-type) tubes, are especially tasty.

EQUIPMENT

In addition to the food processor, the following equipment will prove helpful:

Kitchen scale (with dual American/metric measurements if desired)
Thermometers—mercury-type oven thermometer and instant-registering meat/yeast thermometer (both very important)
Pots and pans including:
    small (1- to 1½-qt./1- to 1½-L) saucepan
    medium (2- to 2½-qt./2- to 2½-L) saucepan
    large (3- to 4-qt./3- to 4-L) saucepan
    medium (8- to 10-inch/20- to 25-cm) skillet
    large (11- to 12-inch/27½- to 30-cm) skillet
    6-qt./6-L soup kettle or Dutch oven
    12-qt./12-L stockpot
    8-inch (20-cm) ovenproof omelette pan

For pâtés and terrines, enameled cast-iron loaf pans or French porcelain terrines of desired capacity

For baking, long narrow loaf pans with black finish; lightweight aluminum cookie sheets; metal pie and tart tins; jelly roll pan

Pasta machine with changeable cutting heads

Food processor accessories including:
Funnel attachment
Slicing guide or spear
French-fry disk
Thin and thick slicing disks
Expanded feed tube lid accessory and special disks (make adjustments in recipes when using)

4
Basic Techniques

CONTROLLED TIMING WITH THE METAL KNIFE BLADE

The *metal knife blade* is the workhorse that processes cooked and uncooked foods by chopping, mincing, pulverizing, puréeing, and grinding. Also use this blade to mix, knead bread dough, "rapid-sift," beat, stir, churn, and purée. Always insert the blade before the food.

Mastering the technique of controlled timing is critical to the successful use of your food processor which operates on a single speed. The longer the blade turns, the more the food is processed. Therefore, the basic controlled timing technique is called "pulsing" or processing with an on/off turn of the lid or the pulse button. In this book an on/off turn is simply called a "pulse."

Controlled timing is measured in fractions of a second or seconds. There are three basic units.

The half-second on/off turn or pulse is an immediate, split-second burst that gives maximum control. Use half-second on/off turns or pulses when mixing, adding dry ingredients to a batter, or chopping soft or sticky foods or those which have a high water content such as onions.

After 4 half-second pulses, a batch of firm vegetables such as carrots is barely chopped.

The one-second on/off turn or pulse is best measured with the sweep hand of a wristwatch or clock until you become accustomed to the rhythm, or by slowly counting "one thousand one." Use one-second on/off turns for processing medium- to firm-textured foods, mixing ingredients into loose liquid mixtures, and chopping (but not grinding) meat, vegetables, or fish.

The two-second on/off turn or pulse may be timed on a clock or by slowly counting "one

9

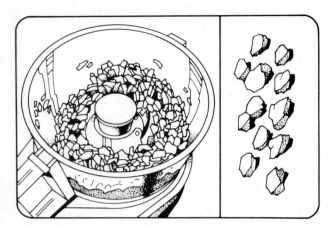

After 4 one-second pulses, carrots are coarsely chopped.

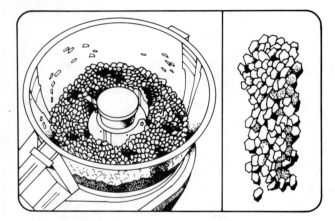

A batch of carrots processed with 4 two-second pulses is finely chopped.

thousand one, one thousand two." Use two-second pulses for chopping or mincing firm foods, for grinding meat or fish, or for sustained but controlled mixing.

Two consecutive five-second on/off turns or pulses are used only for "rapid-sifting" or mixing dry ingredients.

Controlled timing may be deceptive at first, even if you are accustomed to using the processor. For best results, use the timing indicated in recipes. If in doubt about how long to process or if your machine performs slightly differently from the recipe standard, use the general guidelines above and check your progress by stopping and removing the lid frequently.

OTHER PROCESSING FACTORS

In addition to controlled timing there are several other factors which will affect food processing.

Size. Cut food into uniform size before processing. One-inch (2½-cm) cubes or lengths are best.

Texture. Never process any food that is too hard to be pierced easily with the tip of a small sharp knife or the end of the metal knife blade. Hard foods can lodge themselves on the edge of the blade and cause jamming, or they may be pushed around the container and overheat the motor or damage the blade. Never process firmly frozen foods. Before processing meat, remove all bones, tough gristle, tendon, and fiber. Always remove the rind from hard cheese such as Parmesan.

Amount. The maximum quantity of dry ingredients for standard-size machines is 3 to 3½ cups (¾ L). Large-capacity models may handle more. Liquid capacity varies according to the thickness of the liquid and the design of the container. Most machines accommodate 1½ cups (3½ dL) of a thin liquid like broth or 4 cups (1 L) of a thick liquid like cheesecake batter. For most fruits, vegetables, meat, fish, and nuts, a 1- to 1½-cup (¼-L) batch gives best results. Always verify the capacity of your food processor by consulting the instruction booklet that comes with the machine.

Note on large-capacity machines: In general, very small quantities, such as a single garlic clove or one small carrot cut into cubes, will take slightly longer to process in large-capacity machines. Standard quantities (those specified in recipes) may be processed with fewer on/off turns or pulses, especially if the foods are soft.

For best results, adjust quantities to machine capacity following manufacturer's guidelines. Follow controlled timing techniques according to textures of food and increase the number of pulses as needed. For example, a medium onion processed with 4 to 6 half-second pulses in a standard machine may require 6 to 8 or 8 to 10 half-second pulses in larger machines. You may wish to note variations on the Conversion Chart (page 164).

Moisture. Dry ingredients for baking require a dry container and blade. Other foods which require a dry container and blade include parsley (first towel-dried), nuts, bread crumbs, garlic, shallots, onions, and Parmesan and Romano cheese.

Processing in sequence. The recipes in this book are written in a convenient working sequence. Dry ingredients and those which require a dry container and blade (even if used for garnish) are frequently processed before wet or messy ingredients. It will not be necessary to wash the container and blade after every task. Clean them well with a rubber spatula and do not worry about small bits of leftover foods. It may be helpful to wipe the container and lid with paper toweling or rinse and dry it quickly from time to time. When it is absolutely necessary to wash, the recipe will specify a clean, dry container and blade or disk.

To empty container of most machines without removing blade, first unlock container. Insert the longest finger on your left (or right) hand into the hollow core of the blade. Scrape container clean with a spatula.

ADDITIONAL USEFUL TECHNIQUES WITH THE METAL KNIFE BLADE

- To process less than 1 ounce (30 g) garlic, shallots, onion, or hard cheese, drop food through the chute while machine is running. When minced, sound will change slightly.

- To make bread crumbs, "grate" hard cheese, or purée cooked or soft uncooked foods, cut food into cubes, and process to desired consistency.

- To "grate" lemon, orange, lime, or grapefruit zest or rind, strip off the rind or zest with a vegetable peeler. Grind rind strips with a minimum of 3 tablespoons sugar until fine.

- "Grate" onion by grinding with ¼ cup (½ dL) water until pulverized.

- To "juice" citrus fruits such as lemons, limes, or oranges, first peel fruit completely removing all the white pith. Cut fruit into quarters or sixths depending on size. Process until liquefied, then strain, pressing pulp with a spoon to extract all juice. Discard pulp.

- To whip cream for frosting or filling, first refrigerate container, blade, and lid for 5 minutes and always use chilled (refrigerator-cold) cream. Process 15 to 20 seconds, then check consistency every 5 seconds, scraping down sides of container as necessary until cream is whipped to desired texture. See page 5 for additional information on cream.

- For grinding meat consult techniques on page 77.

- For creaming shortening and sugar, consult techniques on page 132.

USING THE DISKS

The disks are used for slicing, shredding, and cutting foods into elongated french-fry "finger" shapes. Processing is controlled by push or pressure—a steady force exerted on the food in the chute so that it passes through the disk at the optimum pace.

Push or pressure can be difficult to gauge at first and most people exert too much force on the pusher. Recipes specify which push to use on foods or you may consult the Conversion Chart on page 164.

Types of Pressure

Three directions are used to describe push or pressure required for processing.

Gentle push. This is enough pressure to keep the food in place against the revolving disk. Because the force of the disk causes food to bounce slightly, light foods, such as mushrooms, will turn somersaults until a gentle push is applied. Slice mushrooms, tomatoes, or bananas to practice the gentle push.

Moderate push. Best control is obtained with this pressure. It is more force, but not much more than the gentle push. Slice pears, apples, or a whole peeled lemon to practice.

Firm push. Use this for firm or fibrous foods which naturally tend to resist less firm pressure. Shred zucchini, or slice a whole lime (with the peel) to practice the firm push.

The softer the food, the softer the push required. Chilled cheese, such as mozzarella, however, always requires a gentle push. *Never use a hard push.* Very hard foods such as pepperoni, however, require a moderate push.

Too much pressure can jam or bend a disk. It is often necessary to release the pressure slightly if the food resists processing.

Loading the Food Chute

Whether your processor has a standard size or an expanded food chute or feed tube, loading the chute will be easiest when there is little trimming or adjustment to be done.

Food is assembled in the chute only when disks are to be used. Always insert disk before food.

Food loaded upright in the chute will be processed across the grain (crosswise). Food

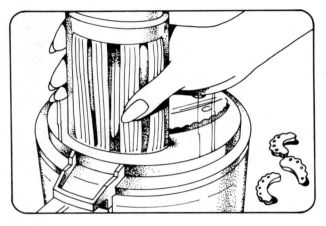

To cut foods such as celery into short slices, load upright in chute.

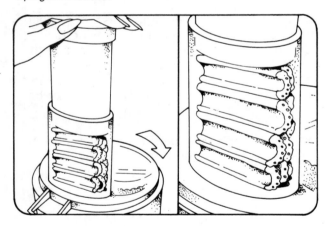

To make long slices with celery or other vegetables, load in food chute sideways. Chute may be packed three-quarters full.

loaded sideways will be processed with the grain (lengthwise).

Prepare food for processing by cutting it into even lengths, wedges, or rectangular chunks to fit the food chute. Use the pusher as a size guide. Trim or halve foods as necessary.

It is not essential to cut the ends of food blunt (straight across) before processing. However, blunt-cut foods process more evenly and are less likely to twist, thereby leaving waste on top of the disk because the blunt ends permit the food to rest firmly between the disk and the pusher.

Load slim foods, such as carrots or celery, from the top of the chute and pack snugly to prevent twisting. Cut small amounts into short even lengths which fill the area of the chute. An accessory such as a slicing guide, which has a short spear on the end, can be a convenient implement to use to prevent food from twisting. A slicing guide or spear also will permit you to process a single slim food across the grain without cutting either end blunt or positioning it as described below.

Foods that are too large to be inserted from the top of the chute may frequently be loaded from underneath as the base of the chute on many machines is slightly larger than the mouth. Large size or expanded food chute attachments solve many of these problems. *Never* force food into the chute either from the top or the bottom.

Never use a disk to process any food which is firmly frozen or cannot be pierced with the tip of a small, sharp knife. Damage to the disk may result.

The Medium Slicing Disk

The slicing disk that comes packaged with your machine is called the *medium slicing disk.* Exact thickness of the slices varies with machines from 2 to 4 millimeters. Some machines have optional slicing accessories such as thin slicing disks (usually 1 to 2 millimeters), thick slicing disks (5 to 6 millimeters), or ripple-cut disks. All the disks are used in exactly the same way as the *medium slicing disk.*

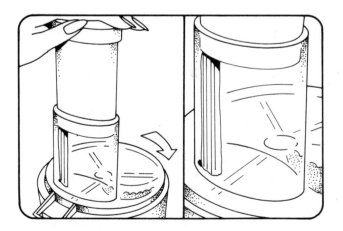

Position a single piece of food such as celery against the side of the chute opposite the direction of the oncoming disk. The force of the disk holds the food in place. Use this technique for slicing larger foods in "expanded" food chutes. Single foods require the same push as a full chute.

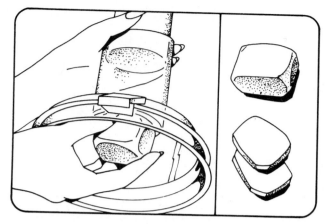

Insert large whole foods such as potatoes, turnips, chunks of cheese, meat, or fruit such as whole lemons or limes from underneath food chute, trimming as necessary to fit. When slicing, push varies with textures of food.

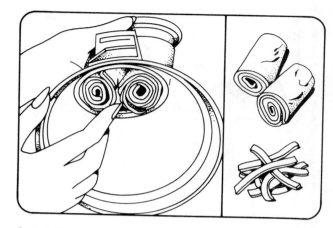

Soft julienne strips or coarse shreds are made from soft foods such as sliced meats, roasted bell peppers, or spinach leaves by a "stack and roll" procedure. If small, cut rolls crosswise to fit snugly in base of chute. Insert side-by-side as rolls expand to hold food in position as lid is replaced.

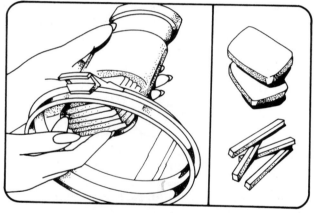

Julienne (matchstick) strips are made from firm sliced food by "double slicing." Gather slices together; invert lid. Assemble slices in base of chute with cut edges resting against pusher. Pack slices snugly to hold in position as lid is replaced.

Some tricks with the slicing disk. A firm push on an apple, which normally requires a moderate push, will give slightly thicker slices because the increased pressure causes it to pass more quickly through the disk. With a gentle push the apple can be sliced somewhat thinner than usual. This works best with medium-texture foods.

Note on slicing with large-size or expanded food chute accessories: A large-size food chute attachment will in many cases eliminate the need to trim or cut foods in half before slicing. Such an accessory also may eliminate the need to load foods from the base of the chute as illustrated. Recipe directions do not include instructions for using such an accessory, however, and must be adjusted accordingly.

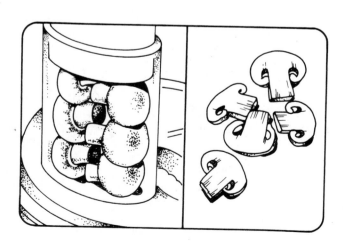

Mushrooms slice best when loaded sideways in food chute with caps alternating. For larger-than-standard food chutes, load mushrooms sideways and three abreast.

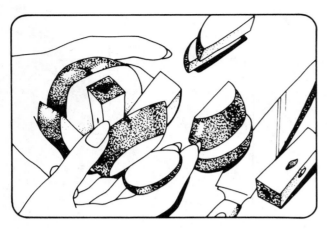

To prepare apples or pears for decorative slicing, cut fruit on each side of core to form 4 pieces. Discard core. Remove rounded sides of the 2 large outside pieces and halve each lengthwise. Six flat segments result. Prepare pineapple and melons for slicing as described; then trim as necessary to fit food chute.

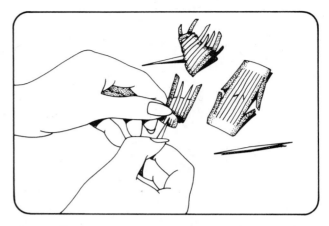

Carrot flowers require long thin carrot slices. With a sharp knife make narrow parallel cuts in carrot slices to within ½ inch (1½ cm) of each short end. Free outside edges and 1 or 2 center strips by cutting on a diagonal. Curl carrot slice, overlap ends slightly, and fix with a toothpick. Place in ice water to hold.

To make decorative slices. Decorative slices work best with the *thin slicing disk* (1 to 2 millimeters).

The French-Fry Disk

This disk is standard equipment with many machines. In addition to cutting potatoes into slightly curved french fries, it may be used to process fruit, such as melon or pineapple, firm vegetables, such as turnips and beets, or soft-layered foods, such as onions and tomatoes. Results vary according to size, texture, and interior structure of the food.

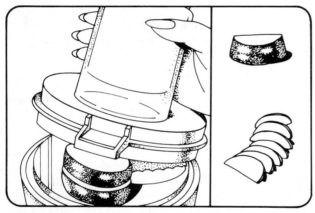

To make decorative slices, stack fruit segments directly on disk. Replace lid so fruit fits snugly in bottom of chute before slicing.

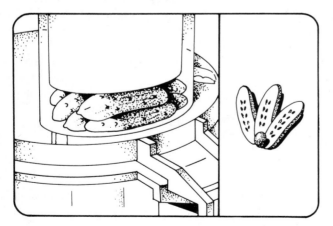

To make gherkin fans, position whole gherkins sideways in chute directly on disk. Place lid over; slice. Arrange thin slices in 3 overlapping pieces to form fans; garnish with a dot of pimiento.

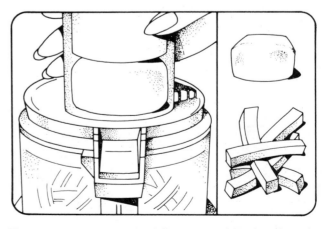

To cut potatoes or round firm vegetables into french fry or finger shapes, load food sideways in chute and slice with the grain.

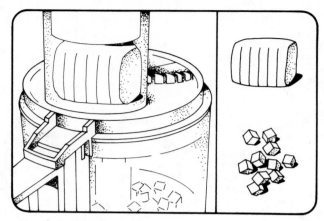

To cut firm foods such as potatoes or turnips into coarse dice, make vertical slits in food about ¼ inch (¾ cm) apart leaving pieces attached at top. Insert food so that slits are perpendicular to surface of disk before cutting.

- Fruits such as pineapple or melon can be cut into thick matchstick pieces of varying lengths for use in fruit salads or pie (see page 148. Length of pieces will depend on *width* of food. If food is cut into a chunk as wide as the food chute, thick matchsticks will be long. If two pieces are inserted upright and side-by-side, thick matchsticks will be shorter.

- Onions, cabbage, or lettuce (layered foods)

may be cut into coarse pieces using the *french-fry disk.* Onions cut with this disk can be browned whereas onions chopped with the *metal knife blade* generally do not brown.

- Tomatoes may be coarsely diced by cutting across the grain with the *french-fry disk.* Italian plum tomatoes work especially well.

- Other medium and firm-textured vegetables and fruits may be coarsely "chopped" by loading cubes in food chute randomly and cutting with the *french-fry disk.*

The Medium Shredding Disk

The shredding disk packed with your machine is called the *medium shredding disk.* Exact size of shreds varies slightly from machine to machine. Some processors have additional accessories such as fine or coarse shredding disks, all of which are used in the same way. You may find that shredding disks work best when pressure on food is increased slightly.

- Shreds will be short when food is loaded upright in food chute and processed across the grain.

- Shreds will be long and elegant when food is loaded sideways and shredded with the grain.

5
Mini-Lessons

If you have never before used a food processor, here is the place to begin. This section is a brief crash course designed to teach basic techniques while you prepare something quick and delicious to eat. When you have made all eight of these recipes, you will have used the basic *metal knife blade* as well as each of the special disks. You will have mastered timing the on/off turns or pulses, and you will have had your first experience using correct pressure while slicing and shredding.

If you have any questions about technique after completing these mini-lessons, consult Basic Techniques, pages 9 to 15.

PITA OREGANATA
Makes 6 to 8 servings

Store-bought pita breads tend to be larger than home-baked loaves; adjust ingredients accordingly.

4 Pita Breads, page 121
½ **lb. (225 g) mozzarella cheese, chilled**
2 **to 3 oz. (60 to 85 g) Parmesan cheese (room temperature), cut into 1-inch cubes**

⅓ **to ½ cup (¾ to 1 dL) olive or vegetable oil**
Salt and pepper to taste
2 **teaspoons dried oregano leaves or 4 teaspoons snipped fresh oregano**

1. Split bread rounds to form 2 circles. Place cut side up on baking sheets; set aside. Cut mozzarella into rectangular chunks to fit food chute. Insert the *medium shredding disk*. Shred mozzarella with a gentle push; set aside. Change to the *metal knife blade*. With the machine running, drop Parmesan chunks one at a time through food chute. Process until cheese is powdery; set aside.

2. Generously brush each bread round with oil. Sprinkle lightly with salt and pepper. Top each with ¼ teaspoon oregano, ¼ cup (½ dL) mozzarella, and 1 tablespoon Parmesan. Drizzle ½ teaspoon of the remaining oil over top of each bread round.

3. Heat broiler 5 minutes. Broil breads on baking sheets as close as possible to heat source until cheese is lightly browned. Cut into wedges and serve piping hot.

YAKITORI
Makes about 12 servings

Yakitori is a Japanese snack food that also makes a great hors d'oeuvre. This is an expandable recipe (the number of portions depends on how much meat is threaded on each skewer) and it doubles beautifully.

½ **medium flank steak (¾ lb./340 g), well trimmed**
1 **medium garlic clove, peeled**
½ **inch fresh ginger root, peeled and halved, or** ½ **teaspoon powdered ginger**
½ **medium onion, peeled, cut into 1-inch cubes**
⅓ **cup (¾ dL) teriyaki sauce**
1 **tablespoon honey**

1. Cut steak lengthwise in half. Cut halves crosswise or as necessary into even lengths to fit upright in food chute so that when sliced, meat will be cut across the grain. Wrap and partially freeze.

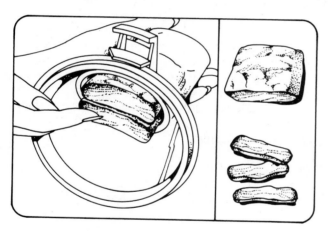

2. When steak is partially frozen, insert *medium slicing disk* in processor container. Place 1 or 2 steak pieces in food chute from underneath. Slice across the grain with a moderate push; remove to a shallow baking dish.

3. Change to the *metal knife blade*. With machine running, drop garlic, ginger, and onion pieces one at a time through food chute. Process until minced. Scrape down sides of container. Add teriyaki sauce and honey. Process 5 seconds to mix. Pour over steak slices; cover and refrigerate 2 to 6 hours, tossing frequently.

4. Just before cooking, soak 8-inch (20-cm) bamboo skewers in hot water for 30 minutes. Loosely thread 5 or 6 steak slices through both ends on each skewer. Broil immediately, about 3 minutes per side, or refrigerate until ready to broil. Serve hot.

TUNA FISH SALAD
Makes 4 to 6 servings

White meat water-pack tuna may be substituted, if desired.

¼ **cup (½ dL) firmly packed parsley leaves**
3 **medium shallots or ½ medium onion, peeled, cut into 1-inch cubes**
1 **medium celery rib, cut into 1-inch lengths**
2 **medium sweet gherkins, halved**
1 **teaspoon fresh lemon juice**
¾ **cup (1¾ dL) mayonnaise**
¼ **teaspoon salt, or more to taste**
2 **cans (6½ oz./195 g each) chunk light tuna, oil packed, well drained**

Insert the *metal knife blade*. Process parsley until finely minced. Add shallots and mince with 3 or 4 one-second on/off turns or pulses. Add celery and gherkins. Process to chop with 4 half-second on/off turns or pulses. Scrape down side of container. Mix in lemon juice, mayonnaise, salt, and tuna with 7 or 8 half-second on/off turns or pulses. Adjust seasoning to taste.

Variation:

Tuna Salad with Green Peppers and Capers
Cut ½ green bell pepper into 1-inch (2½-cm) squares and add to container with celery. Proceed with recipe, adding 2 tablespoons drained capers to container with tuna.

CHOPPED STEAK
Makes 4 servings

This recipe provides a delicious introduction to all three processing times: half-second, one-second, and two-second on/off turns or pulses.

1½ lbs. (675 g) boneless sirloin steak, well
  trimmed, cut into 1-inch cubes, chilled
1 medium garlic clove, peeled
½ medium onion, peeled, cut into 1-inch cubes
3 tablespoons (45 g) butter, chilled
¼ teaspoon salt, or more to taste
Pepper to taste
Pinch dried thyme leaves
2 teaspoons Worcestershire sauce
1 egg

1. Insert *metal knife blade* in a dry container.
Coarsely chop half the meat cubes with 4 one-
second on/off turns or pulses; remove to waxed
paper. Repeat with remaining meat; remove to
waxed paper. With machine running, drop garlic clove and onion cubes one at a time through
food chute. Process until minced.

2. Melt 1 tablespoon butter in a small skillet.
Cook garlic and onion until soft but not brown;
set aside to cool. Place remaining butter, salt,
pepper, and thyme in processor. Mix with 2
two-second on/off turns or pulses; scrape down
sides of container. Add chopped meat, Worcestershire sauce, cooked onion mixture, and egg
to container. Process with 10 to 12 half-second
on/off turns or pulses to mix all ingredients and
chop meat to hamburger consistency.

3. Divide meat mixture into 4 equal parts. Form
each into a thick oval. Cover and refrigerate 1
to 4 hours to allow butter to firm. To cook,
preheat broiler and broil chopped steaks close
to heat source 3 to 4 minutes on each side for
rare. They also may be pan fried.

CRUDITES
Yield varies according to amount

Crudités, or raw vegetable pieces for dips or
snacks, may be prepared in any quantity. Serve
crudités with Pesto, or Summer Herb Vinaigrette, pages 110 and 113.

Carrots
Broccoli
Zucchini
Cucumber
Turnips or kohlrabi
Green, red, or yellow bell peppers

1. Carrots. Peel and cut into even lengths to fit
sideways in food chute. Insert *medium slicing
disk* and slice into strips with a firm push.

2. Broccoli. Remove flowerets. Peel stems with
sharp knife or vegetable peeler. Cut stems into
even lengths to fit sideways in food chute.
Insert *medium slicing disk* and slice into strips
with a gentle push.

3. Zucchini. Rinse and dry. Strip with vegetable
peeler if desired. Cut ends blunt. Cut into even
lengths to fit upright in food chute. Insert *thick
or medium slicing disk*. If large, insert zucchini
from underneath food chute. Slice into coins
with a firm push.

4. Cucumber. Prepare as for zucchini. Slice
into coins with a gentle push.

5. Turnips or kohlrabi. Peel with vegetable
peeler and place in lemon water to avoid dis-
coloration. Trim as necessary to fit sideways in
food chute and insert from underneath. Attach
french-fry disk. Cut into strips with a firm push.

6. Bell peppers. Halve peppers lengthwise and
remove core and seeds. Cut ends blunt and
halve crosswise. Insert 1 or 2 halves (depending on size) upright in food chute from underneath, curling slightly if necessary. Insert *thick
or medium slicing disk*. Slice into half rounds
with a gentle push.

THOUSAND ISLAND DRESSING
Makes 1¼ cups (3 dL)

When inserting pepper strips from underneath
the food chute, hold pusher in place and rest
ends of strips on pusher.

½ medium green bell pepper, cut into 1-inch
  strips
1 medium dill pickle, cut into 1-inch lengths
1-inch cube onion or 1 medium shallot, peeled
2 tablespoons sour cream or plain yogurt
½ cup (1 dL) mayonnaise, page 114
¼ cup (½ dL) ketchup
2 dashes cayenne pepper

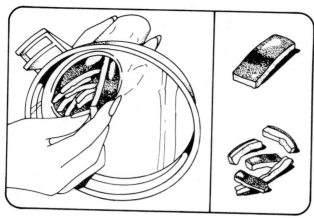

Cut green pepper strips into even lengths to fill food chute. Turn lid over and wedge in strips upright from underneath food chute. Insert the *medium slicing disk.* Slice peppers with a gentle push. Move pieces aside and insert the *metal knife blade.* Add pickle and onion. Process to chop with 4 or 5 half-second on/off turns or pulses; scrape down sides of container. Add remaining ingredients. Process with 3 or 4 one-second on/off turns or pulses or until mixed. Serve immediately or store in an airtight container up to 5 days.

POTATOES ANNETTE
Makes 4 to 6 servings

Cutting ends of potatoes straight or blunt allows them to shred evenly and minimizes waste. Potatoes will discolor slightly in the towel but will whiten again when cooked.

1¼ lbs. (565 g) **medium russet potatoes, peeled, ends cut blunt**
Cold water
2 tablespoons vegetable oil
Salt and pepper to taste
3 tablespoons (45 g) butter
½ cup (1 dL) sour cream (optional)
2 tablespoons fresh snipped chives or parsley, to garnish

1. Trim potatoes if necessary to fit in food chute. Attach the *medium shredding disk.* Insert each potato from underneath food chute and shred with a moderate push. Transfer to a large bowl and fill with water to cover. Set aside 30 minutes, changing water once. Drain

and pat potatoes dry in 2 cloth towels. Refrigerate, rolled up in towels, until ready to cook.

2. Heat oil in a medium omelette pan or skillet. Add potatoes, pressing together gently to form a mound. Cook over medium heat until bottom is browned and crusty, about 4 to 5 minutes. Season top lightly with salt and pepper. Cover and cook over low heat about 8 minutes.

3. With a metal spatula, loosen potatoes around edges so that they slide freely in pan when shaken gently. Invert onto a flat pot lid or baking sheet. Place butter in skillet. Carefully slide potatoes off lid or baking sheet into the skillet, browned side up. Salt and pepper lightly. Continue cooking on medium heat until bottom is browned well, about 6 to 8 minutes longer. Transfer to a heated serving dish. Mound sour cream in center, if desired. Garnish with chives or parsley. Serve piping hot.

BROWNIES
Makes 16 two-inch (5-cm) square brownies

The walnuts are mixed into the batter and simultaneously chopped.

½ **lb. (225 g) semisweet chocolate, broken into ½-inch pieces**
4 eggs
1 teaspoon vanilla extract
¼ **cup (½ dL) vegetable oil**
¾ **cup (145 g) sugar**
3 tablespoons unbleached all-purpose flour
¼ **teaspoon salt**
¼ **teaspoon baking powder**
1 cup (4 oz./115 g) shelled walnut pieces

1. Adjust the oven rack to middle position. Heat oven to 350° F (175° C). Lightly oil an 8-cup (2-L) baking dish; set aside. Insert the *metal knife blade.* Place half the chocolate in the container. Process until chocolate forms small beads; remove to waxed paper. Repeat with remaining chocolate; then return all chocolate to container.

2. Add eggs and vanilla. Process 15 seconds. Heat oil in a small saucepan to almost bubbling; then with machine running, pour hot oil

through food chute within 10 seconds. Scrape down sides of container. Process 20 seconds longer. Do not worry if small bits of chocolate remain undissolved.

3. Attach funnel if desired. Process, gradually adding sugar within 10 seconds. Scrape down container sides. Sprinkle flour, salt, baking powder, and walnut pieces evenly over top of batter. Process to mix in walnuts and flour with 6 or 7 half-second on/off turns or pulses or until flour is mixed into batter. Do not overprocess or walnuts will become too finely ground. Pour batter into prepared dish. Bake 45 minutes. Cool on cake rack to room temperature. Cut into squares.

WHAT WENT WRONG?

Common Processing Problems and Their Solutions

- Texture of food is too fine. Proper timing of on/off turns or pulses was not used.

- Puréed food retains lumps after several minutes of processing. Food was not cut small enough or into uniform size before insertion.

- Parsley does not mince. Parsley was not sufficiently towel-dried, or container or blade were wet.

- Butter does not become smooth. Butter was too cold.

- Onions become mushy and lose texture when chopped. They were processed too long or without proper timing of pulses.

- Liquid leaks out of container. Container was filled too full.

- Machine stops during processing. It was overloaded and overheated so that automatic turn-off mechanism was activated.

- Slices are uneven. Food chute was improperly or unevenly packed, or incorrect push was used while slicing.

- Foods in chute twist while slicing. Food chute was not snugly packed or ends of food were not cut blunt.

- Slicer jams on partially frozen food. Food

was too firmly frozen to have been sliced. Always pretest with a sharp knife.

- Slices are broken or edges are not clean. Food was too soft or unchilled, or push was incorrect.

- Peel of whole fruit or vegetable detaches and is left on top of disk. Peel was not facing the cutting or shredding edge of the oncoming disk, or ends were not cut blunt.

- Food inserted from underneath food chute sticks in chute. Food was too large to insert; trim to fit chute snugly.

- Texture of a batter is lumpy after mixing. Scrape down sides of container more frequently.

- Machine twists on counter while slicing firm food. Food may be caught in slicing disk. Remove food from chute, clean disk, and reinsert disk and food.

- Lid becomes stuck to bowl and is difficult to turn. A common occurrence when sugar is lodged between lip of lid and bowl. Wipe off bowl; rinse lid with hot water, and dry before continuing.

- Machine stops while kneading bread dough. Gluten is activated and load is too great for machine. Remove half of dough from container. Add 1 tablespoon flour. Restart motor as soon as possible and continue kneading. Repeat to knead remaining half of dough. If problems persist, divide dough into 3 parts and knead each separately. Recombine by hand before placing dough in bowl to rise.

- Pie crust dough is very dry and falls apart even after it is chilled. Additional liquid is required; add 1 to 2 teaspoons cold water to container. Break dough into 3 pieces and reprocess with half-second on/off turns or pulses until water is absorbed and dough begins to clump.

- Butter for pastry does not slice evenly. Butter is too warm; chill it thoroughly.

- Rind strips, Parmesan cheese, or bread crumbs do not mince fine in specified time. This is caused by variations in age and texture; run machine longer to obtain desired results.

6

Hors d'Oeuvres

The food processor has inexorably changed the manufacture of hors d'oeuvres by cutting preparation time drastically and opening new avenues of exploration. The machine is a master at whipping up butters and spreads, slicing ingredients for canapés (including bread), mincing meat and fish for "tartares," and beating dough for *chou* pastry puffs. Fillings of every description are quickly made in the processor, and fancy garnishes, such as gherkin fans or olive rings, are a snap.

Apart from Guacamole, which I adore passionately, I have chosen to exclude dips from this book. Let me grit my teeth and say it straight out: In my opinion gooey dips are boring, fattening, and generally worthless. Crudités, page 18, make a great low-calorie snack, and I prefer to pair them with one of the light fresh salad dressings in Chapter 14.

Canapés, or little open-face finger sandwiches, are traditional cold fare for parties, weddings, and teas. The best are made with homemade French white bread called *pain de mie*—the word *mie* means "crumb" in French. *Pain de mie* is a shaped bread that requires a special hinged mold. Two molds are made specially for use with the food processor, and the finished breads, either round or oval, neatly

fit into the food chute for slicing. The recipe appears on page 123. This bread may be baked several weeks in advance and frozen. If you wish to slice it a day or two in advance, be sure that the slices are double wrapped in plastic and refrigerated. Unfortunately, not all slicing disks do a perfect job on *pain de mie*, although most I've tested will. Test yours to be sure.

Pâtés and terrines are fast becoming standard party props, and their Americanization has already begun. Yet they still retain an aura of sophistication and difficulty that most guests appreciate. A homemade pâté proves that the cook really has gone all out. Now pâtés can be made reliably and easily in the food processor using controlled timing techniques—even by a relatively inexperienced cook.

I am often asked to explain the difference between pâtés and terrines. Basically the words are used interchangeably; although in principle, according to *Larousse Gastronomique,*

The word pâté should apply only to meat or fish dishes enclosed in pastry and baked in the oven. The term, however, is also used to describe any preparation put in a pie dish lined with strips of bacon and baked in the oven. The correct name of this type of dish is terrine, and they should always be referred to as such, but common usage has applied the term pâté to these preparations, which, by the way, are always served cold, whereas the real pâtés can be served hot or cold.

The impact of the new French cooking has blurred such distinctions even further, and today many pâtés and terrines are made without any *lining* of fat whatsoever. Actually these are nothing more than ground mixtures of meat, poultry, liver, fish, or vegetables bound with eggs and fat, seasoned, and frequently baked in sturdy loaf pans or oval porcelain dishes in which they also may be served. Fat is absolutely essential to the mixture, and if removed the pâté or terrine will be dry.

The real significance of pâtés and terrines, however, has little to do with nomenclature. They, perhaps more than any other French food, represent the mastery of restaurant or professional quality preparations by the home cook of moderate means and attest to our excitement and expanded sense of confidence in the kitchen.

GUACAMOLE
Makes 2½ cups (6 dL) or 6 to 8 appetizer servings

Guacamole is a mélange of strong flavors well merged through the use of the processor and heightened by fresh coriander. The proper texture for Guacamole is much disputed. Like many Mexicans, I like mine chunky. However, 1 or 2 additional two-second pulses will give smoother results.

2   medium garlic cloves, peeled
1   medium onion, peeled, cut into 1-inch cubes
2   medium tomatoes, cored, cut in eighths
2   (½ lb./225 g) avocados, peeled and pitted, rinsed
½ teaspoon salt or more to taste
5   dashes Tabasco, or more to taste
½ tablespoon lemon or lime juice, or more to taste
Fresh snipped coriander leaves to taste (optional)
Tortilla chips

1. Insert the *metal knife blade*. With machine running, drop garlic cloves through food chute; process until minced; scrape down sides of

container. Add onion and 1 tomato and process with 5 one-second pulses to chop. Add avocado and process with 4 or 5 two-second pulses for chunky texture. Add salt, Tabasco, lemon juice, and remaining tomato. Process with 2 one-second pulses to coarsely chop tomato. Adjust seasonings to taste.

2. Transfer Guacamole to bowl. Cover with plastic wrap and refrigerate until chilled. Just before serving, stir in snipped coriander leaves, if desired. Serve with tortilla chips.

ONION AND OLIVE CANAPES
Makes about 2 dozen

Good-quality black olives have a full rich taste because they are picked when the fruit is ripe. The best are sold in bulk at Italian or Greek markets, but always taste before buying to be sure they are not bitter or old.

6   oz. (180 g) pitted black olives
3-inch length round Pain de Mie, page 123
3   small (1½-inch diameter) white onions, peeled, ends cut blunt
⅛ cup (¼ dL) firmly packed parsley leaves, plus additional sprigs for garnish
2   packages (3 oz./85 g each) cream cheese, at room temperature, cut into 1-inch cubes
1   teaspoon lemon juice, or more to taste

1. Insert the *medium slicing disk*. Pat olives dry; stand 6 or 8 close together on disk, pitted ends down. Replace lid. Slice olives with a moderate push; set aside. Cut ends of bread

flat. Insert bread from underneath food chute placing it against the side of the chute opposite the direction of the oncoming disk (see page 12, lower right illustration). Slice with a firm push; set bread aside. Stand onions directly on disk. Replace lid and slice onions with a moderate push; set slices aside.

2. Change to the *metal knife blade* and wipe container dry. Process parsley until finely minced. Add remaining olives and process to chop with 4 half-second pulses; set aside. Process cream cheese and lemon juice 15 seconds; scrape down container sides. Add parsley and olives. Process to mix with 4 half-second pulses, stopping to scrape down container sides as necessary.

3. To assemble canapés, lightly spread cream cheese mixture on bread slices. Cover with onion slices. Top with 1 tablespoon cream cheese mixture, completely covering onion. Garnish with an olive ring and a parsley leaf. Assemble on platters or cookie sheets and cover tightly with plastic. Refrigerate until ready to serve.

CUCUMBER CANAPES
Makes about 3 dozen

These canapés are reminiscent of English cucumber sandwiches, and I very much like them with dill butter. Before slicing the bread, test with a small piece to be sure your medium slicer does a good job; if not, you may wish to slice the bread by hand.

2 3-inch lengths round Pain de Mie, page 123
**1 medium cucumber, ends cut blunt (use
      seedless English type, if desired)**
2 large hard-boiled eggs, peeled and quartered
Dash salt
Pepper to taste
¾ teaspoon Dijon mustard
1 or 2 dashes Tabasco
**4 to 6 tablespoons (60 to 80 g) Herb Butter,
      page 113, slightly softened**
Pimiento strips, for garnish

1. Cut ends of bread flat. Insert the *medium slicing disk.* Insert bread from underneath food

chute, placing it against the side of the chute opposite the direction of the oncoming disk (see page 12, lower right illustration). Slice each length with a firm push; set bread aside.

2. Score cucumber lengthwise and cut into even lengths to fit upright in food chute. If desired, change to *thin slicing disk.* Insert cucumber from underneath food chute and slice with a moderate push. Repeat as necessary (if thin slicer is used, it may not be necessary to slice the entire cucumber). Carefully remove cucumber slices and place in ½-inch (1½-cm)-high stacks. Remove seeds from center with a small round cookie cutter or by cutting around the seeds with the tip of a sharp knife. Set cucumber slices aside; discard seeds.

3. Change to the *metal knife blade.* Wipe container dry. Process hard-boiled eggs with salt, pepper, mustard, and Tabasco with 4 one-second pulses until egg is chopped fine and seasonings are combined. Remove to a bowl. Prepare Herb Butter (page 113).

4. To assemble canapés, butter each bread slice generously with Herb Butter. Sprinkle each lightly with salt and pepper. Place a cucumber round on the bread slice over butter. Place a level ½ teaspoon firmly packed chopped egg mixture in the center of each seeded cucumber round. Garnish top of egg with a small strip of pimiento.

5. Place canapés on platters or baking sheet. Carefully cover with plastic and refrigerate several hours or until ready to serve.

SPINACH AND CHEESE BOREKS
Makes 2 to 2½ dozen

These delicious little envelopes of crisp, flaky phyllo dough enclose a classic spinach and white cheese mixture common to at least two cuisines—Italian and Greek. However, such filled pastries are found throughout the Mediterranean world, whether shaped into flat rectangles, cylinders (like rolled-up rugs), or triangles. *Borek* is the Turkish name; in Morocco these are called *braewats,* in Tunisia *briks,* and in Greece *tiropetes.*

Borek Filling:

1 tablespoon (15 g) butter
½ lb. (225 g) fresh spinach, stemmed, rinsed, drained
1 oz. (30 g) Parmesan cheese, cut into cubes
¼ cup (½ dL) firmly packed parsley leaves
1 medium garlic clove, peeled
1 medium onion, peeled, cut into 1-inch cubes
2 tablespoons olive or vegetable oil
½ lb. (225 g) ricotta cheese, kneaded lightly in a towel to remove excess moisture
1 egg
Salt and pepper to taste

Borek Wrappers:

1 lb. (450 g) fresh or thawed frozen phyllo pastry
1 to 1½ cups (¼ to 3½ dL) vegetable oil
Egg Glaze, page 5

1. To prepare borek filling, heat the butter in a large skillet. Add spinach leaves with water that clings. Stir well to coat spinach with butter. Cover and cook over medium heat until wilted, stirring from time to time. Let spinach cool. Squeeze tightly in a cloth towel to remove all excess liquid; set spinach aside.

2. Insert the *metal knife blade.* With machine running, drop Parmesan cheese through food chute. Process until powdery; remove to waxed paper. Process parsley until finely minced. Add spinach to container and chop with 4 or 5 half-second pulses. Set spinach mixture aside with Parmesan cheese. With machine running, drop garlic clove through food chute. Add onion to container and chop with 4 to 6 half-second pulses. Remove onion mixture to a small skillet; add oil and cook until soft but not brown; set aside to cool.

3. Place ricotta cheese, egg, salt, and pepper in processor container. Process 10 seconds; scrape down container sides. Return spinach, Parmesan cheese, and onion mixture to container. Process to mix with 5 or 6 half-second pulses. Taste and adjust seasonings. Refrigerate until ready to use.

4. To assemble boreks, unwrap phyllo pastry. If slightly dry and crumbly, place between 2 barely damp towels and keep covered while working. If moist and pliable (when dough is fresh), place between 2 dry towels. Cut 1 sheet of phyllo in half lengthwise; return other half to towels. Brush remaining half with oil. Fold in half lengthwise. Brush again with oil. Place 2 teaspoons borek filling near one short end of the dough strip. Brush 1 long edge and the short edge opposite the filling with Egg Glaze.

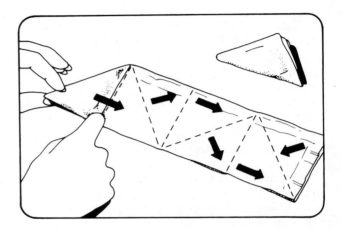

Fold top end of strip over filling, enclosing it and forming a triangle, just as a flag is folded. Fold the triangle down, over itself, and continue folding, maintaining the triangle shape. Press the short glazed end onto the triangle to seal. Set aside on a baking sheet lined with waxed paper to prevent sticking. Repeat to use all filling and phyllo. Cover tightly with plastic and refrigerate until ready to bake. Boreks may also be frozen at this point; defrost in refrigerator.

5. Adjust one oven rack to top third and one to bottom third of oven. Heat oven to 400° F (205° C). Brush baking sheets lightly with oil. Brush triangles with oil. Place boreks directly on baking sheets and bake, 2 sheets at a time, until boreks are puffed, brown, and crisp, about 15 to 18 minutes. Serve immediately or keep warm in a 250° F (120° C) oven up to 2 hours.

SALMON TARTARE WITH SCALLOPS
Makes 8 to 10 appetizer servings

The term *tartar* has such a ferocious connotation that the spirit of this appetizer is betrayed by its name. Actually, it is rather mild and more closely related to *ceviche,* the Peruvian marinated fish preparation, than to a true tartare.

Insist on impeccably fresh fish for this dish; I buy mine at a special market catering to a Japanese trade that demands top quality fish for *sashimi*.

¼ **lb. (115 g) small bay scallops or sea scallops, cut into small pieces**
2 **tablespoons fresh lemon juice**
1½ **lbs. (675 g) skinned fresh salmon or striped sea bass fillets**
¼ **cup (½ dL) firmly packed parsley leaves**
6 **medium shallots, peeled**
2 **flat anchovies, rinsed, patted dry**
2 **teaspoons Dijon mustard**
¼ **cup (½ dL) olive oil**
Freshly ground black pepper
Dash cayenne pepper
½ **teaspoon salt**
2 **tablespoons capers, drained, rinsed, patted dry**
Leaf lettuce
Lemon wedges
Melba Toast, page 124

1. Rinse scallops with cold running water. Drain and pat dry on paper toweling. Place scallops in small shallow glass bowl; sprinkle with lemon juice. Refrigerate covered, turning frequently, until scallops are opaque, about 3 hours.

2. Rinse fish fillets with cold running water. Drain and pat dry on paper toweling. Cut into 1-inch cubes; cover and refrigerate until ready to mince. Insert *metal knife blade*. Process parsley until finely minced; set aside. With machine running, drop shallots one at a time through food chute. Process until minced; scrape down sides of container. Add anchovies, mustard, oil, pepper, cayenne pepper, salt, and 1 tablespoon of the lemon juice from scallops. Process 20 seconds; set aside.

3. Process half the fish at a time with 3 one-second pulses; remove to waxed paper. Repeat and return all chopped fish to container. Add parsley, capers, and shallot mixture; process to thoroughly mix with 5 or 6 one-second pulses.

4. Remove mixture to a bowl. Drain scallops and pat dry; mix thoroughly into the chopped fish. Cover tightly with plastic wrap touching the top of the mixture and refrigerate at least 1 hour but no more than 6 hours before serving. To serve, line a platter with lettuce leaves and

spoon fish tartare on top. Accompany with lemon wedges and Melba Toast.

STEAK TARTARE
Makes 8 to 10 appetizer servings

For perfect results, select the finest quality lean beef, trim it with care, and time the on/off turns or pulses accurately.

¼ **cup (½ dL) firmly packed parsley leaves**
4 **medium shallots, peeled, or ½ medium onion, peeled, cut into 1-inch cubes**
1½ **flat anchovy fillets, rinsed, patted dry**
½ **teaspoon salt, or more to taste**
Freshly ground pepper to taste
2 **tablespoons Dijon mustard**
1 **large egg**
1 **tablespoon olive or safflower oil**
1½ **lbs. (675 g) boneless beef round or sirloin, all traces of fat, gristle, and tendon removed, cut into 1-inch cubes, well chilled**
Leaf lettuce
2 **tablespoons capers, drained, rinsed, patted dry**
Melba Toast, page 124, or toast points

1. Insert the *metal knife blade*. Process parsley until finely minced; remove to a bowl. With machine running, drop shallots and anchovy fillets through food chute. Process until minced; scrape down sides of container. Add salt, pepper, mustard, egg, and oil to container. Process to mix 5 seconds; add to bowl with parsley; stir well.

2. Wipe container and blade with paper toweling. Add half the meat and process to grind with 3 two-second pulses. Transfer half the seasoning mixture from bowl to container. Process to combine and grind meat to medium (hamburger) consistency with 1 or 2 two-second pulses. Remove to waxed paper.

3. Repeat Step 2 with remaining meat and seasoning mixture. Place all seasoned meat in bowl. Taste and adjust seasoning. Mix several times with hands or spoon to evenly distribute flavors. Cover with plastic touching top; refrigerate at least 30 minutes but no longer than 4 hours.

4. To serve, mound mixture on lettuce-lined serving platter. With back of a spoon, make a small well or indentation in top of meat. Fill with capers. Serve immediately with Melba Toast.

CAROLINES
Makes about 4 dozen

Think of these as savory miniature puffs filled to the brim with swirls of piquant filling. They bring raves from my guests, which is why I invest the considerable time it takes for their manufacture. Note that a pastry bag and shell border tip are required.

Our testing showed that it takes 2 seconds for *chou* paste to absorb 1 egg and that dough is fully beaten 30 seconds after the last egg has been added—follow Step 2 carefully.

Chou Pastry:

6 tablespoons (85 g) chilled butter
1 cup (¼ L) cold water
1 cup (150 g) unbleached all-purpose flour
Pinch salt
4 eggs
Egg Glaze, page 5

Salmon Filling:

¼ medium onion, peeled, cut into 1-inch cubes, or 2 medium shallots, peeled
1 tablespoon fresh lemon juice
Freshly ground pepper to taste
¼ lb. (115 g) sliced smoked salmon
¾ lb. (340 g) cream cheese, room temperature, cut into 1-inch cubes
1 tablespoon plain yogurt or sour cream
Dash each: Worcestershire and Tabasco sauces

1. To prepare the chou puffs, insert the *medium slicing disk.* Slice the butter with a moderate push; transfer to a large saucepan. Add water to saucepan; heat to boiling. Remove from heat and add flour and salt all at once. Return saucepan to medium heat, stirring until mixture forms a ball. Cook over medium heat, working and flattening dough with a wooden spoon or spatula, until dough tightens slightly and makes a light film on the bottom of the pan, about 4 minutes.

2. Change to the *metal knife blade.* Transfer hot dough to container. Break eggs into a glass measuring cup. With machine running, pour 1 egg through food chute every 2 seconds. After eggs are added, process 15 seconds and scrape down sides of container. Process 15 seconds longer to knead thoroughly. Dough will be thick, gluey, and sticky.

3. Cut parchment paper or brown paper bag to fit 2 baking sheets. Insert a #5 plain tip into a pastry bag or have on hand 2 teaspoons and a glass of cold water in which they may be dipped. Secure paper to baking sheet with a dab of chou dough at each corner to prevent paper from sliding. Pipe or drop 1-inch (2½-cm) mounds of dough at least 1½ inches (4 cm) apart on the paper liners. With a wet index finger, press each mound gently, making a rounded shape like a miniature bun. Brush each with Egg Glaze.

4. Meanwhile, heat oven to 425° F (220° C). Bake 1 baking sheet at a time in the middle of the oven for 17 to 20 minutes. Remove from oven and pierce each puff with the tine of a kitchen fork or with a small sharp knife. Set aside until all puffs are baked; then return them to turned-off oven and let stand 10 minutes with oven door ajar. Remove puffs from paper and cool to room temperature. Fill immediately, or close in a plastic bag and set aside overnight at room temperature, or double-wrap and freeze puffs.

5. To prepare filling, insert the *metal knife blade.* With machine running, drop onion through food chute; process until minced. Add lemon juice and pepper. Pat salmon dry in paper toweling and add to container. Process 15 seconds; scrape down sides of container. Add cream cheese, yogurt, Worcestershire, and Tabasco. Process until completely smooth, about 1 to 2 minutes, scraping down sides of container as necessary.

6. To assemble Carolines, fit a pastry bag with a #32 or #99 shell border tip. Fill bag half-full with salmon mixture; set aside. Make a little hinged top for each pastry puff by cutting the top third of each puff nearly all the way through. Carefully place the tip of the pastry bag into the puff. Squeeze in enough filling so that it shows a swirled pattern and supports the top of the puff. Place puffs on platters or

baking sheets. Cover with plastic wrap and refrigerate no longer than 6 to 8 hours. Serve cold.

Filling Variations:

Port-Wine Cheddar Filling

Substitute 6 oz. (180 g) Port wine cheddar cheese, at room temperature, for the salmon.

Watercress Filling

Reduce onion or shallot to one cube or use 1 medium shallot. Substitute 1 bunch (4 oz./ 115 g) of watercress for the salmon. Remove watercress stems before processing; add salt to taste.

COLD SCALLOP TERRINE

Makes 10 to 12 appetizer servings

This is a deceptively easy-to-make terrine with a wondrous silky texture, a beautiful layering of colors and a haunting fresh scallop flavor. The technique of tinting the scallops with twin infusions of saffron and tomato creams comes from a two-star French chef. The painterly slices may be served with a small amount of Cold Tomato Sauce (page 112) or with a more traditional green mayonnaise. Either way the terrine is a knockout.

3 cups (¾ L) chilled whipping cream
⅛ teaspoon powdered saffron
3 tablespoons tomato paste, see page 7
¼ cup (½ dL) firmly packed parsley leaves or
**   1½ tablespoons fresh snipped chives**
1 to 1¼ teaspoons dried tarragon leaves or 1
**   teaspoon fresh minced tarragon**
¾ lb. (340 g) sea or bay scallops, rinsed, patted
**   dry, thoroughly chilled**
1 egg
1 teaspoon salt, or more to taste
Freshly ground white pepper
Dash nutmeg
2 dashes Tabasco sauce
Butter

1. Place ½ cup (1 dL) cream with saffron in a small saucepan. Stir over low heat until saffron dissolves; place in a cup; cover and refrigerate until chilled. Place ½ cup (1 dL) cream with tomato paste in same saucepan. Stir over low heat until tomato paste dissolves evenly. Refrigerate until chilled.

2. Insert the *metal knife blade.* Process parsley with dried tarragon leaves until finely minced; remove to waxed paper. Wipe out container and dry blade with paper toweling. Return container and blade to processor base. Place scallops in container; process until minced, about 30 seconds; scrape down container sides. Add egg, salt, pepper, nutmeg, and Tabasco. Process until smooth, about 1 minute scraping sides and bottom edge of container as necessary. With machine running, pour 1 cup (¼ L) cream through food chute within 40 seconds; scrape down sides and bottom edge of container. Adjust seasonings to taste slightly salty and peppery or terrine will be bland when served. Process until scallop cream is completely smooth and no streaks remain, 40 to 60 seconds; scrape down container sides often.

3. Remove half the contents of container to a bowl; cover and refrigerate. With machine running, pour the remaining 1 cup (¼ L) cream through food chute within 40 seconds. Correct seasonings and put container, with contents and blade in place, in refrigerator.

4. Adjust oven rack to middle position. Heat oven to 350° F (175° C). Generously butter a 6-cup (1½-L) enameled cast-iron terrine. Cut parchment paper to fit over top of terrine; butter parchment generously; set aside.

5. Spoon half the refrigerated contents of the processor container into the terrine. Tap on counter to remove air bubbles and smooth top with the back of a spoon. Return processor container and blade to base. Add parsley mixture to scallops remaining in the container. Process to mix, about 10 seconds, scraping down sides of container as necessary. Spoon herbed scallop mixture over plain layer in terrine, cleaning out container well with a spatula; smooth herbed mixture with back of spoon.

6. Without washing container, place half the reserved, refrigerated scallop mixture in the container. With machine running, pour the saffron cream through the food chute within 20 seconds; scrape down container sides and process until thoroughly mixed, about 10 seconds longer. Spoon saffron mixture over herbed layer in terrine; smooth with spoon.

7. Repeat Step 6, using remaining scallop mixture and the tomato cream. Spoon into terrine on top of saffron layer. Cover with parchment paper but do not cover terrine.

8. Place terrine in a pan of hot but not boiling water that comes one-half to two-thirds up the outside of the terrine. Bake until puffed and a sharp knife carefully inserted into the center is withdrawn clean, about 1¼ hours. Remove terrine carefully from water. Place on cake rack and cool to room temperature. Scallop mixture will settle as it cools. Carefully remove and discard parchment paper. Cover with plastic wrap and refrigerate overnight but no longer than 3 days before slicing.

CHICKEN LIVER PATE
Makes 8 to 10 servings

A truly voluptuous parsley-flecked pâté with a heady rich taste that demands French bread and a good bottle of wine.

⅓ **cup (¾ dL) firmly packed parsley leaves**
8 **medium shallots, peeled (2 oz./60 g), or 1 medium onion, peeled, cut into 1-inch cubes**
½ **medium onion, peeled, cut into 1-inch cubes**
¼ **lb. (115 g) butter, slightly softened**
1½ **lbs. (675 g) chicken livers, rinsed, trimmed, well drained**
3 **tablespoons cognac or brandy**
Béchamel Sauce, page 112, made with 1 cup (¼ L) whipping cream
¾ **teaspoon salt, or more to taste**
Freshly ground pepper to taste
Dash nutmeg
½ **teaspoon dried marjoram leaves**
½ **teaspoon dried rubbed sage**
Melba Toast, page 124, or French Bread, page 119

1. Insert the *metal knife blade.* Process parsley until finely minced; set aside. With machine running, drop shallots one at a time through food chute. Scrape down sides of container; add onion and chop with 6 to 8 half-second pulses. Transfer onion mixture to a large skillet with 3 tablespoons of the butter. Cook over medium heat until soft but not brown; transfer to a plate and refrigerate. Return blade to processor container.

2. Pat chicken livers dry. Heat 3 tablespoons butter in same skillet until hot and bubbling. Add chicken livers and sauté over high heat until firm, about 4 minutes. Remove skillet from heat. Warm cognac and ignite; pour over chicken livers. Shake skillet until flames subside. Remove livers from skillet with a slotted spoon. Place in a strainer set over a bowl. Reserve pan juices. Discard juices that accumulate in bowl.

3. Prepare Béchamel Sauce, substituting whipping cream for milk. Place sauce in container fitted with *metal knife blade.* Add salt, pepper, nutmeg, and remaining 2 tablespoons butter. Process 30 seconds. Add half the livers, the reserved onion mixture, and the pan juices. Process 45 seconds, stopping several times to scrape down container sides. Add remaining livers, reserved parsley, marjoram, and sage. Process 1 minute longer or until smooth, scraping down sides of container as necessary.

4. Adjust seasonings to taste slightly salty and peppery or pâté will be bland when served. Spoon into a 4- to 5-cup (1- to 1¼-L) covered terrine or dish. Tap dish on work surface to remove air bubbles. Smooth top; cool to room temperature. Cover with plastic wrap touching top of pâté; add lid and refrigerate overnight or as long as 3 days before serving. Spread on Melba Toast or French Bread.

COUNTRY TERRINE
Makes 10 to 12 servings

Not so many years ago, such a coarse-textured country terrine or pâté was beyond the reach of all but the most skilled and diligent cook because the preparation was so demanding. The food processor has changed all that, and with its assist, professional quality pâtés are accessible to everyone. Concentrate on timing when processing each batch of the meat mixture so the texture remains uniform. Pay careful attention to seasoning so the flavor will be just right when the terrine is chilled.

½ **cup (1 dL) firmly packed parsley leaves**
¾ **lb. (340 g) boneless veal shoulder, well trimmed, cut into 1-inch cubes**
¾ **lb. (340 g) boneless pork shoulder, well trimmed, cut into 1-inch cubes**

½ lb. (225 g) fresh pork fat, cut in ½-inch dice
2 teaspoons salt
⅛ teaspoon freshly ground black pepper
1 teaspoon Mixed Herbs, page 6
½ teaspoon ground mace
Dash nutmeg
Pinch ground cloves
2 medium garlic cloves, peeled
2 medium onions, peeled, cut into 1-inch cubes
3 tablespoons (45 g) butter
¼ lb. (115 g) chicken livers, rinsed, well trimmed
1 chunk (6 oz./180 g) boiled ham, chilled, cut to fit food chute
2 eggs
¼ cup (½ dL) cognac or brandy
3 tablespoons dry bread crumbs
½ cup (75 g) shelled and blanched natural pistachios (optional)
1 bay leaf
Parsley or watercress, for garnish
Cornichons (sour gherkins), for garnish
French Bread, page 119
Unsalted butter

1. Insert *metal knife blade.* Process parsley until finely minced; remove to a large bowl. Mix veal, pork, and fat cubes together and place on 1 large sheet of waxed paper in single layer. Sprinkle salt, pepper, herbs, mace, nutmeg, and cloves evenly over meat. Add one-third of the meat to processor container and grind with 5 or 6 two-second pulses to just finer-than-hamburger consistency. Transfer ground meat to bowl with parsley. Repeat, adding to bowl any seasoning left on the paper.

2. Turn on the empty machine and drop garlic through food chute. Scrape down container sides and add onion. Process to chop with 6 to 8 half-second pulses. Place onion mixture with 2 tablespoons butter in a medium skillet. Cook over medium heat until soft but not brown. Remove to a plate and refrigerate. Melt remaining butter in skillet. Add chicken livers and toss over high heat until firm, about 3 to 4 minutes. Transfer livers to strainer set over bowl and place in refrigerator. Discard pan juices and juices that accumulate in bowl.

3. Fit processor container with *french-fry disk.* Cut ham with a moderate push or fine dice by hand. Add ham to mixture in bowl. Fill food chute with chicken livers. Coarsely cut with a very gentle push or finely dice by hand. Add livers to bowl. Add chilled onion mixture, eggs, cognac, bread crumbs, and pistachios to bowl. With clean hands, mix lightly but thoroughly and take care not to overwork meat mixture or terrine will be tough.

4. Cook 1 to 2 tablespoons meat mixture in a small skillet until juices run clear when meat is pierced. Taste. Adjust seasonings as necessary so mixture tastes slightly oversalted and over-spiced (otherwise terrine will be bland when served cold). If desired, cover tightly and refrigerate overnight.

5. Adjust oven rack to middle position. Heat oven to 350° F (175° C). Spoon meat mixture into a 4- to 5-cup (1- to 1¼-L) enameled cast-iron terrine, mounding meat slightly. Place bay leaf on meat. Cover tightly with aluminum foil. Place terrine in a pan of hot but not boiling water that comes one-half to two-thirds up the outside of terrine (do not allow terrine to float). Bake 1½ hours. Remove foil and bake 30 minutes longer.

6. Remove pan from oven but leave terrine in hot water. Cut a piece of cardboard that just fits to top edges of terrine. Cover with foil and place on top of meat. Press firmly. Hold in place with 5 pounds of canned goods placed on cardboard. Let stand 45 minutes and remove weights. Lift terrine out of water. Cool on a cake rack to room temperature. Cover with foil and refrigerate at least 2 but preferably 4 days.

7. To serve, cut a ½-inch (1½-cm)-thick slice at 1 end and remove slice with pancake turner (it may break). Lift off bay leaf and any congealed fat and discard. Slice and serve directly from terrine. If desired, top may be sprinkled with chopped parsley or slices may be served with parsley sprigs, cornichons, French bread, and butter. Be sure terrine is thoroughly chilled before slicing to keep slices from crumbling.

HOT VEGETABLE TERRINE
Makes 6 to 8 servings

This terrine is a spectacularly elegant first course for an important dinner. The texture is gossamer and the three fresh vegetable purées, bound lightly with hollandaise (a technical *tour de force* by the processor), harbor wonderful flavors. The delicate taste of the terrine is matched only by the beauty of eating a vegetable rainbow. Leftovers are delicious or the terrine may be served cold.

1½ lbs. (675 g) fresh spinach, washed, stems removed, drained
½ lb. (225 g) fresh cauliflower, core and leaves removed
½ lb. (225 g) carrots, peeled, cut into 1-inch chunks
4 tablespoons (60 g) softened unsalted butter
3 eggs
3 egg yolks
3 teaspoons fresh lemon juice
Salt and freshly ground white pepper to taste
Several dashes each: nutmeg and Tabasco sauce
½ cup (115 g) hot melted unsalted butter
¼ teaspoon sugar
3 tablespoons whipping cream
Beurre Blanc, page 108 (double recipe)

1. Place spinach leaves in a medium skillet with water that clings. Cover and cook over medium heat, stirring frequently, until spinach wilts; set aside to cool.

2. Place a vegetable steamer basket in a large saucepan. Add enough water to barely touch bottom of steamer basket. Place cauliflower and carrots in basket. Cover and steam until carrots are very tender when pierced with a knife, 15 to 20 minutes. Transfer hot vegetables to a cloth towel; set aside to cool. If desired, cover and refrigerate all vegetables overnight.

3. Cut a sheet of parchment paper large enough to line the bottom and long sides of a 4- to 5-cup (1- to 1¼-L) enameled cast-iron terrine and to extend 1 inch (2½ cm) above the top edges. Heavily butter ends and along the top edges of the terrine. Butter parchment paper and place it in the terrine, buttered side up. Smooth to remove any creases; refrigerate. Adjust oven rack to lower position. Heat oven to 350°F (175°C).

4. To prepare vegetables, work as indicated below. Return container and blade to processor base each time without washing (clean well with spatula) and do not wash skillet (clean

with spatula). Insert the *metal knife blade*. Purée cauliflower 40 seconds. Place in a medium skillet with 1 tablespoon softened butter. Stir over medium heat to remove all excess moisture, about 4 minutes.

5. Place 1 egg, 1 egg yolk, 1 teaspoon lemon juice, a scant ½ teaspoon salt, white pepper, and 1 dash each nutmeg and Tabasco in empty processor container. With machine running, pour 2½ tablespoons hot melted butter through food chute. Process 5 seconds. Add cauliflower purée to container and purée until smooth, about 30 seconds, scraping down container sides as necessary. Adjust seasonings to taste. Spoon cauliflower purée into terrine; gently smooth to make an even layer; set aside.

6. Purée carrots 40 to 50 seconds and transfer to skillet. Add 1 tablespoon softened butter and sugar. Stir over medium heat to remove excess moisture, about 4 minutes. Repeat Step 5, substituting carrot for cauliflower.

7. Squeeze spinach dry with hands. Place in a cloth towel and wring as dry as possible. Unless spinach still feels very wet, do not dry out in skillet. Repeat Step 5, adding whipping cream to container before butter is added and substituting spinach for cauliflower. Smooth top of spinach in terrine and cover with a sheet of buttered parchment paper cut slightly larger than the terrine opening; do not bend down edges or ends. If desired, the terrine may be refrigerated several hours. Before baking, let terrine warm to room temperature.

8. Place terrine in a pan and add enough hot tap water to come one-third to one-half up the outside of the terrine. Carefully place pan in oven. Bake until vegetables are firm in center and have risen slightly, about 1 hour. Turn off oven; open door and pull out rack partway. Remove parchment from top. Let stand 10 minutes. Remove terrine from water bath and set it aside 5 minutes before unmolding.

9. To unmold, place a serving platter or foil-lined board over terrine. Gently invert. Remove parchment paper. Spoon hot Beurre Blanc sauce in center of heated serving plates. Cut terrine into ¾- to 1-inch (2- to 2½-cm)-thick slices and transfer to serving plate with pancake turner. Place each slice over sauce. Serve immediately. Leftovers may be served cold.

7

Soups

Soup is universal, a dish found in every cuisine. A cornmeal soup called *puls* nourished the Roman legions. Rich savory consommé graced noble tables in the courts of kings; hearty soups composed of foraged scraps sustained American pioneers over their long journeys across the plains.

Today, homemade soup is enjoying a new vogue, and vegetable soups are in the limelight. Borrowing techniques from the new French cooking, vegetables are transformed by the food processor into purées with a dual role: flavoring and thickening. The results are soups which are purer in taste, lighter in body, and lower in calories than ever before.

The role of the processor in soup making is not restricted to puréeing, however. Chopping and slicing take place in a flash; green beans are frenched at record speed, and with patience and careful arrangement of slices, julienne or square matchstick strips can be cut in seconds.

Great soup begins with a rich broth made from poultry, meat, or fish bones and no self-respecting cook should ever be without a supply in the freezer. Since chicken and beef broths simmer all day, I frequently begin a pot on Saturday morning and leave it to cool uncovered overnight. The next day I decant the amount I need and freeze the remainder for other uses. Fish stock, which cooks in less than an hour, is hardly any trouble at all.

Here are some general guidelines for making soups in this chapter:

- Simmer soup over low heat but do not allow it to reach a rapid boil.

- Cook soup in a kettle or Dutch oven of the correct size to guarantee the number of servings specified in the recipes. Too large a pot may yield less soup; too small a pot can slow the cooking. A good quality stockpot with a capacity of 12 or more quarts (12 L) is essential for stock. A 6-quart (6-L) soup kettle or Dutch oven will accommodate most soups.

- Add salt and freshly ground pepper to soup during the last few minutes of cooking.

- Soup made with canned broth requires far less salt than those made with homemade broth.

- Taste soup just before serving to make last-minute adjustments in seasoning. Never serve soup (or anything else for that matter) that you have not tasted.

- Milk or half-and-half may be substituted for cream; however, the flavor and texture will be less intense.

- To substitute green onions (scallions) for leeks, use 4 whole green onions to equal 1 small leek, 6 to equal a medium leek, and 8 to equal a large leek.

- Uncover soup before cooling to prevent spoilage. Refrigerate or freeze only after it has come to room temperature.

- If a soup is prepared in advance, omit delicate vegetables, such as green beans and peas, or seafood, such as clams or shrimp, from it until the last moment because these foods will toughen when overcooked.

- Shorten chilling time of uncooked soups, such as Gazpacho, by beginning with chilled vegetables.

All cooked soups and stocks may be frozen. If either is leftover longer than 2 days, however, first simmer slowly for 5 minutes, then cool and refrigerate until cold before freezing. Be sure freezer containers have at least 2 inches (5 cm) of headroom into which soup may expand when frozen.

Defrost frozen soup in the refrigerator, uncovered at room temperature, or slowly in the microwave. Defrosted puréed vegetable soups often separate. To restore their texture, fit the processor container with the *metal knife blade* and purée 1½- to 2-cup (3½-dL to ½-L) batches for 30 seconds.

Several recipes call for attaching the funnel to the food chute and pouring hot liquid and vegetables into the machine to purée. In general, I have found this to be a safe procedure, but, from time to time, a drop of hot soup can jump up the chute, so keep your face at a distance. A 2-cup (½-L) glass measure with pouring spout will facilitate the pouring process and a fork is useful for regulating the speed at which solids are poured from the cup. Most processors will handle 2 cups of liquid without overflowing; some large-capacity models hold even more. Check the instruction manual for your machine to verify liquid capacity.

CUCUMBER SUMMERSOUP
Makes 6 servings

I consider this a "throw together" soup because absolutely no cooking is required and prepara-

tion time is so minimal. As such, it is perfect for lazy days in hot summer kitchens.

1 medium avocado, peeled, pitted, rinsed
3 lbs. (1,350 g) cucumbers, peeled, seeded, cut into 1-inch chunks
¼ medium onion, peeled, cut into 1-inch cubes
1 cup (¼ L) Chicken Broth, page 40
½ teaspoon salt
2 tablespoons fresh lemon juice
¾ cup (1¾ dL) plain yogurt
Freshly ground white pepper to taste
Plain yogurt, for garnish

1. Insert the *metal knife blade* in the processor container. Place avocado, 1 cup (¼ L) cucumber pieces, and onion in container. Purée 45 seconds; then with machine running, pour half the chicken broth through the food chute within 10 seconds. Stop and scrape down sides of container. Purée 1 minute longer or until smooth; remove to a large bowl.

2. Place 1½ cups (3½ dL) cucumber pieces in container and purée 15 seconds. With machine running, pour remaining chicken broth through food chute within 10 seconds. Stop and scrape down container sides. Purée until smooth and add to bowl.

3. Place remaining cucumber in container and purée 15 seconds. Add salt, lemon juice, yogurt, and pepper. Purée 1 minute or until smooth, stopping to scrape down container sides as necessary. Add contents of container to bowl; stir well and adjust seasonings to taste. Refrigerate until thoroughly cold, about 1 hour. Taste to be sure seasonings are correct before serving. If desired, garnish with additional yogurt.

TOMATO GAZPACHO
Makes 4 to 6 servings

Red gazpacho is a cultural hybrid that melds a fruit of the Americas—the tomato—with an Arabic name meaning "soaked bread" and the Spanish predilection for garlic and onions.

¼ cup (½ dL) firmly packed parsley leaves
2 medium garlic cloves, peeled

1 medium onion, peeled, cut into 1-inch cubes
1 cup (¼ L) Brown Beef Broth, page 40
2 lbs. (900 g) ripe tomatoes, peeled, seeded, quartered
2 tablespoons red wine vinegar
3 tablespoons olive or vegetable oil
½ teaspoon chili powder, or more to taste
¼ teaspoon salt, or more to taste
¼ teaspoon paprika
⅛ teaspoon cayenne pepper

Garnishes:

1 (4 oz./115 g) cucumber, quartered lengthwise
1 (4 oz./115 g) green pepper, cored, quartered lengthwise
1 large (8 oz./225 g) tomato, core removed
1 cup (¼ L) croutons

1. To prepare the soup, insert the *metal knife blade* in the dry container. Process parsley until finely minced; transfer to a large bowl. Place garlic and onion in container. With machine running, pour broth through food chute within 40 seconds. Purée until fine, about 30 seconds longer.

2. Add half the tomatoes and purée until fine, about 30 seconds. Transfer contents of container to the bowl; return blade and container to processor base. Place remaining tomatoes, the vinegar, oil, chili powder, salt, paprika, and cayenne pepper in the container. Process until puréed, about 40 seconds; add to bowl; stir well. Chill; then adjust seasonings to taste.

3. To prepare garnishes, rinse and dry container. Insert the *medium* or *thin slicing disk.* Insert cucumber upright in food chute from underneath and slice with a gentle push; set aside. Turn lid over and firmly wedge green pepper strips upright in food chute from underneath. Slice with a gentle push; set aside separately. Change to the *french-fry disk.* Halve tomato lengthwise. Insert tomato halves from underneath food chute (so they will be cut across the grain). Cut with a gentle push and repeat until all tomatoes are roughly diced.

4. Place tomatoes, croutons, cucumber, and green pepper in separate serving bowls. Cover and refrigerate until ready to serve soup. Pass separately as garnishes.

BARBARA KAFKA'S GREEN GAZPACHO
Makes 4 to 6 servings

The classic gazpacho repertory includes condiment-studded tomato and almond flavors. Here, Barbara Kafka, the gifted cook, editor, and restaurant consultant, adds a hot and spicy green version that packs a wallop of fresh coriander flavor.

½ cup (1 dL) firmly packed parsley leaves
1½ small onions, peeled, quartered
2 jalapeño peppers, seeds and stems removed, cut into ¼-inch pieces
3 medium garlic cloves, peeled
1 teaspoon salt
1 cup (¼ L) olive oil
3 slices white bread, crusts removed
2 medium green bell peppers, peeled and cored, cut into 1-inch chunks
2 medium cucumbers, peeled, seeded, cut into 1-inch lengths
¼ cup (½ dL) firmly packed fresh coriander (*cilantro*) leaves
1½ cups (3½ dL) ice water or Chicken Broth, page 40

1. Insert the *metal knife blade* in container. Process parsley until finely minced; remove to a large bowl. Chop onions with hot peppers using 8 to 10 half-second pulses; add to bowl. With machine running, drop garlic cloves through food chute; scrape down sides of container and add salt. Process, pouring oil through the food chute in a steady stream within 30 seconds; add to bowl.

2. Tear bread into 1-inch (2½-cm) pieces and place in container; add green peppers. Process to chop with 6 one-second pulses; add to bowl.

3. Chop cucumber with coriander using 6 one-second pulses; add to bowl. Stir in ice water and adjust seasonings to taste. Chill 1 hour before serving and correct consistency to a coarse thick soup by adding water, if necessary.

JADE SOUP
Makes 4 to 6 servings

The term "jade" refers to the mottled green color this soup assumes when puréed. In addition to spinach and watercress, variations could include Swiss chard and kale soups. It is equally good hot or cold.

1 lb. (450 g) medium potatoes, peeled
3 medium celery ribs, strings removed
1 medium garlic clove, peeled
4 whole green onions, cut into 1½-inch lengths
1½ qts. (1½ L) Chicken Broth, page 40
1½ lbs. (675 g) Boston lettuce, washed, cored
½ cup (1 dL) whipping cream
¼ teaspoon salt, or more to taste
Freshly ground pepper to taste
1 teaspoon fresh lemon juice
½ teaspoon dried basil leaves or 1 teaspoon chopped fresh basil
¾ cup (1¾ dL) sour cream or plain yogurt

1. Attach the *medium* or *thin slicing disk.* Insert potatoes one at a time from underneath food chute and slice with a moderate push. Place slices in a 6-quart (6-L) soup kettle. Slice celery with a gentle push and add to soup kettle.

2. Change to the *metal knife blade.* Turn on the empty machine and drop the garlic clove through the food chute. Process until minced. Add green onions and chop with 4 to 6 one-second pulses; add contents of container to soup kettle. Return blade and container to processor base.

3. Add broth to kettle and heat to boiling. Cover and simmer 35 minutes or until vegetables are very soft. Add lettuce leaves to soup kettle; push down. Continue simmering until leaves are very soft, about 20 minutes longer.

4. Attach the funnel to food chute, if desired. Remove 2 cups (½ L) cooked vegetables and liquid from soup kettle. With machine running, slowly pour mixture through food chute. Process until smooth; set aside. Repeat until all soup is puréed. Return purée to clean kettle or saucepan. Stir in cream, salt, pepper, lemon juice, and basil. Heat thoroughly. Adjust seasonings to taste and stir well. To serve cold, refrigerate 6 hours or overnight; then correct seasoning. Before serving, garnish each bowl with 2 tablespoons sour cream or yogurt.

Variations:

Spinach Soup
Omit lettuce and basil. Substitute 2 pounds

(900 g) fresh spinach, washed and stemmed (10 cups [2½ L] firmly packed leaves), and a dash of nutmeg.

Watercress Soup
Omit lettuce, basil, and sour cream or yogurt. Substitute 3 large bunches fresh watercress (5 cups [1¼ L] lightly packed). Reserve 1 sprig for each bowl to be garnished. Add several dashes Tabasco.

CREAM OF CARROT SOUP
Makes 6 to 8 servings

Called *Purée Crècy* by the French, this soup is said to be the sole survivor of a 14th-century battle that took place near that town.

2 lbs. (900 g) fresh carrots, peeled, stemmed
1 medium garlic clove, peeled
2 medium onions, peeled, cut into 1-inch cubes
1½ qts. (1½ L) Chicken Broth, page 40
½ to ¾ teaspoon ground sage or 1 teaspoon fresh chopped sage leaves
1½ cups (3½ dL) half-and-half
½ cup (1 dL) whipping cream or half-and-half
½ teaspoon salt, or more to taste
Freshly ground pepper to taste
2 dashes Tabasco sauce

1. Cut carrots to fit upright in food chute. Insert the *medium* or *thin slicing disk.* Slice carrots with a firm push; repeat as necessary. Place carrot slices in a 4- to 6-quart (6-L) soup kettle.

2. Change to the *metal knife blade.* With the machine running, drop garlic through food chute. Process until minced. Add onions to container and chop with 4 to 6 half-second pulses. Add contents of container to soup kettle. Add broth. Heat liquid to boiling. Cover and simmer about 55 minutes, or until carrots are very soft. Return blade and container to processor base.

3. Attach the funnel to food chute, if desired. Remove 2 cups (½ L) cooked vegetables and liquid from soup kettle. With machine running, slowly pour mixture through food chute. Pro-

cess until smooth; set aside. Repeat until all soup is puréed.

4. Return purée to a clean kettle or saucepan. Stir in sage, half-and-half, cream, salt, pepper, and Tabasco. Heat thoroughly. Adjust seasonings to taste and stir well. Serve immediately. To serve cold, refrigerate; then correct seasonings.

Variation:

Cream of Cauliflower Soup
Substitute 2½ pounds (1¼ kg) fresh cauliflower for carrots. Trim cauliflower into flowerets. With the *medium slicing disk,* slice flowerets with a gentle push. Garnish with fresh minced chives, if desired.

MUSHROOM VELVET SOUP
Makes 8 servings

I include this soup in homage to the late cooking teacher Dione Lucas, whom I never knew. Her Crème Olga nourished me, and her dedication to solid culinary values remains a constant inspiration.

1½ lbs. (675 g) mushrooms, wiped clean with a damp cloth
2 medium bunches whole green onions
2 small garlic cloves, peeled
4 medium shallots, peeled, or ¼ peeled medium onion
1 qt. (1 L) Chicken Broth, page 40
1 teaspoon fresh lemon juice
½ teaspoon salt, or more to taste
4 tablespoons (60 g) butter
Pepper to taste
¾ cup (1¾ dL) whipping cream

1. Set aside 4 firm mushrooms for garnish. Insert the *medium slicing disk* in the processor container. Fill food chute with mushrooms; slice with a gentle push. Repeat until all mushrooms are sliced, emptying container into a 6-quart (6-L) soup kettle as necessary. Cut green onions into even lengths to fit upright in food chute and slice with a gentle push; add to soup kettle. Change to the *metal knife blade.* With the machine running, drop garlic cloves and shallots one at a time through food chute.

Process until minced; add to soup kettle. Return container and blade to processor base.

2. Add broth, lemon juice, salt, and butter to soup kettle. Heat to boiling. Cover and simmer 50 to 55 minutes or until vegetables are very soft.

3. Attach funnel to food chute, if desired. Remove 2 cups (½ L) cooked vegetables and liquid from soup kettle. With machine running, slowly pour mixture through food chute. Process until smooth; set aside. Repeat until all soup is puréed. Return purée to clean kettle or saucepan. Stir in pepper and cream. Heat thoroughly; adjust seasonings to taste. Halve or slice reserved mushrooms and use to garnish each serving. To serve cold, refrigerate 6 hours or overnight; correct seasonings.

Variation:

Diet Mushroom Soup
Substitute ⅔ cup (6 oz./180 g) plain yogurt and 3 tablespoons ricotta cheese or cottage cheese for cream. Do not let soup boil or yogurt and cheese will curdle.

SHRIMP BISQUE
Makes 4 servings

Simmering the shrimp shells in broth enriches and strengthens the flavor of the soup. The final spike of cognac provides an important flavor boost.

1¼ lbs. (560 g) uncooked shrimp in shells
3 cups (¾ L) Chicken or Fish Broth, pages 40 and 41
2 medium garlic cloves, peeled
6 medium shallots, peeled
2 small carrots, peeled, cut into 1-inch lengths
2 medium tomatoes, peeled, cored, seeded
2 tablespoons (30 g) butter
3 tablespoons flour
½ cup (1 dL) dry white wine
1 tablespoon cognac or brandy
1½ cups (3½ dL) whipping cream
2 dashes Tabasco sauce
Freshly ground pepper
Salt to taste

1. Peel and devein shrimp. Refrigerate meat and place shells in large saucepan. Add broth and heat to boiling. Cover and simmer slowly 20 minutes. Strain, pressing firmly to extract all broth. Discard shells and set broth aside.

2. Insert the *metal knife blade.* Process to coarsely chop half the shrimp with 4 one-second pulses; remove to plastic wrap. Repeat to chop remaining shrimp and refrigerate until shortly before serving. Without washing container, turn on machine and drop garlic, shallots, and carrot pieces one at a time through food chute. Process until minced; remove to waxed paper. Process tomatoes until puréed.

3. Melt butter in a large saucepan. Add flour and whisk over low heat until cooked but not browned, about 2 minutes. Remove saucepan from heat and slowly whisk in broth until liquid is smooth. Add chopped carrot mixture, tomato purée, and wine. Heat to boiling. Cover and simmer 55 minutes, stirring occasionally.

4. With the *metal knife blade* in place, turn on the machine. Attach funnel, if desired, and carefully pour half the hot soup through food chute within 15 to 20 seconds. Process 45 seconds longer or until smooth; empty container into a clean saucepan. Repeat to purée remaining soup. Set aside several hours, if desired, or refrigerate overnight.

5. Shortly before serving, stir in cognac, cream, Tabasco, and pepper. Add chopped shrimp to soup liquid in saucepan. Stir over low heat without allowing mixture to simmer, until shrimp is just cooked and turns white, about 8 to 10 minutes. Adjust seasonings to taste, adding salt if necessary.

NEW ENGLAND CLAM CHOWDER
Makes 8 to 10 servings

Not very long ago, a fresh clam chowder like this one was relatively commonplace. Now, due to the price of fish and shellfish, it has become a delicacy. So why not make it a meal? Just add a mixed green salad, a crusty loaf of French Bread (page 119), and some fresh fruit and cheese.

A few quick notes on clams: Littlenecks and cherrystones vary greatly in size and flavor. Adjust taste and texture by adding half-and-half as needed in Step 5. Discard clams with broken shells. Press those with open shells together; if they remain open, discard as they are probably not alive. A live clam will sputter and close up slowly on its own when pressed. See page 54 about storing fresh clams overnight.

3 dozen fresh littleneck or 12 to 18 cherrystone clams
3 cups (¾ L) cold water
1 cup (¼ L) dry white wine
3 slices bacon, preferably without preservatives
¼ cup (½ dL) firmly packed parsley leaves
2 medium onions, peeled, cut into 1-inch cubes
2 lbs. (900 g) potatoes, peeled, ends cut blunt (6 medium)
3 medium carrots, peeled, ends cut blunt
3 dashes Tabasco sauce
1 tablespoon lemon juice
1½ to 2½ cups (3½ to 6 dL) half-and-half
Salt and pepper to taste

1. Brush clams to clean; then soak about 30 minutes in a basin with enough cold lightly salted water to cover. Drain. Place clams and 3 cups (¾ L) cold water with wine in a 6-quart (6-L) soup kettle (see note). Cover and cook over medium-high heat, shaking pot once or twice until clams are wide open. Check after 8 minutes and take care to remove clams as soon as they open or they will be tough. Transfer open clams with a slotted spoon to a colander and rinse immediately with cold water. Cover and cook any unopened clams until they open. Pull clam meat free and discard shells. Line a strainer with cheesecloth to trap any sand that remains in broth. Strain and set aside 7 cups (1¾ L) clam broth or add cold water to equal 7 cups. Remaining broth may be frozen for use as fish stock.

2. Clean soup kettle. Add bacon and cook until crisp. Remove bacon, leaving drippings in kettle. Pat bacon dry; cool. Insert the *metal knife blade.* Process parsley until finely minced; set aside. Process bacon 5 seconds; set aside. Chop onions with 6 to 8 half-second pulses; add to bacon drippings in kettle. Process clams

in 2 portions until coarsely chopped with 6 one-second pulses. Cover and refrigerate chopped clams.

3. Cook onions in soup kettle over low heat until soft but not brown. Add clam broth and heat to simmering. Meanwhile, insert the *medium slicing disk*. Slice half the potatoes with a moderate push, inserting each from underneath food chute; add to soup kettle. Halve 3 remaining potatoes lengthwise. Slice and set aside in a bowl of cold water. Cut carrots in even lengths to fit upright in food chute. Slice with a firm push; set aside.

4. Simmer liquid in kettle until potatoes are completely tender, about 40 minutes. Remove onions and potatoes from soup with a slotted spoon. Replace *metal knife blade*. Place 1 to 1½ cups (3½ dL) potatoes and onions in container and purée until smooth, about 30 seconds. Repeat, returning purée to soup kettle. Stir in carrots. Drain raw potatoes well and stir into kettle.

5. Cover and simmer until potato slices are soft, about 30 minutes. Stir in parsley, Tabasco, lemon juice, and half-and-half as needed to make a medium-thick soup. Add bacon and chopped clams. Heat thoroughly, stirring constantly, but do not simmer or clams will toughen. Adjust seasonings to taste before serving.

Note: If clams are very large, open them in 2 or 3 batches rather than 1.

CUBAN BLACK BEAN SOUP
Makes 8 servings

This hearty and economical one-dish meal requires the potency of salt pork, an ingredient found at good butcher shops or stores specializing in Mexican products. Unfortunately bacon does not work well as a substitute here.

12 oz. (340 g) dried black turtle beans, rinsed
3 qts. (3 L) cold water
1 medium green pepper, cored, seeded
¼ lb. (115 g) salt pork, rinsed, rind removed, cut into ½-inch cubes
5 medium garlic cloves, peeled
3 medium onions, peeled, cut into 1-inch cubes
1½ teaspoons ground cumin
1½ teaspoons oregano
¾ teaspoon salt, or more to taste
Freshly ground pepper to taste
2 tablespoons white wine vinegar

1. Place beans in a large bowl. Add 1 quart (1 L) water; cover and soak overnight.

2. Cut green pepper ends blunt and cut lengthwise into 1-inch (2½-cm) strips. Insert *medium slicing disk*. Turn lid over and pull pusher back. Wedge green pepper strips upright in food chute from underneath. Slice with a gentle push; set aside. Change to the *metal knife blade*. Grind salt pork with 5 two-second pulses; set aside. With machine running, drop garlic cloves one at a time through food chute; process until minced. Add 2 onions and chop with 6 to 8 half-second pulses; set aside.

3. Cook salt pork in 6-quart (6-L) soup kettle until crisp and brown. Add onion mixture and cook over medium heat until onions are lightly colored. Add green pepper slivers. Stir until peppers are wilted. Stir in cumin and oregano.

4. Drain, rinse, and add beans to soup kettle. Add 8 cups (2 L) cold water. Heat to boiling. Cover and simmer 4 to 5 hours, stirring occasionally, until beans are completely soft when pressed with a spoon.

5. Using the *metal knife blade,* chop remaining onion with 4 to 6 half-second pulses; set aside for garnish. Remove 4 cups (1 L) vegetables and liquid from kettle. Purée 2 cups (½ L) vegetables and liquid until smooth; repeat. Return purée to soup kettle and stir in salt, pepper, and vinegar. Heat thoroughly and adjust seasonings to taste. Garnish each serving with 1 tablespoon reserved chopped onion.

FRENCH ONION SOUP
Makes 6 servings

The anemic liquid posing as onion soup in so many restaurants these days has nothing whatever to do with the rich, steeped-in flavors of the real thing, which can be brewed so easily at home.

¼ lb. (115 g) chunk Gruyère or Swiss cheese, rind removed, chilled
2 oz. (60 g) Parmesan cheese, cut into 1-inch chunks
6 medium garlic cloves, peeled
3 lbs. (1,350 g) yellow onions, peeled, halved lengthwise
¼ lb. (115 g) butter
2 tablespoons olive or vegetable oil
2 tablespoons flour
1 tablespoon Dijon mustard
1 cup (¼ L) dry white wine or vermouth
2 qts. (2 L) Brown Beef Broth, page 40
6 slices (1-inch-thick) dry French or Italian bread
2 tablespoons brandy or cognac
Salt and pepper to taste

1. Insert the *medium shredding disk.* Shred Gruyère with a gentle push; set aside for garnish. Change to the *metal knife blade.* With machine running, drop Parmesan cheese through food chute. Process until powdery; set aside. With machine running, drop garlic cloves through food chute. Process until minced. Measure 1 tablespoon garlic and place in a large skillet; reserve remainder.

2. Change to the *medium slicing disk.* Slice all onions with a gentle push, emptying container into skillet as necessary. Add 4 tablespoons butter and oil to skillet and stir over high heat for several minutes to melt the butter and start the onions cooking. Then turn heat to medium and saute onions, stirring frequently, until golden brown. Sprinkle flour over the onions and stir until flour browns. Stir in mustard. Remove skillet from heat. Immediately add white wine and scrape browned flour off skillet bottom with a wooden spatula or spoon. Return skillet to high heat and cook until wine evaporates, stirring frequently.

3. Transfer onions and any pan juices to a 6-quart (6-L) soup kettle. Add broth. Heat liquid to a rapid simmer. Set cover slightly ajar and adjust flame to slowly simmer soup 2 to 2½ hours, stirring occasionally. Set soup aside several hours or cool to room temperature and refrigerate as long as 3 days.

4. Heat oven to 350° F (175° C). In a small

saucepan cook remaining minced garlic with remaining 4 tablespoons butter over low heat for 3 minutes. Remove from heat and dip both sides of each bread slice in garlic butter. Transfer bread to a baking sheet and bake 10 minutes. Turn and bake 10 minutes longer. Keep bread warm.

5. Heat soup thoroughly to boiling. Stir in brandy. Adjust seasonings to taste. Spoon soup into oven-proof bowls. Add a heaping tablespoon of grated Parmesan cheese to each bowl and stir. Place a toasted slice of bread in each bowl and top bread slices with 2 heaping tablespoons Gruyère. Place bowls on a baking sheet and brown cheese under broiler close to heat source until bubbling, 4 to 6 minutes. Serve immediately.

SCOTCH BROTH
Makes 8 to 10 servings

Another relatively inexpensive, hearty one-dish meal that profits from advance preparation.

3 lbs. (1,350 g) lean lamb shoulder or neck meat, with bone in, cut up
3 qts. (3¾ L) Brown Beef Broth, page 40
⅔ cup (1½ dL) barley
2 medium garlic cloves, peeled
1 medium onion, peeled, cut into 1-inch cubes
White part of 1 medium leek or 4 green onions
3 medium celery ribs, cut into even lengths to fit upright in food chute
2 medium turnips, peeled, ends cut blunt
2 medium carrots, peeled

¼ teaspoon dried thyme leaves or ½ teaspoon chopped fresh thyme
⅛ teaspoon dried crushed rosemary leaves or ¼ teaspoon chopped fresh rosemary
½ lb. (225 g) fresh green beans
½ teaspoon salt, or more to taste
Pepper to taste

1. Place lamb on broiler tray. Broil until well browned, turning frequently so that edges do not singe, about 20 minutes. Transfer lamb to a 6-quart (6-L) soup kettle; discard drippings. Add beef broth to kettle. Heat to a rapid simmer over high heat. Remove any scum that appears on surface. Cover and simmer over low heat 1½ hours, skimming as necessary.

2. Transfer meat to a bowl with a slotted spoon. Cut by hand into bite-size cubes; set aside. Discard bones. Strain; then return 10 cups (2½ L) broth to a clean soup kettle. Add barley. Heat to a rapid simmer. Cover and simmer over low heat 20 minutes.

3. Insert the *metal knife blade*. With machine running, drop garlic cloves through food chute. Process until minced. Add onion and process to chop with 4 half-second pulses. Halve leek crosswise. Change to the *medium slicing disk*. Insert leek and celery together upright in food chute. Slice with a gentle push. Add contents of container to soup kettle. Cover and simmer 30 minutes. Replace disk in container.

4. Insert turnips from underneath food chute and slice each with a firm push. Gather slices together and tightly wedge them in from bottom of food chute with cut edges perpendicular to pusher (see page 13, center left illustration). Slice into matchsticks with a firm push. Cut carrots to fit upright in food chute and slice with a firm push. Add contents of container to soup kettle. Add lamb cubes, thyme, and rosemary. Simmer 20 minutes.

5. Return slicing disk to container. Trim green beans to fit sideways in food chute. French slice beans with a gentle push and add to kettle. Simmer until beans are just tender, about 15 to 20 minutes. Adjust seasonings to taste, adding salt and pepper as necessary. Serve immediately or cool to room temperature and refrigerate as long as 2 days.

LIGURIAN VEGETABLE SOUP
Makes 6 to 8 servings

Zuppa di Verdure was the first course of a memorable lunch in San Remo, and my introduction to the gentle vegetable flavors of the Italian Riviera. Quite unlike an American vegetable soup and looser than a minestrone, its true taste can be recreated only when the herbs are fresh, vegetables are at their peak, and a thin slice of soft butter is swirled in at the last moment.

½ lb. (225 g) butternut squash, seeded, peeled
Salt

1 small leek, well cleaned, roots removed
2 medium celery ribs, leaves removed
2 medium carrots, peeled, halved lengthwise
1 cup (¼ L) firmly packed stemmed spinach or Swiss chard leaves
¼ lb. (115 g) mushrooms, wiped clean
¼ lb. (115 g) green beans, tips removed
1 medium zucchini, tips removed
1 medium potato, peeled
2 medium tomatoes, peeled, halved, seeded
2 oz. (60 g) Parmesan cheese, cut into 1-inch chunks
1 medium onion, peeled, cut into 1-inch chunks
⅓ cup (¾ dL) olive or vegetable oil
1½ tablespoons Mixed Herbs (page 6), or 3 tablespoons chopped fresh herbs including basil, marjoram, savory, and sage
1½ qts. (1½ L) Chicken Broth, page 40
1 qt. (1 L) cold water
Freshly ground pepper to taste
Softened butter

1. Insert the *medium slicing disk*. Cut squash into even lengths to fit food chute and slice with a firm push. Transfer to a colander and salt lightly. Set aside 20 minutes. Cut leek into even lengths to fit upright in food chute (use both white and green parts) and slice with a gentle push. Repeat with celery. Empty container into a 6-quart (6-L) soup kettle. Insert carrots upright in food chute and slice with a firm push; add to kettle.

2. Divide spinach or chard leaves into 2 batches and stack. Roll up stacks tightly. Insert rolls upright from underneath food chute (see page 13, upper right illustration) and slice with a gentle push. Stack mushrooms, alternating caps, in food chute; slice with a gentle push; add to kettle.

3. Change to the *french-fry disk*. Cut green beans into even lengths to fit upright and fill food chute snugly; slice with a gentle push. Repeat with zucchini, potato, and tomatoes, inserting each as necessary from underneath food chute. Cut zucchini with a firm push, potato with a moderate push, and tomato with a gentle push; add each to soup kettle.

4. Wipe container dry and insert the *metal knife blade*. Process Parmesan cheese until powdery; reserve for garnish. Rinse squash under cold running water to remove all traces of salt. Add

squash to container and process to mince with 4 to 6 one-second pulses; add to kettle. Chop onion with 4 to 6 half-second pulses; transfer to kettle.

5. Add oil to kettle and toss to coat vegetables. Stir over very low heat until all vegetables begin to soften. Cover and cook over low heat, stirring frequently, until all vegetables have softened and given up juices, about 30 minutes.

6. Add herbs, broth, and water. Heat liquid to simmering. Place cover slightly ajar and very slowly simmer soup until flavors meld, about 2½ to 3 hours. Add salt and pepper to taste. Swirl a thin slice of butter into each serving and pass grated cheese.

CHICKEN BROTH
Makes about 5 quarts (5 L)

Stock may be refrigerated longer than two days if it is boiled briefly every other day to prevent souring.

6 to 7 lbs. (2¾ to 3¼ kg) chicken backs, necks, wings, giblets, and carcasses, if available, or preferably a 5- to 7-lb. (2¼- to 3¼-kg) stewing hen, cut up, fat removed
6 to 7 qts. (5½ to 6½ L) cold water, or more as needed
2 medium onions, peeled, halved
Green leaves from 2 medium leeks
4 carrots, peeled
6 medium celery ribs, with leaves
2 unpeeled garlic cloves, crushed
1 cup (¼ L) firmly packed parsley with stems
1 teaspoon dried thyme leaves
1 bay leaf, crushed
½ teaspoon salt
2 whole cloves

1. Place chicken in a 12-qt. (12-L) stockpot; reserve liver for another use. Add enough water to cover by 1 to 2 inches (2½ to 5 cm). Cover and heat liquid to a rapid simmer over high heat. With a large spoon, remove all fat and scum that rises to surface. Cover and simmer slowly for 3 hours, skimming as necessary.

2. With the *medium slicing disk,* slice onion

halves with a gentle push. Pack leek greens loosely in food chute and slice with a gentle push; add contents of container to stockpot. Slice carrots with a firm push and celery with a gentle push; add to stockpot with garlic, parsley, thyme, bay leaf, salt, and cloves. Replace cover and simmer slowly 4 to 5 hours longer.

3. Uncover and cool finished stock to room temperature. Set a large strainer over a bowl. Remove vegetables with a slotted spoon; place in strainer and press firmly to extract all liquid. Discard vegetables.

4. Remove chicken with slotted spoon to strainer. Discard skin and bones. Pick over and reserve meat for soups, salads, or casseroles. Clean strainer and line with cheesecloth. Strain broth from stockpot and bowl into freezer containers, leaving several inches at tops of containers for broth to expand when frozen. Refrigerate 2 days or freeze up to 6 months.

Substitutions:

To substitute canned broth for 2 cups (½ L) broth, remove fat from a small (13¾ oz./4 dL) can chicken broth. Add ⅓ cup (¾ dL) cold water and stir. Broth is ready to use.

To substitute canned broth for 2 quarts (2 L) broth, remove fat from 1 large (1 qt. 14 oz./1½ L) can chicken broth. Add 2 cups (½ L) cold water and stir. Broth is ready to use.

BROWN BEEF BROTH
Makes about 5 quarts (5 L)

Soup bones are most often sections of the shank (leg) and should include at least one knuckle or knee bone, which is rich in natural gelatin, to give body to the broth.

3 lbs. (1,350 g) beef soup bones, cut up
2 lbs. (900 g) beef shank or neck bones with meat
1 medium oxtail (about 2 lbs./900 g), cut up
7 qts. (7 L) cold water
3 medium onions, peeled, halved
4 carrots, peeled
3 medium ribs celery with leaves
2 unpeeled garlic cloves, crushed

1 cup (¼ L) firmly packed parsley with stems
1 teaspoon dried thyme leaves
1 bay leaf, crushed
½ teaspoon salt

1. Heat oven to 425° F (220° C). Roast beef soup bones, shank bones, and oxtail on broiler tray or roasting pan until golden brown, about 45 minutes. Turn once or twice, taking care not to let edges of bones singe. Transfer bones to a 12-quart (12-L) stockpot. Pour off and discard the fat. Place the roasting pan or broiler tray on the stove over medium heat until browned matter in pan sizzles. Add 1 cup (¼ L) cold water all at once, scraping pan juices well with wooden spatula. When pan is clean of brown matter, pour liquid into stockpot. Add 7 quarts (7 L) or enough cold water to cover bones by 1 to 2 inches (2½ to 5 cm).

2. Cover and heat liquid to a rapid simmer over high heat. With a large spoon, remove any fat or scum that rises to surface. Cover and continue simmering slowly for 4 to 6 hours, skimming as necessary.

3. Insert *medium slicing disk.* Slice onion halves with a gentle push; add to stockpot. Slice carrots with a firm push and celery with a gentle push. Add contents of container, garlic, parsley, thyme, bay leaf, and salt to stockpot. Cover and slowly simmer 4 to 6 hours longer.

4. Uncover and cool finished stock to room temperature. Set a large strainer over a bowl. Transfer vegetables with a slotted spoon to strainer and press firmly to extract all liquid. Discard vegetables.

5. Add bones and meat to strainer; drain well. Discard bones and reserve meat for another use. Clean strainer and line with cheesecloth. Strain broth from stockpot and bowl into freezer containers, leaving several inches in tops of containers for broth to expand when frozen. Refrigerate 2 days or freeze up to 6 months.

Substitutions:

Follow guidelines for Chicken Broth, page 40, using canned beef broth.

FISH BROTH
Makes about 3 quarts (3 L)

The best bones to use are from nonoily flat fish, such as sole and flounder. Salmon, whitefish, or red snapper bones are not usually suitable for stock or broth.

2 lbs. (900 g) fresh fish frames (heads and bones) from striped bass, sole, pike, or flounder, cut into large chunks
¼ cup (½ dL) firmly packed parsley with stems
1 medium onion, peeled, halved
1 small leek or 4 whole green onions, roots removed, well cleaned, cut into even lengths to fit upright in food chute
¼ lb. (115 g) mushrooms, wiped clean
¼ cup (½ dL) vegetable oil
Pinch thyme
½ bay leaf
½ cup (1 dL) dry white wine
3 qts. (3 L) cold water

1. Place fish bones in a large bowl and cover with cold water. Set aside several hours or overnight, changing water several times to whiten bones and remove all blood.

2. Insert *metal knife blade.* Process parsley until finely minced; empty into a 6-quart (6-L) soup kettle. Change to the *medium slicing disk.* Slice onion, leek, and mushrooms each with a gentle push. Add to soup kettle. Add oil, thyme, and bay leaf to kettle. Place a sheet of aluminum foil touching top of the vegetables; cook very slowly, stirring occasionally, until vegetables soften and begin to give up juices, about 25 minutes.

3. Remove foil and add wine all at once. Stir well. Drain bones well. Add bones to kettle and add 3 quarts (3 L) or enough cold water to cover bones by 2 inches (5 cm). Heat liquid almost to boiling and remove scum from surface with a large spoon. Set cover ajar and simmer rapidly (but do not boil) for 20 minutes.

4. With a slotted spoon, remove, drain, and discard all vegetables and bones. Strain broth through a fine sieve or a cheesecloth-lined strainer. Broth is ready to use. It may be refrigerated or frozen.

8

Pasta and Pizza

Pasta and pizza are the beautiful daughters of Italian cuisine, adopted by good cooks as the focus of a simplified meal—one that increasingly emphasizes one main dish, a green salad and light dessert, yet is still delicious, economical, nutritious, and filling.

Attribute it to a new energy-conscious mentality or to a new gastronomic maturity. Almost nothing seems more satisfying than a steaming bowl of homemade noodles caressed with a made-from-scratch meat sauce. No pasta could be more fragrant than one dressed in pesto made with a fresh-from-the-garden herb like basil. No pizza could be tastier or more stringy with cheese than one made at home for an informal Sunday dinner.

The simple art of preparing pasta and pizza is so easily mastered, they quickly become staples of this new repertory. Yet both are so preparation intensive that without the food processor they would never have obtained their current prominence, and they would be prepared and enjoyed at home far less frequently.

PASTA

Fresh pasta will spoil you. Once tasted, you can never go back to just plain spaghetti. Take the case of my friend Bob Cooper, a young journalist and budding food maven who was assigned a story on pasta and instructed by his editor to learn to make it from scratch and then report on the best method. Cooper's only problem was that he had never before tasted fresh pasta. The beginning of his story says it all.

It was like nothing he had ever eaten. Before him was a bowl of steaming fettuccine bathed in an ambrosial cream sauce studded with strips of bright red peppers. Each noodle was magnificent—perfectly formed, long and slinky . . . offering the barest resistance to the teeth. . . . It was just unbleached flour, fresh eggs, and perhaps the slightest hint of oil and water. So simple; yet he wanted more—much more. . . . He left knowing he had just had his first taste of what he had been born to eat.

Purists will tell you that the best pasta is handmade and hand-rolled, and no doubt that is true. Yet few of us have either the time or the training it takes to acquire those skills. Pasta dough can be made in the food processor in less than 10 seconds; rolled out and ready to cook 20 to 30 minutes later with the aid of a relatively inexpensive hand-cranked pasta machine.

Italians traditionally use pasta three ways: for noodles, to enclose a filling, or to garnish soup, but it is always served as an appetizer, never as a main course. Americans break this rule with spaghetti, and I see no reason why it should not also be broken with respect to homemade noodles.

With so many authentic Italian sauces based on vegetables or fish, main-course pastas tend to place less emphasis on meat, thus reducing calories. While it may have a reputation for being fattening, one serving of pasta (based on these recipes) contains a surprisingly low number of calories, about 160 to 165.

Pasta made with high-protein bread flour by the "pulse and bead" method: I make most of my pasta doughs with higher gluten bread flour (14 grams nutritional protein per ¼ pound/ 140 g) that mixes perfectly and yields wonderfully light, tender noodles that cook in 2 to 3 minutes. Bread flour (where specified) and large eggs are important to the success of these doughs.

My "pulse and bead" technique for mixing pasta dough in the processor is the reverse of the traditional hand method. I mix eggs and flavoring ingredients together first and then add the flour. One-second on/off turns or pulses are used so that the pasta dough is mixed with a cutting action—a pastry technique—rather than the traditional kneading associated with handwork methods for pasta and bread. This cutting-in process forms small irregular "beads" of dough that resemble a crumbly pie crust; so I call the method "pulse and bead." When pressed together and set aside to relax, the crumbly "beads" form a strong, high-protein dough with an even texture. Once mixed, pasta dough may be well-wrapped and refrigerated overnight, but it will require slightly more flour when rolled.

PIZZA

The food processor is probably the best thing to happen to pizza since the invention of cheese. Kneading the dough takes less than a minute. Shredding the cheese takes only seconds. All the cutting and chopping of ingredients for tomato sauce is done in a flash.

The following three pizza recipes reflect my taste—light on the dough, heavy on the tomatoes and cheese—but feel free to embellish, and to impose your preferences on them.

Before making pizza, I suggest that you read the introduction to Yeast Breads for information about handling the dough as well as using the oven stone for baking it. Because the preparation of the dough is so quick and easy, I would not like to see anyone discouraged by the combined rising time for the starter and the dough. Remember that the starter can be prepared as long as three days in advance, which cuts the waiting time considerably on the day the pizza is to be made.

Pizza, like chili, cheesecake, tuna salad, and apple pie, is a cult food. Cult foods are those often deeply associated with childhood taste memories and the "best"—in anyone's opinion—is usually the one that tastes most like that which your mother or grandmother or favorite aunt made. But as we all know, you can't go home again.

PLAIN PASTA DOUGH
Makes ½ pound (225 g) dough or 2 to 4 servings

This dough is called "plain" because it contains only the natural colorings of white flour and fresh eggs. It is the basic noodle dough that should be used if you are making pasta for the first time, and it marries beautifully with each of the five sauces for pasta.

2 large eggs, room temperature
1 large egg yolk, room temperature
½ teaspoon olive or vegetable oil
¼ teaspoon salt
1¼ cups (180 g) bread flour, or slightly more as needed

1. Insert the *metal knife blade*. Combine eggs, egg yolk, oil, and salt in container; process 10 seconds. Add flour and process to mix with 4 one-second pulses or until small beads that

hold together when pinched and the mixture resembles crumbly pie crust. If beads do not form, add 2 tablespoons flour and process with several additional one-second pulses to mix. Repeat, if necessary, until beads form.

2. Empty container on a sheet of plastic wrap and press dough together. Neatly fold plastic wrap around dough and set aside at room temperature for 20 minutes. Dough is ready to roll.

WHOLE WHEAT PASTA DOUGH
Makes about ½ pound (225 g) dough or 2 to 4 servings

Rough in texture, slightly fibrous, and extra nutritious, this dough best lends itself to noodles that go well with any of the pasta sauces. These noodles make an especially handsome presentation when paired with noodles of another color.

This is made with part cake flour as a tenderizer because whole wheat flour tends to make very stiff dough. The unsweetened cocoa powder, a seemingly odd ingredient, is used purely as a coloring agent and is otherwise undetectable.

2 large eggs
1 large egg yolk
1 teaspoon unsweetened cocoa powder
½ teaspoon olive or vegetable oil
¼ teaspoon salt
¾ cup (100 g) whole wheat flour (*not* stone ground)
¼ to ⅓ cup (25 to 35 g) cake flour, or slightly more as needed

1. Insert the *metal knife blade.* Combine eggs, egg yolk, cocoa, oil, and salt in container; process 10 seconds to mix. Add whole wheat flour and ¼ cup (25 g) of the cake flour. Process to mix with 4 one-second pulses or until small beads form that hold together when pinched and texture of the mixture resembles crumbly pie crust. If beads do not form, add 2 tablespoons cake flour and process with additional one-second pulses to mix. Repeat, if necessary, until beads form.

2. Empty container on a sheet of plastic wrap

and press dough together. Neatly fold plastic wrap around dough and set aside at room temperature for 20 minutes. Dough is ready to roll.

SPINACH PASTA DOUGH
Makes about ¾ pound (340 g) dough or 2 to 4 servings

Beautiful, bright-green, and flecked with fresh spinach, this dough is especially moist. As a result it takes almost twice as long as plain or whole wheat dough to dry to the leathery but supple consistency necessary for cutting. It goes well with four of the five sauces for pasta (I would not pair spinach with clam), and it may be stretched thin enough to enclose a ravioli filling.

Frozen spinach may be substituted; however, the color will be deep and grayish rather than bright green. Defrost frozen spinach but do not cook; pick over and discard tough stems; then drain, squeeze, and measure as described in Step 1.

1 lb. (450 g) fresh spinach, rinsed, drained, stems removed
2 large eggs
½ teaspoon olive or vegetable oil
¼ teaspoon salt
1¼ cups (180 g) bread flour, or slightly more as needed

1. Place spinach with water that clings to leaves in a large skillet. Cover and cook over medium heat, stirring frequently, until spinach wilts. Transfer to a colander and drain well. Squeeze to remove liquid; then place in a dry cloth towel and wring well to remove all remaining liquid. Measure ¼ cup (½ dL) firmly packed spinach, and set any remainder aside for another use.

2. Insert the *metal knife blade.* Combine spinach, eggs, oil, and salt in processor container; process 10 seconds to thoroughly mix. Add 1¼ cups (180 g) flour and process to mix with 5 or 6 one-second pulses or until small beads form that hold together when pinched and texture of mixture resembles crumbly pie crust. If small beads do not form, add 2 tablespoons flour and process with several additional one-second

pulses to mix. Repeat, if necessary, until beads form.

3. Empty container on a sheet of plastic wrap and press dough together. Neatly fold plastic wrap around dough and set aside at room temperature for 20 minutes. Dough is ready to roll.

CARROT PASTA DOUGH

Makes about 1 pound (450 g) dough or 4 to 6 servings

The delicate color of carrots is strengthened by tomato paste, and the taste is sparked by the acidity of Tabasco sauce. This pasta is best suited to noodles and most dramatic when paired with spinach or whole wheat. Carrots provide a good deal of moisture so this recipe yields a larger amount of dough than others (be sure to cut dough into 4 pieces for rolling). Plan an hour or more for pasta to dry to cutting consistency.

¼ lb. (115 g) carrots, peeled, cut into 1-inch lengths
1 tablespoon good-quality tomato paste
¾ teaspoon salt
Several dashes Tabasco sauce
2 large eggs
1 large egg yolk
2 to 2¼ cups (300 to 330 g) bread flour, or slightly more as needed

1. Place carrots in a vegetable steamer basket. Fill a medium saucepan with 1 inch (2½ cm) of water. Place basket in pan; cover and steam carrots over high heat until soft-tender, about 15 to 18 minutes. Remove carrots to a towel to cool.

2. Insert the *metal knife blade*. Combine carrots, tomato paste, salt, and Tabasco in container. Process until carrots are chopped, scraping down container sides as necessary. Add eggs and egg yolk and process until carrots are completely puréed and virtually no small chunks remain; scrape down container sides as necessary. Mixture will turn pale orange and may become foamy.

3. Add 2 cups (300 g) flour and process with 5

or 6 one-second pulses until small beads form that hold together when pinched and texture of mixture resembles crumbly pie crust. If beads do not form, add 2 tablespoons flour and process with several additional one-second pulses to mix. Repeat, if necessary, until beads form.

4. Empty container on a sheet of plastic wrap and press dough together. Neatly fold plastic wrap around dough and set aside at room temperature for 20 minutes. Dough is ready to roll.

BASIC PROCEDURES FOR USING A PASTA MACHINE

Pasta-making is not an exact science. It is an art, or a craft, based on keenness of eye and touch and experience. Pasta is almost as much fun to make as to eat, and you should have perfect results on the first try if you follow directions carefully. However, some cooks find that it takes several attempts to get a good feel for the dough. As you become accustomed to handling dough, the quality of the pasta will improve and the process will take progressively less time.

A great deal also depends on the flour used, the size of the eggs, ingredients, humidity, room temperature, and even mood. Allow at least an hour or more the first few times and do not attempt to roll out pasta in a hurry.

There are specialized ways of rolling pasta dough by hand, but using a relatively inexpensive hand-cranked machine with six settings and interchangeable cutters is the simplest and fastest way I know.

My machines have removeable cutting heads that allow me to switch cutters. In addition to fettuccine or *tagliatelle* (ribbon noodles) and *tagliarini* (thin noodles), I have cutters to make the lovely zigzag *pappardelle* and even fresh spaghetti. Rolled-out dough strips can be cut by hand into wrappers for ravioli.

General instructions for rolling any of the four pasta doughs follow. My machines have 6 settings; therefore, the directions are given for machines like mine. Adjust accordingly; if your machine is different you may already know how to use it and can proceed directly to cutting instructions contained in the following recipes.

I have found that flour differs greatly from region to region. For best results, always use large eggs and exactly the type of flour specified in the recipes (see page 5 for further information on flours); adjusting amounts will then be a matter of feel.

Here are a few tips for rolling out pasta dough:

- Check texture after dough has rested in plastic wrap. If it glues itself to the wrap, that is a sign it will need to have flour worked in during the rolling. Otherwise, dough will be smooth and easy to handle.

- If dough shreds when rolled initially, either you are putting too large a piece through the machine, or dough is too wet and requires slightly more flour. The less flour worked into the dough, the more tender the pasta, however.

- Have 3 dry cloth towels (not terry cloth) on hand. Spread them flat on a counter or table before you begin working to avoid opening drawers and unfolding towels with floury hands.

- Dough strips are fragile; handle them gently. Remember that dough swells after cooking and will be thicker than it actually looks after stretching.

1. Place pasta machine on a flat work surface and secure with the clamp. Open rollers to widest setting (#1). Unwrap and cut dough into 3 pieces (cut carrot dough into 4 pieces). Remove one piece to roll. Rewrap and set remainder aside. If dough is soft and wet enough to glue itself to the plastic wrap, sprinkle 2 tablespoons flour on the work surface. Otherwise, coat a work surface (preferably wood) with 1 tablespoon flour. More flour may be added to work surface as necessary for rolling. Insert the crank handle into the gear that controls the smooth rollers.

2. Flatten the piece of dough with the heels of your hands. Flour both sides, pinch one edge, and roll dough quickly through the rollers. If you have difficulty catching the dough in the rollers, pinch again and roll faster. Once started, do not stop rolling and do not reverse direction of the rollers. Carefully remove rolled dough from underneath pasta machine as it falls.

3. Flour both sides of dough lightly; brush off excess. Fold dough in half crosswise; gently press folded end to flatten. Place folded end in roller opening; roll dough through machine. Repeat flouring, removing excess flour, folding and rolling dough through machine once more if dough is smooth. Roll through twice more if dough is sticky. If it shreds, it may need more flour and as many as 4 "turns" through the machine to bring it to a smooth, workable consistency for stretching. When dough is ready to be stretched, it will feel smooth and tender. *After this point, do not fold dough again.*

4. Change to next widest opening (#2). Flour dough lightly. Roll through machine, allowing dough strip to pass over top of machine (like laundry through a wringer. If dough is held up in the air, it tends to pass less evenly through rollers.) Carefully remove dough from underneath machine as it falls and place it flat on work surface. Repeat flouring lightly and rolling dough through machine changing settings each time, through #3 and #4.

5. Change to setting #5. Cut dough crosswise in half. Lightly flour and roll each strip through the machine. Place dough strips flat on cloth towels and do not overlap. Begin again at Step 2 to roll out additional pieces of dough, adding additional flour to work surface as needed. (For filled pastas, such as ravioli, proceed directly to Step 6; do not allow dough strips to dry.) After all dough is rolled, allow dough strips to dry to a leathery, but supple, consistency needed for cutting. Turn dough strips frequently so they dry evenly on both sides. Plain and whole wheat dough strips usually will dry to a leathery consistency in a warm kitchen within 20 to 30 minutes. Spinach and carrot dough strips usually will dry to leathery consistency in a warm kitchen in 1 to 2 hours. While waiting to cut dough strips, proceed to desired recipe for cutting instructions.

6. For ravioli, dough strips must be rolled very thin. Proceed as before, carefully flouring dough lightly and rolling it through the thinnest setting (#6). Cut dough crosswise into workable lengths if it proves difficult to handle. It will be very stretched and paper thin. To prevent sticking, remove dough quickly and carefully as it falls from machine. Handling this thin dough takes some experience and confidence. These thin dough strips should be rolled and then filled one by one because they dry out very

quickly. If necessary to hold them, place them on cloth towels and cover with plastic wrap to prevent drying. Proceed to desired recipe for filling and cutting instructions.

Note: **Never wash your pasta machine!** After using, no matter how messy it gets, brush or wipe it off; do not rinse.

FETTUCCINE, TAGLIATELLE, TAGLIARINI, or PAPPARDELLE
Makes 2 to 4 servings

Tagliatelle are perhaps the most common homemade noodles found in Italy, although fettuccine is the name best known to Americans. The words *tagliatelle* and *tagliarini* come from the Italian verb *tagliare* meaning "to cut"; the "ini" suffix is a diminutive. Fettuccine, which comes from the noun *fettuccia* (tape, ribbon, or small slice), are slightly narrower than *tagliatelle*, but for practical purposes they can be cut to the same size. *Pappardelle* have been traditionally served with hare; the verb *pappare* means "to gulp down, or gorge"; the noodles have zigzag edges, and indeed, you won't be able to eat just one.

½ **lb. (225 g) pasta dough**
4 to 6 qts. (4 to 6 L) water
1 teaspoon salt
A large bowl of warm water mixed with 1 teaspoon oil
3 tablespoons olive oil or melted butter
Pasta sauce, as desired
Grated Parmesan cheese, if appropriate

1. Roll out pasta dough according to Basic Procedures, beginning on page 45. Proceed through Step 5 of Basic Procedures. Dough strips are ready to cut when they are slightly dry and leathery on the surface but still supple. Do not allow dough to dry until brittle or it will break when cut. However, dough cut before it is sufficiently dry and leathery can clog cutters and noodles tend not to separate properly.

2. Before cutting, insert crank handle into desired cutter gear. For fettuccine or *tagliatelle* (ribbon noodles), use the ¼-inch- to ⅜-inch (1-cm)-wide cutter; for *tagliarini* (thin noodles), use the ⅛-inch (½-cm)-wide cutter. *Pappardelle*

(zigzag noodles) are ½-inch to ⅝-inch (1½-cm) wide, and a special cutting head is required for these. However, they may be cut by hand using a ravioli wheel guided by a ruler.

3. To cut noodles, roll each dough strip through cutter. Catch noodles as they fall and place on a pasta drying rack or flat on cloth towels (noodles may be placed in bunches on towels if they are to be cooked within 2 hours). Noodles are best if cooked within several hours, but they may be left to dry out completely on pasta rack as long as 1 week. After 2 days it is usually wise to transfer noodles to an airtight container or bag, as they become brittle and tend to break.

4. To cook pasta, heat 4 to 6 quarts (4 to 6 L) water to a rolling boil in a 6- to 8-quart (6- to 8-L) soup kettle or larger stockpot. Add salt and noodles to boiling water; stir once and boil 2 to 3 minutes or until noodles are just tender (taste one to be sure). Dried noodles take slightly longer to cook than just made noodles. Drain in a colander.

5. Transfer noodles to the warm water mixed with oil and stir well to remove excess starch. Immediately drain again in colander. Place 3 tablespoons oil or melted butter into the empty pot. Add noodles and toss over low heat using wooden spatula or pasta forks and taking care not to break noodles as you work. If noodles are to be served directly from the kitchen, add sauce to the pot. Toss carefully and serve noodles in heated rimmed soup bowls. If noodles are to be served at table, do not add sauce to pot. Transfer noodles to a heated serving bowl. Spoon sauce over and toss at table. Serve immediately with cheese, if desired.

RAVIOLI
Makes 4 servings

Say the word *ravioli* and my mind wanders back to a small beachfront restaurant in the little town of Laigueglia on the Italian Riviera, where we stopped one day for lunch. The proprietor was Sardinian and so were his triangular ravioli, called *culurzones* in that dialect. Filled with a white cheese mixture similar to the one that follows, they were feather light and sauced with a delicate, vegetable-rich Marinara.

Square ravioli of Genovese origin are more familiar, however, and pose fewer assembly problems; so I am suggesting them here. According to food historian Waverly Root, they were originally called *rabiole* (meaning leftovers). Modern stuffings may include leftovers, but I believe these really do merit one of the suggested fillings. They may be tossed in a sauce or more simply with butter or oil and grated cheese.

This recipe poses the challenge of working with dough stretched parchment thin, and therefore I do not recommend it to beginners. While a thicker noodle is easier to handle, the results are no match for these transcendently light little bundles that seem to float into your mouth.

Some practical notes: It is best to assemble and hold these at room temperature no longer than 3 hours before cooking. I have made them a day in advance and refrigerated them overnight, but the rate of attrition is high because moisture from the filling often causes them to stick, then tear. If you are working with a small pasta machine (narrower than 5 inches) an additional batch of dough may be required to use up all the filling. Cutting and sealing ravioli is a simultaneous process; work on a generously floured surface and then quickly transfer them to a floured cloth towel. A considerable quantity of nonusable dough scraps will accrue from the cutting process; discard them.

½ lb. (225 g) pasta dough, preferably plain
Cheese or Meat Filling (following page)
3 to 4 cups (¾ to 1 L) Marinara Sauce (page 109), or Meat Sauce (page 110)
Warm water mixed with 1 teaspoon oil
4 qts. (4 L) boiling water
Salt
Grated Parmesan cheese, for garnish

1. Prepare pasta dough and filling. Roll out dough one piece at a time through thinnest pasta machine setting according to Basic Procedures, beginning on page 45; quickly unfold dough on a generously floured work surface. Cut dough lengthwise in half unless it is narrower than 5 inches (13 cm), and if necessary cut into workable lengths. Set half aside and cover to keep moist. Place remainder on work surface. Work as quickly as possible.

2. Center a heaping teaspoon of filling on 1

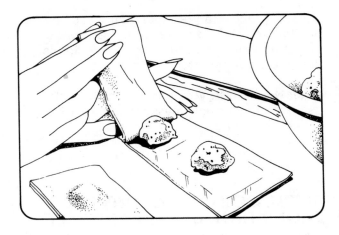

dough strip about 1 inch from the end. Continue placing teaspoons of filling 1½ inches (4 cm) apart along the center of the strip.

3. Lightly moisten dough strip between mounds of filling and along edges. Carefully cover with a reserved strip of dough and press between each mound of filling so doughs stick together. Press around each mound to remove wrinkles and as much air as possible.

4. Use a fluted ravioli wheel to seal and cut apart ravioli so that each measures approximately 2 × 2¼ inches (5 cm) or slightly smaller if desired. Discard scraps. Transfer ravioli to a generously floured cloth towel set on a baking sheet. Cover with another cloth towel and set aside until ready to cook. Repeat to fill, seal, and cut remaining dough strips.

5. Shortly before cooking, reheat sauce. Place oily water near sink. Add 1 teaspoon salt to

boiling water, stir, and add ravioli. Boil uncovered about 2 minutes or just until edges of dough are tender. Drain in a colander. Transfer to oily water to remove excess starch; drain well in colander. Transfer to warm serving dish; top judiciously with sauce; garnish with grated cheese.

CHEESE FILLING
Makes filling for about ½ lb. (225 g) pasta dough

This mild filling is lightly scented with onion and herbs.

1 oz. (30 g) Parmesan cheese, cut into 1-inch chunks
¼ cup (½ dL) firmly packed parsley leaves
¼ teaspoon Mixed Herbs, page 6
1-inch cube peeled onion
½ tablespoon butter
½ lb. (225 g) ricotta cheese, kneaded in towel to remove excess moisture
1 egg yolk
Salt and freshly ground pepper to taste

1. Insert the *metal knife blade.* With machine running, drop Parmesan cheese chunks through food chute; process until powdery and remove to waxed paper. Process parsley with herbs until finely minced; remove to waxed paper. With machine running, drop onion through food chute; process until minced and transfer to a small skillet.

2. Add butter to skillet and cook onion until soft but not brown; set aside to cool. Return blade to container. Process ricotta cheese with egg yolk, salt, pepper, Parmesan cheese, parsley mixture, and cooled onion using 3 or 4 one-second pulses to thoroughly mix. Adjust seasonings to taste. Cover and refrigerate until ready to fill pasta, as long as overnight if desired.

MEAT FILLING
Makes filling for about ½ lb. (225 g) pasta dough

This filling may be prepared as long as three days in advance provided that the egg yolk is omitted.

½ oz. (15 g) Parmesan cheese, cut into 1-inch cubes
⅛ cup (¼ dL) firmly packed parsley leaves
1 small garlic clove, peeled
½ small onion, peeled, cut into 1-inch cubes
1 small carrot, peeled, cut into 1-inch lengths
½ small celery rib, strings removed, halved
4 medium mushrooms, wiped clean
2 tablespoons (30 g) butter
¼ lb. (115 g) boneless pork shoulder, cut into 1-inch cubes
¼ lb. (115 g) boneless beef chuck, cut into 1-inch cubes
2 tablespoons dry bread crumbs
Salt and pepper to taste
Pinch nutmeg
1 egg yolk

1. Insert the *metal knife blade* in dry container. Process cheese by dropping through food chute and grinding until powdery; transfer to waxed paper. Process parsley until minced; add to waxed paper with cheese. With machine running, drop garlic and onion cubes through food chute. Process until minced. Add carrot, celery, and mushrooms to container. Process to mince with 5 one-second pulses. Empty container into a medium skillet; return blade and container to processor base.

2. Add butter to skillet and cook vegetables over low heat until softened. Meanwhile, add pork and beef cubes to container and process to coarsely chop with 3 two-second pulses. Add meat to skillet and stir over medium heat until meat is gently but thoroughly cooked. Transfer contents of skillet to a plate and refrigerate until cold.

3. Clean blade and container and return them to processor base. Add chilled meat and vegetables to container with bread crumbs, salt, pepper, nutmeg, parsley, cheese, and egg yolk. Process to thoroughly mix with 4 or 5 one-second pulses. Adjust seasonings to taste. Cover and refrigerate until ready to use, as long as overnight if desired.

PIZZA
Makes 6 to 8 servings

Distinguished by a thin crisp dough, abundant

sauce, and extra cheese, this pizza may be enhanced by processor-sliced mushrooms, green pepper, or pepperoni. In summer, when plum tomatoes are plentiful, inexpensive, and ripe, substitute about three pounds (1,350 g) fresh tomatoes (peeled) for canned tomatoes; then make and freeze several batches of the sauce mixture.

Pizza Dough, page 129
1 rectangular chunk (6 oz./180 g) mozzarella cheese, chilled
1 oz. (30 g) Parmesan cheese, cut into 1-inch chunks
3 medium garlic cloves, peeled
2 cans (1 lb. 12 oz./790 g each) Italian plum tomatoes, drained
6 tablespoons (¾ dL) olive or vegetable oil
1½ teaspoons dried oregano
½ teaspoon dried basil
3 tablespoons (45 g) butter
Salt

1. Begin Pizza Dough at least 4 to 5 hours in advance.

2. Insert *medium shredding disk.* Shred mozzarella with a gentle push; set aside. Change to *metal knife blade.* With machine running, drop Parmesan cheese chunks through food chute. Process until finely ground; set aside. Turn on machine and drop garlic cloves one at a time through food chute. Process until finely minced; set aside.

3. Make an X in bottom of tomatoes and squeeze gently to remove seeds. If desired, reserve liquid for another purpose, see page 7. Fit processor with *french-fry disk.* Fill food chute with tomatoes and cut with a gentle push. Repeat, emptying container as necessary. (Or, divide tomatoes into 2 even batches. Using *metal knife blade,* chop each batch with 4 half-second pulses.) Set tomatoes aside.

4. Heat 4 tablespoons oil in a large skillet. Add garlic and cook over low heat until soft but not brown. Add tomatoes. Cook over high heat, stirring frequently, until all liquid has evaporated and tomatoes have thickened to a spreadable consistency, lowering heat as necessary. Stir in butter, oregano, basil, and salt as needed; cool.

5. Adjust oven rack to lower position and place oven stone on rack, if desired. Heat oven to 450° F (230° C) for 30 minutes.

6. Generously flour a baker's paddle or set an ungreased baking sheet or pizza pan aside. Flour the work surface. Roll out prepared dough to a 16-inch (40-cm) circle. Trim to a 14-inch (35-cm) circle. Transfer dough to paddle, baking sheet, or pizza pan. Sprinkle dough with 2 tablespoons oil. Salt and pepper lightly. Leaving a narrow blank border around edge of dough, spread remainder evenly with tomato mixture. Top with mozzarella, then Parmesan cheese.

7. Carefully loosen dough from paddle and test to be sure dough moves freely by shaking gently (loosen again if necessary). Slide dough onto oven stone. Or place baking sheet or pizza pan directly onto oven rack. Bake until cheese is brown and bubbling, 10 to 12 minutes. To remove pizza from oven stone, slide baker's paddle or baking sheet underneath. Serve immediately.

RED ONION FOCACCIA
Makes 8 to 10 servings

This is an odd but delicious thick-crusted pizza eaten as a breakfast snack in many parts of Northern Italy. We tasted it early one morning in the San Remo market—as usual, I was starving. I'm sure that Italians would be horrified to learn that I often cut focaccia into squares to serve with white wine as an informal hors d'oeuvre for a very simple meal. Choose a nonaluminum (nonreactive) skillet for cooking the onions, otherwise they can discolor.

Pizza Dough, page 129
1¾ lbs. (800 g) red onions, peeled, halved lengthwise
⅓ cup (¾ dL) olive oil
1 teaspoon anchovy paste
1 tablespoon white vinegar
3 tablespoons water
Additional olive oil
Salt and freshly ground pepper

1. Begin Pizza Dough (and its starter) several hours in advance.

2. Insert the *medium slicing disk.* Slice onion halves with a gentle push; transfer to a large nonreactive skillet. Add olive oil and toss over low heat until onions begin to soften. Dissolve anchovy paste in vinegar and water; stir well. Add to onions and cook over medium heat until onions are very soft and all the liquid has evaporated. Set onions aside to cool.

3. Punch down risen dough. Generously flour a work surface and roll out dough to fit a 15- × 10-inch (38½- × 25-cm) baking sheet or a 12-inch (30-cm) round pizza pan. Place dough on pan and cover with a dry cloth towel. Set dough aside to rise until it is about ½-inch (1½-cm) thick, about 30 to 40 minutes.

4. Adjust oven rack to lower position. Heat oven to 400° F (205° C). Brush slightly risen dough with oil. Sprinkle with salt and pepper. Adjust seasoning of onions, adding salt and pepper as needed. Spread onions gently over top of risen dough leaving a ½-inch (1½-cm) border. Bake 30 to 35 minutes until puffy, crisp, and very lightly browned. Serve warm; cut into triangles if round or into 2-inch (5-cm) squares if rectangular.

CHICAGO STUFFED PIZZA

Makes 6 to 8 servings or one 14-inch (35-cm) round double-crust pizza

Stuffed pizza is a gooey two-crusted wonder baked in a special 14-inch deep-dish pizza pan (available at specialty cookware stores) and believed to be indigenous to the city of Chicago. It almost defies description, but if you can imagine pounds of cheese, tomato, sausage, mushrooms, and onions stuffed into, rather than on top of, a pizza you'll get the idea.

This is a labor of love, and without the processor I would never have attempted to develop the recipe. Prepare the components of the filling a day or two in advance. The pizza then may be assembled and refrigerated for several hours or frozen for a week. If I do say so myself, it's a guaranteed show-stopper.

Stuffed Pizza Dough, page 130

Filling:

2 medium garlic cloves, peeled
3 tablespoons olive or vegetable oil
4 cans (1 lb. 12 oz./790 g each) Italian plum tomatoes, drained, seeded, juice reserved, or 6 lbs. ripe tomatoes, peeled, seeded, halved
1 teaspoon dried basil leaves
1½ teaspoons dried oregano leaves
2 tablespoons olive or vegetable oil
1 tablespoon (15 g) butter
2 medium onions, peeled, halved
Salt and freshly ground pepper
1 lb. (450 g) fresh mushrooms, wiped clean
3 tablespoons olive or vegetable oil
1 lb. (450 g) Sweet Italian Sausage, page 79
¾ teaspoon ground fennel seeds (optional)
¾ lb. (340 g) chilled mozzarella cheese, cut into chunks to fit food chute

Topping:

2 tablespoons olive or vegetable oil
2 oz. (60 g) Parmesan cheese, cut into chunks

1. Begin preparing dough (and its starter) at least 4 to 5 hours in advance.

2. To prepare filling, insert the *metal knife blade.* With machine running, drop garlic cloves through food chute and process until minced. Transfer garlic to a large skillet and add 3 tablespoons oil. Cook garlic over low heat until soft but not brown; set skillet aside. Change to the *french-fry disk.* Fill food chute with tomatoes and process with a gentle push. Empty container as necessary into skillet and repeat until all tomatoes are cut into small pieces. Cook in skillet over medium heat until tomatoes are slightly thickened and nearly all the liquid has evaporated, about 40 to 45 minutes. Stir in basil and oregano leaves; remove to a bowl to cool.

3. Add 2 tablespoons oil and the butter to skillet; set aside. Change to the *medium slicing disk.* Slice onion halves with a gentle push; transfer to skillet and cook over medium heat until onions soften, about 10 to 15 minutes. Add salt and pepper to taste; set onions aside in a bowl.

4. Slice mushrooms with a gentle push. Heat 3 tablespoons oil in same skillet; add mushrooms and sauté until dry. Season with salt and pepper and set aside in a bowl to cool.

5. If necessary, remove sausage from casings or place bulk sausage in skillet. Add fennel if desired. Cook over medium heat until sausage has turned pale in color and is thoroughly cooked; remove with slotted spoon and set aside.

6. Change to the *medium shredding disk*. Shred mozzarella cheese with a gentle push; empty container into a bowl as necessary. Remove dough from bowl without kneading. Divide into 2 portions, one equal to one-third of the total dough; the second equal to two-thirds.

7. To assemble pizza, lightly flour a work surface. Roll out larger ball of dough to a 20-inch (50-cm) circle. Place in an ungreased deep-dish pizza pan, allowing excess dough to hang over pan sides. Brush dough with 1 tablespoon oil and sprinkle lightly with salt. Spread 1 cup (¼ L) shredded mozzarella cheese over dough. Scatter sausage pieces evenly over cheese. Distribute mushrooms over sausage; add onions; top with three-quarters of the tomato mixture spread in an even layer. Finish with 1⅓ cups (3¼ dL) shredded mozzarella cheese.

8. Brush sides of dough and overhanging part with water; set pan aside. Roll out remaining dough to a 14-inch (35-cm) circle. Place it over filling and carefully stretch it to touch and adhere to bottom dough. Press all around to seal, and trim bottom dough so that it hangs over pan rim by ½ inch (1½ cm). Brush overhang with water and fold inward onto top of pizza; pinch to form a raised edge. Cut an X in the center of the top dough to make a steam vent. (If pizza is to be frozen, double wrap and freeze at this point; freeze tomato topping separately. Store leftover mozzarella cheese in an airtight container. Defrost pizza in refrigerator for 24 hours; place at room temperature 1 hour before baking.)

9. Return *metal knife blade* to dry container. Process Parmesan cheese until powdery. Brush top of dough with remaining tablespoon oil. Spread with remaining tomato mixture; top with remaining mozzarella and the Parmesan cheese. Brush edge of crust with cold water. (Pizza may now be refrigerated for 2 hours before baking, if desired.)

10. Adjust oven rack to lower position. Heat oven to 450° F (230° C). Bake until well browned and thoroughly hot, 30 to 40 minutes. Serve immediately from pan, first cutting into wedges. If no breaks occur in bottom crust, pizza may also be removed from pan and placed on a board for serving.

9

Fish and Shellfish

How far we have come since the rigid days when fish was never seriously appreciated as a main course, when eating fish was a kind of penance and serving it was a weekly ritual. People who are health and calorie conscious are cooking and eating more fish and shellfish than ever before, not only because these foods are high in protein and vitamins and low in calories, fat, and cholesterol but also because fish is absolutely delicious and quickly prepared.

I have been a fish eater since childhood, and I likely owe my love for fish to my father, who took us trout and deep-sea fishing at early ages and allowed us to participate in the filleting and cooking of the catch. The sights and smells of absolutely fresh-boned, butterflied trout as they emerged golden brown and crisp from the skillet still remain vivid in my memory.

The food processor performs many routine tasks of fish and shellfish cookery by slicing and chopping vegetable ingredients, mincing fish, mixing lump-free batters for frying, and combining cooked ingredients for stuffings and toppings. It excels at adventuresome preparations like my Scallop Mousseline appetizers, page 55, which, but for the processor, would be otherwise unknown. *Mousselines* formerly took

hours to prepare since the fish was pounded to a pulp in a marble mortar using a wooden pestle!

Young French chefs who practice the "new" cooking (or *nouvelle cuisine*) are largely responsible for the popularity of formal fish appetizers and first courses. The *nouvelle cuisine* is *not* diet cooking. It is a rich but lighter style that stresses fresh ingredients, flourless sauces, imaginative combinations, and artistically arranged plates. Therefore, appetizers in this style, such as *mousselines* or Coquilles St. Jacques Nouvelles, page 55, are delicious openers for an important dinner and best when served with a fine dry white wine.

A French chef like Gérard Rouillard of the two-star *La Marée* restaurant in Paris does not cook strictly in the *nouvelle* style. He nonetheless utilizes his *robot coupé* (as commercial-size food processors were originally, and are still called, in France) for myriad preparations served at *La Marée,* a restaurant that specializes in fish and seafood.

I first met Chef Rouillard in Chicago when he came to spend a week as a guest chef in a local restaurant. I was assigned by the *Chicago Tribune* to cover his visit—but that is another story. Suffice it to say that the kitchen was shorthanded, I was pressed (gladly) into service, and I had the opportunity to prepare, under Chef Rouillard's close supervision, the dish from which I adapted the main course Baked Scallops of Fish with Tomato and Basil on page 58. Several months later I visited the kitchen at *La Marée*, where I acquired the recipe for Scallops of Fish in Lettuce Leaves and the *sabayon* technique for the extra-light processor hollandaise that accompanies it, page 108.

BASIC PROCEDURES FOR HANDLING FISH AND SHELLFISH

Buy fresh fish whenever possible. It is also important to trade at a clean, reliable fish market or supermarket where fish and shellfish are displayed and stored on a bed of crushed ice to keep them extra fresh. Both fish and shellfish should be odorless, save for the clean fresh smell of the sea. A strong "fishy" odor is a sure sign of age. Fresh shellfish must be alive—that means oysters, clams, and mussel shells must be tightly closed or must close when shells are pressed together—if wide open, pass them by.

Be sure frozen fish is well wrapped and solidly frozen at the time of purchase. Avoid pieces with torn or open wrappers, edges that have a crusty or dry look, and boxes in which ice crystals have formed.

Storage

Use fresh fish and shellfish within 24 hours of purchase; use frozen fish immediately after defrosting. Before refrigerating fresh fish or seafood, unwrap and rinse under cold running water to remove loose scales, dirt, and preservatives. Always remove fish from paper wrapping since the fish becomes dry and sticks to paper while refrigerated.

Refrigerate fish and delicate shellfish, such as scallops, on a bed of crushed ice placed on a jelly-roll pan, covered with plastic wrap. Live shellfish, such as clams, mussels, and oysters, are stored differently, however. First rinse them in cold water (do not soak); drain well in a large colander or strainer. Place in a bowl and cover with a cold, damp cloth towel.

Never cover live shellfish with plastic wrap and never leave them wrapped in a plastic bag—they cannot breathe. Rinse, drain, and

place cooked and uncooked shrimp or salad crabmeat in a plastic bag in which several air holes have been made; otherwise an unpleasant gas accumulates and hastens spoilage.

Freezing and Defrosting

Store fish and shellfish in freezer no longer than three months. To prepare fish for freezing, gut, scale, remove gills and head; cut into fillets or steaks. Rinse in cold water and pat dry on paper toweling; then place fish flat on a sheet of plastic wrap. Wrap tightly; double wrap in aluminum foil. Always mark and date package clearly. I do not recommend freezing shrimp, crabmeat, or lobster tails unless you are absolutely certain they have never before been frozen. Clams, mussels, and oysters do not freeze especially well.

Defrost frozen fish or seafood in its wrapper on a plate in the refrigerator overnight. Before cooking, pat dry on paper toweling. If you must defrost fish in a hurry (this works best with a firm-fleshed shellfish like shrimp), unwrap and place fish in a large bowl of cold water. Set bowl under the faucet and let cold water run into the bowl; never use hot or warm water to defrost fish and do not defrost fish at room temperature.

Removing Scales and Bones

If skin is intact on whole fish or fillets, always check for scales before cooking. Turn fish skin-side up, run the back of a knife over skin with a scraping motion to lift scales; rinse under cold running water.

To check for hidden bones, place the fillets skin side down (shinier side if skinned) on work surface. Beginning at the narrowest end of the fillet, run your index finger up the center toward the widest end. If bones are there, you will feel them. Remove bones with a tweezer or strawberry huller, pulling with the grain. If the flesh tears, you are pulling against the grain; turn the fish around 180 degrees and remove bones from the opposite direction.

Making Fish "Scallops"

Fish "scallops" are nothing more than skinned boned fillets cut on a strong diagonal into 4½-inch (10-cm)-long segments and slightly pounded to equalize the thickness and promote even cooking. It is not strictly necessary to follow this procedure in recipes that call for "scallops," but the method is not time consuming, and I believe it yields excellent results.

SCALLOP MOUSSELINES
Makes 6 appetizer servings

No food better expresses the spirit of the new French cooking than these gorgeous, light, super-rich appetizers paired with the most famous of all the *nouvelle cuisine* sauces, *Beurre Blanc*. If desired, timbale molds may be filled, covered, and refrigerated for several hours before baking *mousselines*.

¾ **lb. (340 g) sea or bay scallops, rinsed**
¼ **cup (½ dL) firmly packed parsley leaves**
1 egg white
¼ **teaspoon salt**
Freshly ground white pepper
2 dashes Tabasco sauce
Pinch curry powder
1½ cups (3½ dL) chilled whipping cream
Beurre Blanc, page 108
Watercress sprigs, for garnish

1. Pat scallops dry and refrigerate until ready to use. Be sure scallops are thoroughly chilled. Insert *metal knife blade* in clean dry container. Process parsley leaves until finely minced, set aside. Add scallops to container and process 30 seconds; scrape down side of container. Add egg white, salt, pepper, Tabasco, and curry powder. Purée 30 seconds longer, stopping several times to scrape down the container sides. Remove container from base, leaving contents and blade in place. Cover and refrigerate 20 minutes.

2. Return container and blade to processor base. With machine running, pour cream through food chute within 60 seconds. After all the cream is added, process 30 seconds longer, stopping several times to scrape sides and bottom edge of container so that no streaks remain. Mix in parsley with 6 half-second pulses. Transfer mixture to a bowl; cover and refrigerate no longer than 6 hours before baking.

3. Adjust oven rack to middle position. Heat oven to 350° F (175° C). Generously butter six ½-cup (1-dL) round or oval timbale (metal) molds or custard cups. Fill each with scallop mixture. Tap gently on counter to remove air bubbles. Cut six 3-inch (8-cm) waxed paper squares and butter each generously. Place 1 buttered paper square over each mold. Arrange molds in a baking dish. Add hot tap water to come one-third to one-half up outsides of molds, but do not allow molds to touch or float. Bake until a sharp knife inserted into center of mixture is withdrawn clean, about 20 minutes.

4. While *mousselines* are baking, prepare *Beurre Blanc*.

5. Remove baking dish from oven. Cover loosely with aluminum foil and let stand 5 minutes. Uncover; remove waxed paper from molds, and run a sharp knife around inside edge of each. Center molds under inverted warmed dinner plates and invert. Remove molds. Spoon hot sauce around, but not over, each *mousseline*. Garnish with watercress and serve immediately.

COQUILLES ST. JACQUES NOUVELLES
Makes 6 appetizer servings

Inspired by an elegant seafood *ragoût* at the Paris restaurant *Dodin-Bouffant*, this old favorite has a new look, a new lightness, and a new *saveur*. The trick, or *truc* as the French say, is to pour the thick foamy *Beurre Blanc Mousseux* into the warm skillet, then carefully heat scallop-vegetable-sauce mixture just until hot (test with your finger to be sure).

Pastry Scallop Shells, page 147, or 6 natural
  scallop shells
1 lb. (450 g) bay or sea scallops, quartered if
  large
¼ **cup (½ dL) firmly packed parsley leaves**
3 medium shallots, peeled
3 tablespoons (45 g) unsalted butter
¼ **lb. (115 g) mushrooms, wiped clean**
Salt and pepper to taste
Beurre Blanc Mousseux, pages 108–109
Fresh snipped chives, for garnish

1. Prepare Pastry Scallop Shells or set natural shells aside. Rinse scallops in cold water and feel to be sure all sand has been removed. Drain well and pat dry on paper toweling. Insert *metal knife blade* in dry container. Process parsley until finely minced; set aside. With machine running, drop shallots through food chute one at a time. Process until minced. Remove shallots to a medium skillet. Add 2 tablespoons butter and cook over medium heat until shallots are soft but not brown.

2. Change to the *medium slicing disk*. Stack mushrooms in food chute with caps alternating; slice with a gentle push. Add to skillet and toss over high heat until liquid evaporates; remove. Melt remaining butter in skillet. Add scallops and toss over medium heat until scallops turn opaque white and are barely cooked through, about 3 to 4 minutes.

3. Remove skillet from heat and pour pan juices into a small saucepan. Reduce by slowly boiling to 2 tablespoons. Prepare *Beurre Blanc Mousseux* and add reduced pan juices to sauce after all butter has been added; leave in container or set aside until ready to serve, no longer than 1 hour.

4. Just before serving, heat Pastry Scallop Shells in a hot (400° F/205° C) oven for 5 minutes to warm or place natural shells on warm serving plates. Return scallops to low heat and add mushroom mixture and parsley. Toss and heat thoroughly, about 4 to 5 minutes; drain off and discard any additional pan juices that accumulate.

5. Pour prepared sauce into skillet with scallops, taking care that skillet is not so hot that sauce simmers or it will separate. Adjust seasonings to taste. Spoon hot mixture into scallop shells. Garnish with chives. Serve immediately.

OYSTERS ROCKEFELLER
Makes 4 to 6 appetizer servings

Oysters are the dowagers of the shellfish family; all neat and pearly gray, they set an elegant tone for any dinner. This recipe, an old New Orleans favorite, has been our Thanksgiving dinner appetizer for years and has received repeated raves. The processor handles the stuffing in a trice, but the oysters, alas, still must be opened by hand. Always be sure oysters are impeccably fresh (see pages 6 and 54).

⅓ **cup (¾ dL) firmly packed parsley leaves**
2 **medium garlic cloves, peeled**
8 **medium shallots, peeled**
1 **small celery rib, strings removed, cut into 1-inch lengths**
4 **tablespoons (60 g) butter, slightly softened**
1½ **cups (3½ dL) firmly packed fresh stemmed spinach or Swiss chard leaves, patted dry**
⅓ **cup (¾ dL) fresh bread crumbs**
1 **tablespoon Pernod, Ricard, or other unsweetened anise liqueur**
Dash each Worcestershire and Tabasco sauces
2 **teaspoons fresh lemon juice**
Salt and freshly ground pepper to taste
18 **fresh medium oysters**
2 **cups (½ L) coarse (kosher) salt**
Lemon wedges, for garnish

1. To prepare spinach topping, insert the *metal knife blade*. Process parsley until finely minced; set aside. With machine running, drop garlic cloves and shallots through food chute one at a time. Process until minced; scrape down sides of container. Add celery and mince with 4 half-second pulses.

2. Heat butter in a medium skillet. Add minced vegetables and stir over medium heat until soft. Add spinach or chard leaves; stir over medium heat until leaves wilt and all juices evaporate. Remove skillet from heat.

3. Wipe out container and replace the blade. Return cooked vegetables to processor container with bread crumbs, parsley, Pernod, Worcestershire, Tabasco, lemon juice, salt, and pepper. Process to mince vegetables, and combine ingredients into a thick paste using 7 or 8 half-second pulses. Adjust seasonings to taste. Transfer mixture to a bowl and refrigerate as long as 2 days, if desired. Let mixture warm to room temperature before stuffing oysters.

4. To open oysters (no longer than 4 hours in advance), rinse under cold running water, brush shells clean, and drain well. Place a dry cloth towel on work surface. Place an oyster, flattest side up on the towel. Wrap towel

around one hand and grasp oyster firmly. Wedge the pointed end of an oyster knife or a bottle opener into the vertex of the oyster (pointed end) between the shells. Press down firmly to pry apart. Shell may break or chip.

5. As the top (flat) shell lifts off, slip the knife horizontally into the opening and scrape against the top shell to free the oyster. Discard top shell, taking care that liquid in bottom shell (oyster liquor) does not run out. Remove any bits of broken shell. Pour liquor into a bowl; slip knife under oyster meat to free it from bottom shell; place meat in a separate bowl and set shell aside. Repeat with all other oysters.

6. Strain oyster liquor through a double thickness of cheesecloth or a paper towel to remove all sand. Pour into bowl with oyster meat; cover as tightly as possible and refrigerate. Rinse and pat shells dry; place in refrigerator.

7. To assemble oysters and filling, place coarse salt in an even layer on a 15- × 10-inch (38½- × 25-cm) jelly-roll pan; set aside. Return 1 oyster and liquor to each shell. Spoon a scant tablespoon filling over each oyster and press so oyster is completely covered and protected. Place oysters on salt. Cover pan tightly with plastic wrap and refrigerate immediately.

8. Thirty minutes before serving, place oysters at room temperature. Adjust oven rack to top position. Heat oven to 500° F (260° C). Remove plastic wrap; bake oysters uncovered just until hot and beginning to bubble gently, about 10 to 12 minutes. Do not overcook or oysters will toughen. Serve immediately, transferring oysters to serving plates lined with napkins or doilies or to oyster plates. Accompany with lemon wedges.

GEFILTE FISH
Makes 8 to 10 appetizer servings

Homemade gefilte fish has nearly become a lost art. Recipes passed from mother to daughter had been largely abandoned because the work of hand chopping the fish in a wooden bowl until perfectly minced was an overwhelming chore.

The food processor has brought a renaissance of this cultural gem, which I could not have failed to include here.

Fish heads will give superior flavor and body to the jellied broth which, if enough heads are added, may not require gelatin.

3 qts. (3 L) Fish Broth, page 41
¾ lb. (340 g) skinned whitefish fillets, chilled
¾ lb. (340 g) skinned pike (pickerel) fillets, chilled
1 medium carrot, peeled, cut into 1-inch lengths
1 medium onion, peeled, cut into 1-inch cubes
⅓ cup (¾ dL) cold water
1 egg
1¼ teaspoons salt
Freshly ground pepper to taste
1½ teaspoons matzo meal
1 tablespoon (package) unflavored gelatin
Pinch salt
2 egg whites
Parsley sprigs, for garnish
Horseradish, for garnish

1. Prepare Fish Broth. Rinse fish fillets under cold running water to remove any scales that might cling. Run your finger down center of fillets to feel for bones; remove any with a tweezer. Pat fillets dry and cut into 1-inch chunks; set aside.

2. Insert the *metal knife blade.* Mince carrots very fine with 4 two-second pulses; set aside. Add onion to container and purée by processing with 3 tablespoons water about 30 seconds; set aside. Add half the whitefish and half the pike to the empty container. Process with 4 to 6 one-second pulses and remove to a bowl. Repeat to process remaining fish. Place egg, remaining water, salt, pepper, and matzo meal in container; mix with 4 half-second pulses. Scrape down sides of container.

3. Add all the chopped fish to the egg mixture in the container. Process to mix with 4 half-second pulses. Add minced carrots and the onion. Process to finish chopping and combining ingredients with 5 or 6 two-second pulses. Return all the mixture to a bowl; check to be sure it is evenly mixed. Cover and refrigerate 30 minutes but no longer than 4 hours.

4. To shape fish balls, cut a large sheet of aluminum foil and place it on work surface. With wet hands, shape ¼ cup (½ dL) of fish

mixture into a football shape; repeat. Place fish balls on foil as you work.

5. Heat broth to a rapid simmer in a 6-quart (6-L) soup kettle. Add fish balls one at a time. Cover and adjust heat so broth simmers rapidly after all the fish has been added. Cook 1½ hours. Uncover and cool to room temperature. Remove fish from cooled broth with a slotted spoon to a dish; cover and refrigerate. Slowly boil broth until reduced to 3 cups (¾ L); place ¼ cup (½ dL) broth in refrigerator to test for jelling while remainder cools. After 45 minutes to 1 hour, check to see if refrigerated broth has jelled. If jelled and clear, omit Steps 6 and 7. If jelled but not clear, omit gelatin from Step 6 but proceed with clarification adding egg whites as described. If not jelled and not clear, proceed as recipe directs, completing Steps 6 and 7.

6. Place cool reduced broth in a large non-aluminum saucepan. Stir in gelatin and a pinch of salt. Return *metal knife blade* to processor container. Process egg whites until very foamy and opaque, about 1 minute. Pour whites into broth, and, stirring frequently, heat broth just to boiling. As the second bubble breaks the surface of the egg whites, remove pan from heat and set aside 5 minutes.

7. Line a strainer with a damp double layer of cheesecloth and set it over a bowl. Slowly pour contents of saucepan through strainer; set aside to allow liquid to drip through undisturbed; do not stir. Place clarified broth in refrigerator to jell.

8. To serve, place fish on a platter or individual plates. Garnish with jellied broth chopped into pieces. Decorate platter or plates with parsley and accompany with horseradish.

BAKED SCALLOPS OF FISH WITH TOMATO AND BASIL
Makes 4 servings

I have adapted this delicate preparation from Chef Rouillard's original recipe and added a garnish of fresh chives. During the summer when herbs are fresh, a *chiffonnade* of (shredded) stemmed basil leaves could replace dried basil and chives without altering the spirit of the dish.

½ **slice (½ oz./15 g) fresh white, whole wheat or seedless rye bread or ¼ cup (½ dL) fresh bread crumbs**
2 **firm but ripe medium tomatoes, cored, halved lengthwise, ends cut blunt**
2 **tablespoons (30 g) softened butter**
1½ **lbs. (675 g) skinned boned fish fillets, such as striped bass, scrod, halibut, or tilefish**
About ¼ **cup (½ dL) Dijon mustard**
Salt and freshly ground pepper
Several pinches dried basil leaves or a small handful fresh stemmed basil leaves shredded into a *chiffonnade* (with scissors or small knife)
Fresh snipped chives, if dried basil is used
Processor Hollandaise, page 108

1. Tear bread into small pieces. Insert the *metal knife blade*. Process to medium-fine crumbs; transfer to waxed paper. Change to the *medium slicing disk*. Insert tomatoes upright from underneath food chute and slice with a gentle push; set aside.

2. Use 1 tablespoon butter to coat a baking dish large enough to hold fish; set aside. Slicing on a strong diagonal, cut fish into 4 "scallops," each about 4½ inches (10 cm) long. With a veal pounder or the flat side of a cleaver, pound each scallop gently to flatten it slightly. Brush each generously with mustard; place in baking dish; sprinkle lightly with salt and pepper.

3. Place tomato slices over mustard in 1 even layer that completely covers fish. Do not overlap tomatoes or they will not cook properly; press gently so that tomatoes adhere to fish. Sprinkle 1 tablespoon bread crumbs over each "scallop"; top with a pinch of crushed dried basil leaves (omit if using fresh basil *chiffonade* for garnish). Dot tops of fillets with remaining butter cut into small pieces; sprinkle salt and pepper lightly over fish. Set fish aside until ready to bake.

4. Heat oven to 425° F (220° C). Bake fish uncovered until crumbs crisp slightly and fish is just cooked through, 15 to 20 minutes. While fish bakes, prepare Processor Hollandaise. Spoon a pool of sauce onto warmed dinner

plates; place a piece of fish on each plate over sauce. Garnish with chives or fresh basil; serve immediately.

SOLE MEDITERRANEO
Makes 6 servings

Fish baked in paper bags or parchment pouches is an old Italian cooking trick for steaming fish in its own juices. The steam in turn causes the bag to puff; so be sure that the foil is properly and tightly double folded. I have broken the "no cheese with fish" rule here, but somehow I don't think anyone will mind.

⅓ **cup (¾ dL) firmly packed parsley leaves**
3 **oz. (85 g) Parmesan cheese, cut into 1-inch chunks**
1 **medium garlic clove, peeled**
1 **medium onion, peeled, cut into 1-inch chunks**
2 **medium tomatoes, cored, peeled, quartered**
1 **teaspoon Mixed Herbs, page 6**
2 **tablespoons Dijon mustard**
1¼ **cups (3 dL) dry white wine**
⅓ **cup (¾ dL) olive oil**
6 **tablespoons (¾ dL) fresh lemon juice**
¼ **lb. (115 g) fresh mushrooms, wiped clean**
2 **tablespoons (30 g) butter**
6 **small (4 oz./115 g) sole or flounder fillets, or 3 large (8 oz./225 g) sole or flounder fillets, split lengthwise**
Salt and freshly ground pepper to taste

1. Insert the *metal knife blade.* Process parsley until finely minced; set aside. Process Parmesan cheese until powdery; set aside. With machine running, drop garlic through food chute; scrape down sides of container. Add onion and process to chop with 4 or 5 half-second pulses; remove onion mixture to a medium skillet; set aside. Chop tomatoes coarsely with 3 or 4 half-second pulses; set aside.

2. Place herbs, mustard, wine, oil, and lemon juice in container. Mix 5 seconds; transfer to a cup with a pouring spout. Change to the *medium slicing disk.* Stack mushrooms in food chute with caps alternating; slice with a gentle push.

3. Add butter to skillet with onion mixture.

Cook over medium heat until onion mixture is soft but not brown; remove skillet from heat; add salt and pepper to taste.

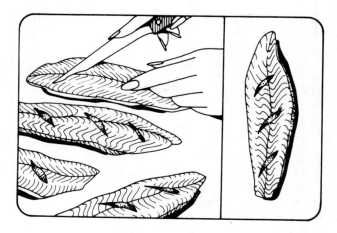

4. Rinse fillets with cold water and pat dry on paper toweling. Place skin (shiny) side up on work surface. Make 3 shallow diagonal slashes on each fillet. Lightly season with salt and pepper. Spoon a scant tablespoon onion mixture over each fillet; roll up and set aside. Cut six 10- × 8-inch (25- × 20-cm) pieces of heavy-duty aluminum foil. Place a rolled fillet in the center of each piece of foil.

5. Cover each fillet with 3 heaping tablespoons sliced mushrooms and 2 tablespoons chopped tomatoes. Top with 1 heaping tablespoon grated cheese and 2 teaspoons minced parsley. Turn up all edges of foil. Stir wine mixture well and pour ⅓ cup (¾ dL) over each fillet. Bring up and match long edges of foil, working carefully so that liquid does not run out.

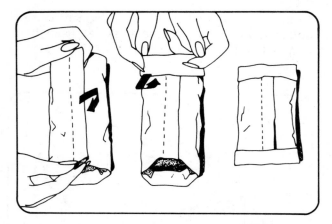

Fold edges over twice to close; press fold tightly. To seal package, fold up open ends twice, again working carefully so no liquid is lost and pressing fold tightly.

6. Bake immediately or refrigerate up to 5 hours. If refrigerated, let packages stand at room temperature 30 minutes before baking. Adjust oven rack to middle position. Heat oven to 525° F (275° C). Place packages on jelly-roll pan. Bake 15 to 20 minutes or until pouches puff. Test 1 for doneness by opening and piercing thickest part of fish with a sharp knife. If knife meets no resistance, fish is cooked. Serve immediately in foil packages or remove from packages and serve in warmed soup bowls.

BAKED STUFFED FISH
Makes 6 servings

This is a neat method for preparing a whole fish; because the fish is boneless, it can easily be cut crosswise for serving. I bake whole fish with the head intact, a classic presentation, but if you object to this, have the fish store remove the head.

1 cup (¼ L) Persillade, page 67
1 oz. (30 g) Parmesan cheese, cut into 1-inch chunks
½ medium onion, peeled, cut into 1-inch cubes
1 medium celery rib, strings removed, cut into 1-inch lengths
1 medium carrot, peeled, cut into 1-inch cubes
1½ cups (3½ dL) firmly packed fresh stemmed spinach or Swiss chard leaves
2 tablespoons (30 g) butter

1 tablespoon olive or vegetable oil
1 (4¼ to 4½ lbs./2 kg) whole fresh fish such as striped bass, bluefish, red snapper, or whitefish, boned through the belly
Salt and pepper to taste

1. Cool or defrost Persillade if frozen; set aside. Insert the *metal knife blade.* With machine running, drop Parmesan cheese 1 chunk at a time through food chute. Process until powdery; set aside. Add onion, celery, and carrot to container. Chop with 4 to 6 one-second pulses. Empty container into a medium skillet. Change to the *medium slicing disk.* Stack and roll spinach leaves (see page 46, upper right illustration) and insert from underneath food chute. Slice with a gentle push; set aside.

2. Add butter to the skillet. Cook vegetables over medium heat until soft but not brown. Add spinach and stir until wilted. Remove skillet from heat; cool slightly and stir in Persillade, grated cheese, and salt and pepper to taste; set mixture aside to cool thoroughly.

3. Adjust oven rack to lower position. Heat oven to 375° F (190° C). Line a jelly-roll pan or shallow roasting pan with aluminum foil. Coat foil with ½ tablespoon oil; set aside.

4. Check fish as described on page 45 to be sure bones and scales are removed. Pat dry inside and out with paper toweling. Sprinkle inside lightly with salt and pepper; coat outside with remaining ½ tablespoon oil. Place in pan, diagonally if necessary.

5. Stuff fish with vegetable mixture. Gently press on outside to distribute stuffing evenly. It is not necessary to sew fish closed; however, sharp toothpicks or short bamboo skewers may be inserted to hold in stuffing, if desired. Bake 35 to 40 minutes or until thickest section of fish flakes easily with a knife and has just turned pale white. Slice crosswise to serve.

SCALLOPS OF FISH IN LETTUCE LEAVES
Makes 6 servings

Like many recipes from professional chefs, this

preparation is involved and the ingredients are expensive. However, this is a beautiful main course for an important dinner, and it can be made and completely assembled ahead of time. If striped bass or salmon are unavailable, another firm-fleshed fish may be substituted.

1 large carrot, peeled, cut to fit food chute sideways
1 large celery rib, strings removed, cut to fit food chute sideways
2-inch length white part of leek or 3 two-inch lengths white part of green onion
2 medium shallots, peeled
1 medium tomato, peeled, seeded, quartered
⅛ lb. (60 g) chilled sea or bay scallops, well rinsed, patted dry
Salt
Dash each: Tabasco sauce and curry powder
Freshly ground white pepper
⅓ cup (¾ dL) chilled whipping cream
2 qts. (2 L) water
6 large Boston lettuce leaves
1½ to 1¾ lbs. (675 to 800 g) skinned, boned fish fillets, such as striped bass or salmon, all small bones removed, rinsed, patted dry
1 tablespoon (15 g) butter, slightly softened
½ cup (1 dL) dry white wine
Processor Hollandaise, page 108, with water omitted

1. To prepare vegetables, insert *medium slicing disk.* Cut carrots and celery into matchsticks by double-slicing (see page 13, center left illustration); set aside. Place leek sideways in chute; slice with a gentle push. Fit a large saucepan with a vegetable steamer basket. Add 1 inch (2½ cm) or enough water to fill space between bottom of saucepan and underside of steamer basket. Cover and steam until vegetables are soft-tender, about 6 to 8 minutes over high heat. Remove to waxed paper and cool to room temperature.

2. Change to the *metal knife blade.* With machine running, drop shallots through food chute. Process until minced; set aside. Coarsely chop tomato with 3 to 5 half-second pulses depending on firmness. Transfer to a strainer to drain. Wipe out container.

3. Add scallops, a generous pinch of salt, Tabasco, curry powder, and white pepper to processor. With machine running, drizzle cream through food chute within 15 seconds, stopping several times to scrape down sides of container. When cream is all incorporated, scrape down sides and bottom edges carefully. Process 5 seconds longer and refrigerate.

4. Heat 2 quarts (2 L) water to a rolling boil. Add 2 lettuce leaves. When water returns to a boil and leaves wilt, remove with a slotted spoon and immediately rinse with cold water. Repeat and set blanched leaves aside.

5. Slicing on a strong diagonal, cut fish fillets into 6 "scallops," each about 4½ inches (10 cm) long. With a veal pounder or the flat side of a cleaver, pound each gently to flatten slightly. Sprinkle with salt and pepper. Spread each generously with scallop *mousseline* and dot evenly with tomato pieces. Carefully place vegetables over *mousseline* and tomatoes; dust with salt and pepper. Unfurl and pat dry lettuce leaves. Cover each piece of fish with a lettuce leaf so that *mousseline* is completely covered; tuck edges of leaves under pieces of fish if necessary to make neat packages.

6. Butter a baking dish large enough to contain all fish in 1 layer. Sprinkle shallots over bottom of dish. Place "scallops" in dish. Cover and refrigerate as long as overnight or bake immediately.

7. If fish has been prepared in advance and refrigerated, remove from refrigerator 30 minutes before baking. Heat oven to 350° F (175° C). Add wine to dish, cover tightly with foil and bake 20 minutes. Test by piercing 1 fillet with tip of a knife. If knife meets no resistance and top of fillet is hot, remove fish from oven. If not, bake 5 minutes longer; check again.

8. Meanwhile, prepare Processor Hollandaise, *omitting water;* cover and leave sauce in processor container. Hold the cooked fish in place with a cloth towel placed over the foil. Turn up a corner of the foil and strain liquid from baking dish into a medium skillet. Cover and keep fish warm. Reduce liquid to 2 tablespoons by boiling.

9. Remove pusher and start the machine. Pour hot reduced liquid into sauce through the food chute. Adjust seasonings of sauce to taste. Place fish on warmed dinner plates. Spoon a small amount of hot sauce over center of fillets;

spoon remainder around fillets. Serve immediately.

BAKED SHRIMP
Makes 4 servings

Tiger shrimp are large meaty creatures from Southeast Asia with a characteristic striped brown and orange coloring. Like nearly all shrimp sold today, they have been frozen; however, their large size and firm flesh causes them to suffer less from freezing than some of their smaller relatives.

Many fish markets have them on hand but they are by no means common and I do suggest ordering them in advance. They will cost a small fortune but their rich taste, further enhanced by garlic, shallots, and butter, makes them a good investment.

6 medium garlic cloves
6 oz. to ½ lb. (180 to 225 g) butter
12 tiger shrimp or prawns (4 to 6 oz./150 g each) in their shells
2 small lemons, scored, ends cut blunt, for garnish
¼ cup (½ dL) firmly packed parsley leaves
⅛ lb. (60 g) shallots, peeled
1 slice (1 oz./30 g) fresh white, whole wheat, or seedless rye bread or ½ cup fresh bread crumbs
Salt and freshly ground pepper to taste

1. Crush 3 of the garlic cloves with the flat side of a knife; it is not necessary to peel them. Place crushed garlic with 4 to 6 ounces (1 to 1½ sticks) of the butter in a small saucepan. Simmer over low heat without allowing garlic to brown, for 6 minutes. Strain; discard garlic and set garlic butter aside.

2. Place shrimp on work surface. With kitchen shears, snip off swimmerets. With a sharp knife, cut lengthwise down the center of the belly beginning at the base of the tail. Cut through the thin belly shell and meat but not through the back shell. Pull sides of shell outward to flatten and expose meat—this will cause back shell to crack. Remove dark vein. With a knife, make a lengthwise slit in the large piece of shrimp meat on each half of the shell to allow shrimp to cook evenly. Do not cut through the back shell. Repeat to open and butterfly all shrimp. Rinse under cold running water and pat dry. Refrigerate until ready to use.

3. Insert the *medium slicing disk*. Place lemons in food chute from underneath. Slice each with a firm push; set aside for garnish. Wipe container dry and change to the *metal knife blade*. Process parsley until finely minced; reserve for garnish. Peel 3 remaining garlic cloves; and with machine running, drop garlic and shallots one at a time through food chute. Process until minced.

4. Melt 4 tablespoons butter in a medium skillet. Add garlic and shallots; return container and blade to processor base. Cook garlic mixture over medium heat until soft but not browned; remove skillet from heat. Meanwhile tear bread into small pieces and process to medium crumbs. Add bread crumbs to skillet, return to medium heat, and stir until butter has been absorbed and crumbs begin to crisp. Add salt and pepper to taste; set skillet aside.

5. Arrange shrimp in a shallow oven-proof skillet or in a paella pan so that shells rest against sides of pan and support the tails which will stand upright. Do not crowd shrimp in pan and spread open thickest part as much as possible (crack back shell if necessary) to allow meat to cook evenly. Wrap tail of each shrimp with a small piece of aluminum foil to prevent burning. Sprinkle shrimps lightly with salt and pepper.

6. Spoon half the garlic butter evenly over shrimp. Place 1 tablespoon shallot mixture on each shrimp to completely cover exposed meat. Drizzle remaining garlic butter evenly over shrimp. Cover skillet or pan with aluminum foil, working carefully so shrimp do not fall or slide. Shrimp are ready to bake. If desired, refrigerate up to 6 hours. Let stand at room temperature for 30 minutes before baking.

7. Adjust oven rack to top position. Heat oven to 500° F (260° C). Bake 12 minutes and test to see that meat nearest bottom shell has just cooked through and turned opaque white. If shrimp is not cooked through, bake 1 to 2 minutes longer; test again, but take care not to overcook or shrimp will be tough.

8. Turn broiler to highest setting. Uncover skillet or pan. Broil shrimp close to heat source until crumbs begin to lightly brown, about 1 to 1½ minutes. Baste with pan juices. Remove foil from tails, sprinkle with parsley, and serve immediately, garnished with lemon slices.

CIOPPINO
Makes 6 servings

This rich seafood chowder is a classic. This version includes a pinch of saffron and leans heavily on shellfish, so it tends to be expensive. Precooked monkfish (also called angler fish) could be substituted for lobster and flounder or tilefish for crabmeat.

⅓ **cup (¾ dL) firmly packed parsley leaves**
4 **medium garlic cloves, peeled**
4 **medium shallots, peeled, or ½ medium onion, cut into 1-inch chunks**
4 **medium tomatoes, cored, peeled, and quartered, or 1 can (1 lb. 12 oz./790 g) Italian plum tomatoes, seeded, drained**
¼ **cup (½ dL) olive or vegetable oil**
4 **tablespoons (60 g) butter**
Large pinch saffron
Salt and freshly ground pepper to taste
1 **teaspoon Mixed Herbs, page 6**
1 **cup (¼ L) dry white wine or dry vermouth**
12 **littleneck clams, rinsed, well scrubbed**
18 **mussels, rinsed, well scrubbed, beards removed**
2 **small lobster tails (about 4 oz./115 g each), with shells, cut into 1-inch chunks**
½ **lb. (225 g) large raw shrimp in shells, rinsed**
½ **lb. (225 g) salad crabmeat, shell fragments removed, rinsed, well drained**
½ **lb. (225 g) bay or sea scallops, rinsed, quartered if large**

1. Insert the *metal knife blade.* Process parsley until finely minced; set aside for garnish. With machine running, drop garlic and shallots one at a time through food chute. Process until minced; set aside. Chop tomatoes coarsely with 4 or 5 half-second pulses, or change to *french-fry disk* and process with a gentle push.

2. Heat oil and butter in a skillet large enough to contain mussels and clams in a single layer. Cook garlic and shallots over medium heat until soft but not brown. Add tomatoes, saffron, a pinch of salt, some freshly ground pepper, the herbs, and wine. Set aside in skillet at room temperature until 30 minutes before you are ready to serve.

3. Arrange clams and mussels in skillet in 1 layer. Cover tightly with lid or heavy-duty aluminum foil. Heat liquid to a rapid simmer; then simmer rapidly until clams and mussels *begin* to open, about 5 to 6 minutes. Add lobster. Replace cover and simmer moderately—not as rapidly as before—until lobster meat *begins* to turn opaque white, about 5 to 6 minutes longer. Add shrimp and crabmeat; stir well; cover and simmer slowly until shrimp turns white, about 4 minutes longer. Add scallops, stir again, and cook until they turn opaque white; check to be sure all pieces of shellfish are hot and tender. Adjust seasonings to taste. Sprinkle with parsley and serve immediately from the skillet or in individual soup bowls.

FISH SOUP
Makes 6 main course servings

Soupe de poissons is a specialty of French seaside cities from Marseilles to the Italian border and each town has its own special version. Although it is called a soup, this dish is a meal in itself and should be served as a main course.

I first tasted this on the beach at St. Tropez and have never forgotten the exquisite flavors of olive oil, garlic, saffron, tomatoes, herbs, and fish blended into a rich but surprisingly low-calorie meal.

Rouille (pronounced roo-ee) is a garlic and red pepper condiment and an essential ingredient. The amount of garlic or peppers may be adjusted to suit your taste. When seeding the cayenne chilis, take special care to wash your hands thoroughly before touching your eyes, nose, or face. Capsaicin, a substance in the chilis, will cause a burning sensation.

A good homemade fish broth (see page 41) is also an essential ingredient. While for most purposes fish broth should not be made with the heads and bones of a strong-flavored fish such as red snapper or one of its many snapper relatives, red porgy, mullet, or red fish, I do recommend including red snapper frames in the broth for this soup.

3 qts. (3 L) fish broth, made with flat fish and snapper heads and bones
2 medium garlic cloves, peeled
2 medium onions, peeled, cubed
⅛ lb. (60 g) boiled ham, cubed (or torn into small pieces if sliced)
2 ripe medium tomatoes, cored, peeled, seeded, quartered
3 tablespoons olive oil
1 tablespoon flour
½ cup (1 dL) dry white wine
¼ teaspoon saffron threads (generous)
1½ lbs. (675 g) skinned, boned red snapper, or other snapper or fish fillets (see above)
½ lb. (225 g) skinned, boned tilefish, scrod, monkfish, or grouper fillets
1 medium celery rib
1 teaspoon dried thyme leaves
1 bay leaf
Small handful parsley (with stems)

Rouille:

1 to 2 fresh cayenne chilis, seeded (these are about 3 inches long and ⅜-inch wide)
2 to 3 medium garlic cloves, peeled
1 slice fresh white or whole wheat bread
Pinch salt
½ cup (1 dL) olive oil

Salt and freshly ground pepper
6 1-inch-thick slices day-old French or Italian bread, toasted golden brown

1. Prepare the fish broth, strain, and set the broth aside. Insert the *metal knife blade* in a dry container. With the machine running drop the garlic cloves through the food chute. Process until minced and add the onions to the container. Chop the onions using 6 to 8 half-second pulses. Empty the container into an 8-quart (8-L) soup kettle. Process the ham until it is finely minced and add it to the kettle. Purée the tomatoes and leave them in the container.

2. Add olive oil to the soup kettle and stir the mixture over high heat until the ham begins to lightly brown. Sprinkle flour over the mixture and continue to cook, stirring frequently until the flour begins to brown. Remove the kettle from the heat. Stir in the white wine and saffron

threads. Replace the kettle, adjust the heat to medium, and bring the mixture to a boil. Boil slowly until mixture thickens slightly. Add the tomato purée.

3. Check over the fish fillets to be sure all bones have been removed as described on page 54. Rinse fillets, then cut them into 3-inch (8-cm)-long chunks. Place them in the soup kettle. Snap the celery rib in half. Place the thyme leaves in the curved part of the rib, cover with the bay leaf and parsley, pressing it so that parsley holds thyme in place. Cover with the remaining piece of celery and tightly tie the mixture in a bundle with string or thread; add to the soup kettle.

4. Add the strained fish broth to the kettle. Cover and bring liquid to a boil. Boil it violently for 15 minutes. Uncover and set soup aside to cool slightly.

5. While soup is cooking and cooling, prepare the *Rouille*. Clean and dry the container and insert the *metal knife blade*. Tear the chili into pieces. With the machine running, drop them through the food chute. Then drop the garlic cloves through the food chute and process until both are minced. Scrape down the side of the container. Tear the bread into pieces, add to container, and process to fine crumbs. Add salt and with the machine running, pour the olive oil through the food chute in a thin stream within 40 seconds. Process 5 seconds longer and transfer the *Rouille* to a small serving dish. Leave the blade in place.

6. Remove and discard the celery bouquet. With a slotted spoon, remove 1½ cups (3½ dL) fish fillets and vegetables from soup kettle to the processor container. Process until fish is completely puréed and with machine running, pour 1 cup (¼ L) of broth through the food chute within 30 seconds. Process 30 seconds longer and empty contents of container into a large mixing bowl. Repeat until all solids are puréed. Strain the remaining broth into the mixing bowl and stir well. Clean the kettle, add the soup, and adjust the seasoning to taste with salt and pepper. Heat soup thoroughly. Place a slice of toasted bread in each large soup bowl. Ladle soup over bread and serve immediately. Stir a spoon or two of *Rouille* into each bowl of soup.

10
Poultry

Culinary fads may come and go, but chicken is always in style. Like a basic black dress, it is suitable for any occasion and is to be found in the wardrobe of virtually every cuisine.

Unadorned, chicken is humble, providing simple nourishment and a sense of well-being. The proverbial chicken in the pot has been such a bird since the 17th century when Henri IV of France declared in a burst of royal humanism that each of his subjects must have chicken in the Sunday *pot au feu.*

Cloak it in truffles, serve it forth with oysters, or bejewel it with aspic, and the humble chicken becomes a thing of exquisite, lively beauty. No wonder it has so staunchly withstood the vagaries of taste and the ravages of history.

Turkey was an American gift to the world. Domesticated in Mexico and eaten well before the *conquistadores* arrived, it was brought to Europe for the first time during the 16th century. That it became the native American symbol of thanksgiving seems particularly appropriate to its origin.

I call this chapter poultry, but actually it is composed of chicken and turkey recipes to which the food processor can give a lightning assist. Chinese stir-fried dishes use boned chicken breasts, which, when partially frozen, can be cut into perfect strips with the slicing disk. Cooked poultry may be quickly shredded for use in casseroles or salads. All manner of batters, stuffings, and toppings can be assembled at record speed. Chicken stews profit mightily from the processor's aid. Even braising liquids, such as coconut milk for the Ceylonese Chicken Curry, can be easily extracted in the processor—a vast improvement over traditional hand-grating methods.

BUYING AND STORING POULTRY

When buying chicken, look for a bird with yellow skin that is free of bruises and soft spots. A plump breast is another sign of a good chicken. Turkey will be paler in color than chicken, but the same rules apply.

Fresh poultry is always odor free—let your nose be your guide. Plan to use it within 48 hours of purchase; if defrosted, use immediately.

Before refrigerating, remove poultry from its wrapper. Remove giblet package from cavity of a whole chicken or turkey and remove neck. Rinse all parts in cold running water. Drain well; pat dry inside and out and rewrap loosely in waxed paper or plastic wrap. Store poultry in the coldest part of the refrigerator.

FREEZING AND DEFROSTING

Fresh chicken and turkey may be frozen as

long as three months. To prepare for freezing, remove from store package. Rinse and pat dry. Cut into serving pieces if desired. If boned chicken breasts are to be frozen, split each and arrange pieces with boned sides facing each other. Wrap chicken breasts individually in plastic wrap; when partially thawed, they will be ready for immediate use.

Double wrap all chicken or turkey, first in plastic wrap, then in a plastic bag or aluminum foil before freezing. Label and date all packages.

Defrost chicken or turkey in wrappings on a plate in the refrigerator overnight. Before cooking, pat dry. Poultry also may be defrosted at room temperature or in the microwave oven, but it may *not* be quick thawed in cold water.

PREPARING BONED CHICKEN BREASTS FOR PROCESSOR SLICING

Boned chicken breasts must be partially frozen before slicing; if floppy, they will not slice perfectly. Remove all skin and cartilage or excess fat that remains; cut out wishbone if necessary. Split chicken breast lengthwise down midline and leave small fillets intact on each side of breast.

Place boned sides facing each other, matching pieces tip to tip. Wrap in plastic and freeze until firm but not solidly frozen. Chicken must be able to be pierced with a sharp knife; if too firmly frozen, the chicken may damage the slicing disk.

Before slicing, cut ends of chicken breast blunt (this prevents twisting). It may also be necessary to cut small breasts in half crosswise and insert them side by side from underneath food chute to fit snugly; a snug fit gives best slicing results.

CUTTING UP WHOLE CHICKENS

It is most economical to purchase chicken whole and cut it apart yourself. Chickens may be cut easily into serving pieces; only a sharp knife is needed. There are several ways to cut apart a chicken, but, for use in these recipes, the eight to ten serving pieces include: two wings, two drumsticks, two second leg joints, one whole breast split into two pieces, and the whole back split crosswise into two pieces. If desired, back may be set aside and frozen for use in stock (if not previously frozen), and each piece of breast meat may be split crosswise so that there will be 4 breast pieces.

Wet chicken or poultry does not brown properly. Pat pieces dry before cooking, using paper toweling or a dry cloth towel. If desired, chicken pieces may be placed directly on refrigerator rack no longer than two hours to allow air to circulate and pieces to dry slightly. Always bring chicken or turkey to room temperature before cooking.

SHREDDING COOKED POULTRY

Any type of cooked boneless poultry may be shredded by slicing. Use the *thick* or *medium slicing disk* or the *french-fry disk*. Before placing poultry pieces in food chute, be sure all bits of bone, tendon, and cartilage have been removed. Like cooked meats, poultry slices best when thoroughly chilled. If a piece should catch on corner of slicing disk causing machine to twist, stop and carefully dislodge the food with a knife; do not use fingers.

CHICKEN BREASTS WITH MUSTARD PERSILLADE
Makes 4 servings

If *Persillade* is kept on hand in the freezer, this is an absolutely no-fuss recipe that is both delicious and economical. Serve with a plain green vegetable, such as broccoli or green beans, and accompany either with a dry white wine or a light red wine.

2 whole chicken breasts (¾ to 1 lb./340 to 450 g each), skin and rib bones left on, breast bone and wishbone removed, split
Persillade (following)
Scant ¼ cup (½ dL) Dijon mustard

1. Rinse chicken breasts under cold running water; pat dry with paper toweling. Heat oven to 425° F (220° C). Spread Persillade in an even layer on a large sheet of waxed paper. Using a pastry brush, paint skin side of each chicken breast generously with Dijon mustard—as much as you would put on a lightly frosted cake.

2. Working carefully, dip mustard sides into Persillade and press firmly to make crumbs adhere. Place chicken breasts crumb side up in a baking dish. Bake until juices run clear when pierced with a skewer and topping is a deep

golden brown, about 20 to 25 minutes; serve immediately.

PERSILLADE
Makes about 1¼ cups (3 dL)

Persil is the French word for parsley, the ingredient which offsets the flavor of garlic in this preparation. Persillade with bread crumbs makes a superb coating for chicken breasts, page 66, or a good stuffing for fish, page 60.

⅓ cup (¾ dL) firmly packed parsley leaves
2 medium garlic cloves, peeled
4 tablespoons (60 g) butter
2 slices (1 oz./30 g each) fresh white, whole wheat, or rye bread, or 1 cup fresh bread crumbs
Salt and pepper to taste

1. Insert the *metal knife blade* in a dry container. Process parsley until finely minced; set aside on waxed paper. With machine running, drop garlic cloves through food chute; process until minced.

2. Place garlic and butter in a medium skillet. Cook on low heat until soft but not brown. Return blade to processor container. Tear bread in pieces and process to medium-fine crumbs. Add bread crumbs to skillet and stir over medium heat until lightly browned. Stir in parsley; salt and pepper to taste. Persillade is ready to use. **Note:** Store in refrigerator in airtight container as long as 5 days. If desired, omit salt and pepper and freeze. Adjust seasonings after defrosting.

BATTER-FRIED CHICKEN
Makes 4 servings

Crisp, moist fried chicken is a great American dish whose reputation has been sadly tarnished by fast-food chains. This recipe recaptures the home-cooked taste of "real" chicken, fried in a delicate batter mixed lump free in the food processor. A deep-fry thermometer is also essential to the success of the dish, since it eliminates guesswork about the temperature of the oil.

Beer Batter (see below)
1 frying chicken (2½ to 3 lbs./1¼ kg), cut into 8 or 10 serving pieces
2 qts. (2 L) vegetable oil
Salt and pepper to taste

1. One hour in advance (or the night before), prepare Beer Batter.

2. Rinse chicken in cold running water. Pat very dry in cloth towels. Heat oil in a 6-quart (6-L) soup kettle or Dutch oven to 350° F (175° C) on a deep-fry thermometer. Heat oven to 250° F (120° C). Place a cake rack on a baking sheet; set aside.

3. Dip chicken pieces in prepared batter. Fry 3 pieces at a time, turning once, until golden brown. Fry wings, backs, and breasts about 8 minutes, legs and thighs about 10 minutes. To keep temperature of oil constant, replace chicken pieces no more than 1 or 2 at a time. Drain on paper toweling for 2 to 3 minutes. Keep drained chicken crisp and hot on cake rack in warm oven up to 1 hour if desired. Before serving, season with salt and pepper.

BEER BATTER
Makes about 1½ cups (3½ dL)

Use draft beer for best taste. Batter also will coat about 2 pounds (900 g) fish fillets.

1 cup (140 g) unbleached all-purpose flour
1 teaspoon salt
Pepper to taste
1 tablespoon (15 g) butter, melted and cooled
1 egg yolk
1 to 1¼ cups (¼ L to 3 dL) flat beer, room temperature

1. Insert the *metal knife blade.* Add flour, salt, and pepper to the container. Process 5 seconds to rapid-sift. Add butter and egg. With machine running pour 1 cup (¼ L) beer through the food chute within 8 seconds. Scrape down sides of container and process 3 seconds longer. Adjust to medium-thick consistency with remaining beer, as needed.

2. Transfer batter to a medium bowl. Cover and refrigerate 1 hour or as long as overnight.

SWEET AND SOUR STIR-FRIED CHICKEN
Makes 4 servings

A popular Cantonese stir-fry made in a wok and a classic food processor dish. Serve with plain steamed rice Chinese style or with Pilaf (omitting vegetables), pages 95–96.

Sauce Mixture:

1 teaspoon all-purpose soy sauce
1 tablespoon dry sherry
2 tablespoons sugar
2 tablespoons rice or white vinegar
1 tablespoon plus 2 teaspoons ketchup
¼ cup (½ dL) reserved pineapple syrup (see below)
¼ cup (½ dL) Chicken Broth, page 40
1 tablespoon cornstarch
1 large raw egg white
1 teaspoon cornstarch
1 skinned, boned, whole chicken breast (½ lb./225 g), partially frozen
6 medium whole green onions
4 large mushrooms, wiped clean
½ small green bell pepper, cored and seeded
½ small red bell pepper, cored and seeded
2 oz. (60 g) drained, rinsed water chestnuts (about 4 large)
1½ cups (3½ dL) peanut oil
½ cup (1 dL) drained, crushed pineapple in heavy syrup, syrup reserved
½ cup (1 dL) moderately packed fresh bean sprouts, rinsed, drained

1. To prepare sauce mixture, insert the *metal knife blade.* Place soy sauce, sherry, sugar, vinegar, ketchup, pineapple syrup, broth, and cornstarch in container. Process 10 seconds. Transfer to large cup; set aside near stove.

2. With *metal knife blade* in place, process egg white and cornstarch 10 seconds. Remove blade, leaving egg white mixture in container. Change to the *medium slicing disk.* Cut end of chicken breast blunt or halve it crosswise and insert it upright in food chute. Slice with a moderate push. Remove disk; toss chicken pieces thoroughly in egg white mixture. Refrigerate in a small bowl 30 minutes or up to 2 hours, tossing occasionally.

3. Replace the disk. Dangle slice white parts of green onions (see page 102); set slices aside,

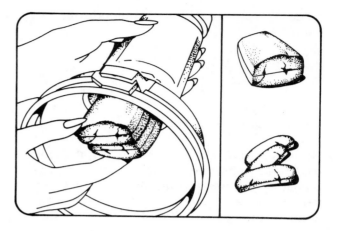

reserve or discard tops. Stack mushrooms in food chute with caps alternating and slice with a gentle push. Cut ends of peppers blunt and halve crosswise. Inserting each piece from underneath food chute, slice with a gentle push; set mushrooms and peppers aside. Slice chestnuts with a moderate push; set aside.

4. Place a large strainer over a medium heat-proof bowl; set aside near stove. Heat peanut oil in a wok or very large skillet over high heat until oil gently bubbles around a dry chopstick when inserted. Add chicken all at once and stir vigorously to separate pieces. When chicken turns white, about 1 minute, carefully pour chicken and oil into strainer.

5. Return 2 tablespoons of the hot oil to wok; heat. Add peppers and mushrooms; stir-fry until crisp-tender about 1 minute; remove from wok with slotted spoon and add to strainer with chicken. Stir sauce mixture well; add to wok; add crushed pineapple. Cook, stirring constantly, until sauce begins to thicken, about 1 to 1½ minutes. Return chicken, peppers, and mushrooms to wok; add water chestnuts, green onions, and bean sprouts. Stir-fry vigorously until thoroughly hot, about 1½ to 2 minutes longer. Serve immediately.

CHICKEN BREASTS TONNATO
Makes 6 to 8 servings

This is a variation on the Italian, *vitello tonnato,* cold sliced veal with tuna mayonnaise, found in the Northern Italian provinces of Lombardy and Piedmont. It is perfect hot weather food, and the lovely pale beige sauce that blankets the chicken offers a smooth background for pretty garnishes, such as Gherkin Fans, page 14, lower left illustration. Thinly sliced cold roast veal may, of course, be substituted for the chicken breasts.

4 whole chicken breasts (½ lb./225 g each), boned, skinned, split
2 to 3 cups (½ to ¾ L) Chicken Broth, page 40
1 medium garlic clove, peeled
½ medium onion, peeled, quartered
½ medium celery rib, cut into 1-inch lengths
½ medium carrot, cut into 1-inch lengths
Pinch each: dried basil, marjoram, sage
½ bay leaf
3 flat anchovy fillets
1 can (6½ oz./195 g) good-quality chunk light oil-packed tuna, well drained
Mayonnaise, page 114, with salt and lemon juice omitted
1 tablespoon white wine vinegar, or to taste
Salt and freshly ground pepper
6 *cornichons* (sour gherkins)
3 tablespoons capers, drained
Pimiento strips, for garnish
Parsley sprigs, for garnish

1. Remove all fat from chicken breasts and cut away any pieces of membrane that cling. Rinse and pat chicken breasts dry. With a veal pounder or the side of a cleaver, pound each breast gently to flatten slightly. Place breasts and broth in a large deep skillet in 1 layer if possible. Add enough broth to cover chicken breasts by ½ inch (1½ cm). Place cover slightly ajar and heat liquid almost to a simmer. Poach chicken breasts by cooking at a slight simmer until they turn pale white and are just cooked through, approximately 8 minutes. Remove 1 and test to be sure that underside of breast between small fillet and large lobe is opaque white and just cooked through. If not, poach several minutes longer. Uncover and cool chicken breasts to room temperature in the poaching liquid. Remove, cover, and refrigerate breasts; strain liquid. Place strained broth in a large clean skillet; set aside.

2. Insert *metal knife blade.* Place garlic, onion, celery, carrot, basil, marjoram, and sage in processor container. Process to chop with 4 or 5 one-second pulses. Add contents of container to skillet with broth. Stir in bay leaf, anchovy, and tuna. Simmer slowly until no liquid re-

mains, taking care not to let mixture burn. Reduce heat if necessary. Remove from heat and cool; discard bay leaf.

3. With *metal knife blade* in place, purée contents of skillet 15 seconds; set aside. Without washing container, prepare Mayonnaise, omitting salt and lemon juice. Return puréed tuna mixture to container with Mayonnaise and add vinegar. Process to thoroughly combine with 5 or 6 one-second pulses, scraping down sides of container as necessary. Adjust seasonings to taste. Refrigerate until thoroughly chilled.

4. To assemble, spoon a third of the chilled tuna mixture onto a serving platter. Arrange chilled chicken fillets on top. Spoon remaining tuna mixture over tops of chicken breasts. Garnish with *cornichons,* capers, pimiento, and parsley. Carefully cover with plastic and refrigerate up to 8 hours. Serve cold.

ARROZ CON POLLO
Makes 4 servings

To call this merely "rice with chicken" gives no hint of the full rich flavor to be found in this traditional Spanish dish. Chorizo is a spicy Spanish sausage that will set the tone of the seasonings. You can make your own or purchase chorizo (either fresh or smoked) at stores carrying Spanish or Mexican foods.

1 chorizo sausage (6 to 8 oz./180 to 225 g), page 80
1 frying chicken (2 to 3½ lbs./900 to 1,500 g), cut into 8 to 10 pieces
¼ cup (½ dL) firmly packed parsley leaves
2 medium garlic cloves, peeled
1 medium onion, peeled, cut into 1-inch cubes
2 medium tomatoes, peeled, cored, quartered
1 medium green pepper, cored, halved lengthwise
2 tablespoons lard or vegetable oil
1½ cups (345 g) raw long-grain rice
3 cups (¾ L) Chicken Broth, page 40
⅛ teaspoon powdered saffron or large pinch saffron threads
¼ teaspoon salt, or more to taste
Freshly ground pepper
2 dashes Tabasco sauce

1. Wrap sausage in plastic and partially freeze about 2 hours. Rinse chicken in cold water and pat dry with paper toweling; set aside.

2. Insert *metal knife blade.* Process parsley until fine and set aside for garnish. With machine running, drop garlic cloves one at a time through food chute. Process until minced. Add onion to container and chop with 4 to 6 half-second pulses; set aside. Chop tomatoes coarsely, using 3 half-second pulses; set aside. Change to *medium slicing disk.* Cut green pepper halves crosswise and cut ends blunt. Inserting each piece from underneath food chute, slice with a gentle push; set aside. Halve sausage crosswise. Place pieces upright in food chute and slice with a firm push; set aside.

3. Heat lard or oil in a large skillet. Brown chicken pieces a few at a time turning once. Do not crowd chicken pieces in skillet. Set browned chicken aside. Remove all but 1 tablespoon fat from skillet. Add minced garlic and onions; stir over low heat until soft but not brown. Add green pepper and cook a minute or two longer. Add rice. Stir until grains turn milky white. Add broth, saffron, salt, pepper, and Tabasco. Stir well.

4. Heat mixture to boiling. Stir well. Place sausage and tomato on rice. Place chicken pieces over sausage in single even layer. Cover with aluminum foil just touching the chicken to ensure all ingredients cook evenly. Cover skillet and simmer until rice has absorbed all liquid and chicken is just cooked through, about 35 to 40 minutes.

5. Before serving, adjust seasonings to taste. Serve from skillet or transfer to a warm serving platter. Garnish with parsley.

CEYLONESE CHICKEN CURRY
Makes 4 servings

Sri Lanka, formerly Ceylon, is an island in the Indian Ocean just off the coast of southern India. This is a typical Ceylonese curry in that it uses coconut milk as the cooking liquid and thickening agent and relies on spices to create the characteristic play of flavors.

The recipe comes from our Sri Lankan friend Merle Phillips, who has always prepared her coconut milk by the traditional hand-grating method. Here is a foolproof method for extracting the milk from fresh coconut that Indian cooking enthusiasts should especially appreciate; heating the coconut in the oven helps to crack the shell.

If desired, prepare the chicken, the omelette, and vegetables for pilaf one day in advance, but prepare the rice at the last moment. Serve this curry with a light red wine and follow it by Fruit Salad with Kiwi, page 105.

1 small fresh coconut (1 lb./450 g)
1½ cups (3½ dL) hot water
1-inch piece (½ oz.) fresh ginger root, peeled
2 medium garlic cloves, peeled
2 medium onions, peeled, cubed
½ cinnamon stick
2 bay leaves, roughly crushed
2 whole cloves
2½ tablespoons Indian curry powder
1½ tablespoons chili powder
1 teaspoon ground cardamom
½ to ¾ teaspoon salt
Juice of ¼ to ½ fresh medium lime
1 frying chicken (2½ to 3 lbs./1¼ kg), cut into 10 serving pieces with breast cut into 4 pieces, well rinsed
Plain Omelette, page 93, cooked and chilled, for garnish
Pilaf with Carrots and Cabbage, pages 95–96

1. Heat oven to 450° F (260° C). Pierce eyes of coconut with a screwdriver or ice pick; drain of and discard the liquid. Bake coconut until shell cracks, about 20 minutes. Pound once or twice with a hammer or veal pounder; remove shell. With a cleaver, split coconut apart. Peel off brown barklike coating with a vegetable peeler. Break coconut meat into pieces to fit processor food chute.

2. Insert *medium shredding disk.* Shred coconut with a firm but not hard push, releasing pressure as necessary; empty container onto waxed paper. Insert the *metal knife blade.* Return coconut to container. Start machine and immediately pour hot water through food chute within 5 seconds. Stop, insert pusher, and let coconut stand 15 minutes.

3. Set a large medium- to fine-mesh strainer over a bowl. Empty coconut into strainer and press with processor pusher to extract all milk,

about 1¼ to 1½ cups (3 dL); set coconut milk aside (or cover and chill overnight).

4. Insert *metal knife blade* in clean dry container. With machine running, drop ginger root and garlic through food chute; process until minced. Add 1 of the onions and process to chop with 6 half-second pulses. Empty contents of container into a 4-quart (4-L) Dutch oven. Return blade and container to base and process to chop remaining onion with 5 or 6 half-second pulses; set aside for use in Pilaf.

5. Add cinnamon, bay leaves, cloves, curry, chili powder, cardamom, salt, lime juice, and chicken to Dutch oven; toss to coat chicken with spices. Add coconut milk, stir well and heat liquid to a simmer. Check to be sure all spices have been stirred into the liquid, otherwise they can scorch on pan bottom. Set cover slightly ajar and simmer until chicken is fork-tender, usually 35 to 40 minutes.

6. Meanwhile, prepare and place omelette in refrigerator to chill. Start rice, using reserved onion; then prepare the vegetables for Pilaf. Leave the *slicing disk* in place. Cut cold omelette into 4 strips and stack up two at a time. Roll up and insert omelette strips in food chute; slice with a gentle push. Repeat and set omelette slivers aside for garnish.

7. Just as chicken is tender, rice should be cooked. If rice is not yet ready, remove chicken from heat and set aside; reheat when rice is cooked and transfer chicken to a heated serving plate. Mound pilaf on a separate warmed serving plate; garnish with slivers of egg.

CHICKEN PROVENÇAL
Makes 4 servings

The robust flavors of garlic, tomatoes, and herbs typify the cooking of *Provence,* and the ingredients cook into a naturally thickened chunky sauce. This recipe is the creation of Leslee Reis, owner/chef of one of Chicago's finest restaurants, Café Provençal in Evanston, Illinois.

¼ cup (½ dL) firmly packed parsley leaves
4 to 5 medium garlic cloves, peeled
¼ lb. (115 g) mushrooms, wiped clean

2 lbs. (900 g) fresh ripe tomatoes, peeled, cored, seeded, halved lengthwise, or 2 cans (1 lb. 12 oz./790 g each) Italian plum tomatoes, well drained, seeded
½ cup (60 g) good-quality black pitted olives or pitted Kalamata olives, well drained
6 tablespoons (85 g) butter
Salt
1 frying chicken (2½ to 3 lbs./1¼ kg), cut into serving pieces, patted very dry
3 tablespoons olive oil
¾ cup (1¾ dL) dry white wine
¼ teaspoon dried thyme leaves
1½ teaspoons Mixed Herbs, page 6
1 bay leaf
12 to 18 pearl onions, peeled, top of each scored with an X
Freshly ground pepper to taste

1. Insert the *metal knife blade.* Process parsley until finely minced; set aside for garnish. With machine running, drop garlic cloves one at a time through food chute. Process until minced; remove to waxed paper. Change to the *medium slicing disk.* Stack mushrooms in food chute with caps alternating and slice with a gentle push; empty container into a large skillet; set skillet aside. Return container to processor base.

2. Change to the *french-fry disk* or leave *slicing disk* in place. Load food chute with tomato halves and cut to coarsely chop with a gentle push, or slice tomatoes; set aside. Place olives in food chute and cut or slice with a gentle push; set aside.

3. Add 1½ tablespoons butter to skillet with mushrooms. Sauté over high heat until excess liquid evaporates and mushrooms just turn color. Transfer mushrooms to a sheet of aluminum foil and salt lightly; set aside.

4. Heat 3 tablespoons of the butter with the oil in the same skillet. When hot and bubbling, add chicken pieces without crowding and sauté until golden brown, turning as necessary. Remove chicken pieces; set aside. Carefully pour off and discard half the hot fat. Add wine to skillet and scrape with wooden spatula to deglaze. Simmer rapidly until wine reduces by half.

5. Add garlic and tomatoes to skillet. Simmer rapidly until some of the excess tomato liquid

evaporates and mixture begins to thicken, about 10 minutes. Add thyme, herbs, and bay leaf; stir well. Add onions and chicken to the sauce mixture and push down so tomatoes cover all ingredients as much as possible. Simmer uncovered until dark meat is fork tender, 20 to 25 minutes longer. Check white meat after 15 minutes by piercing to the bone with a small sharp knife; if juices run clear, remove to a warmed serving platter.

6. Remove chicken pieces to platter and cover loosely with aluminum foil to keep warm. To skillet add remaining 1½ tablespoons butter. Simmer until most of the excess liquid evaporates and the sauce mixture thickens to a chunky consistency. Remove and discard bay leaf. Stir in mushrooms and olives; heat thoroughly. Adjust seasonings to taste. Spoon sauce over and around chicken pieces. Garnish with parsley and serve immediately.

RICHARD OLNEY'S ROAST SPLIT CHICKEN
Makes 4 servings

Richard Olney is one of the world's great cooks, and it was my privilege both to study with him and to have assisted him in cooking classes. With his permission, I have adapted this recipe to the food processor.

The stuffing for this beautiful chicken acts as a layer of insulation, basting and flavoring during roasting. Vegetables, such as sautéed mushrooms or blanched, sautéed, chopped spinach may be substituted for zucchini. Potato Nests, page 95, are a good accompaniment.

Stuffing:

½ lb. (225 g) zucchini, ends cut blunt
1¼ teaspoons salt
1½ oz. (45 g) Parmesan cheese, cut into 1-inch chunks
1 medium onion, peeled, cut into 1-inch chunks
6 tablespoons (85 g) butter, slightly softened
⅔ cup (6 oz./180 g) ricotta cheese, well drained
1 egg
Large pinch chopped fresh marjoram leaves and flowers or ¼ teaspoon dried leaves
Freshly ground pepper to taste

1 whole frying chicken (2½ to 3 lbs./1¼ kg), rinsed, patted dry
1 teaspoon Mixed Herbs, page 6
3 tablespoons olive oil

1. To prepare stuffing, insert the *medium shredding disk.* Shred zucchini with a firm push and spread on a large dish. Sprinkle with 1 teaspoon salt; let stand 30 minutes. Rinse well and taste to be sure all salt is removed. Squeeze well with hands to remove all excess moisture.

2. Wipe container dry and change to the *metal knife blade.* Process cheese until powdery; set aside. Process to chop onion with 3 or 4 half-second pulses; remove to a medium skillet. Return blade and container to base. Add 1 tablespoon butter to skillet and cook onion over low heat until soft; set aside. Heat 2 tablespoons butter in skillet. Add zucchini and sauté, tossing frequently, until moisture has evaporated, usually 8 to 9 minutes; remove skillet from heat.

3. Place remaining 3 tablespoons butter, ricotta cheese, egg, marjoram, Parmesan cheese, ¼ teaspoon salt, and pepper in container. Process to thoroughly combine, about 30 seconds, scraping down sides of container as necessary. Add onion and zucchini to container and process to mix with 3 or 4 half-second pulses, scraping down sides of container as necessary. Adjust seasonings to taste and refrigerate until ready to stuff chicken.

4. To prepare chicken for stuffing, remove visible fat from cavity and neck area. Do not remove neck skin. Place chicken breast-side down on work surface with legs pointing toward you. With heavy scissors or poultry

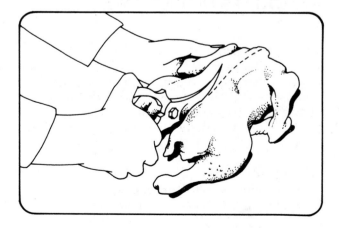

shears, cut through the tail and split chicken down the back, cutting to one side of the neck. Holding each side of the back, pull chicken open and turn it over. With the heel of your hand, firmly whack the top of the chicken breast to break and flatten the bone.

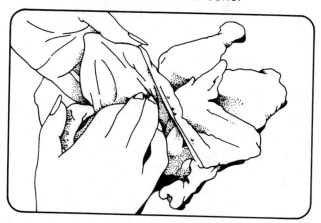

5. Turn chicken so neck end faces you. Lift up neck skin and carefully wedge fingers in between skin and breast meat to make a pocket for stuffing. Break the thin connecting membrane but work carefully to avoid making holes in the skin. Move hand down to loosen skin over each thigh and drumstick. Leave a 1-inch (2½-cm) margin of skin attached at all edges of chicken, otherwise stuffing will fall out.

6. To stuff the chicken, lift up neck skin and push small handfuls of stuffing into place with your fingers. Place stuffing first over drumsticks and thighs, then fill remainder of skin pocket evenly. Press from outside to equalize stuffing over breast and to mold it to contours of chicken. Fold neck skin under and wing tips back and behind to secure neck skin. With the tip of a sharp knife, pierce the apron of skin on each side of the tip of the breast. Make a 1-

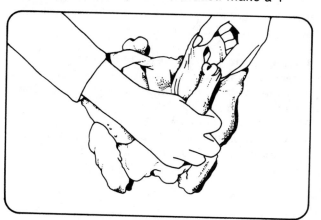

inch-long slit and gently push up drumsticks and insert tips through slits.

7. Place chicken in roasting pan breast side up and sprinkle both sides with herbs. Rub with olive oil. Lightly salt and pepper chicken. (If desired, set the chicken aside at room temperature until ready to roast, as long as 4 hours.)

8. Adjust oven rack to lower position. Heat oven to 450° F (230° C). Roast chicken 10 minutes. Lower heat to 375° F (190° C) and roast 20 minutes longer. Baste with pan juices. Roast 25 to 30 minutes longer, basting once or twice. Cut chicken into 4 serving pieces with a knife or scissors, slicing through the center of the chicken to separate it into 2 pieces and removing each second joint and drumstick in 1 piece. Serve immediately.

SAUSAGE-SAGE TURKEY DRESSING
Makes 10 cups (2½ L)

This is the turkey dressing of my childhood, and, in all modesty, I believe it is one of the best recipes of its type. It may be prepared a day in advance, provided that the eggs are mixed in after the dressing has been brought back to room temperature, just before stuffing the turkey. If too cold, dressing still may be cold in the center when turkey is cooked, juicy, and ready to serve. Leftover Mushroom Bread, page 125, makes especially good dressing.

1 lb. (450 g) day-old unsweetened bread, cut into 1-inch cubes
2 cups (½ L) boiling water
Dianna's Breakfast Sausage, page 79, or 1½ lbs. (675 g) bulk pork sausage (see note on following page)
¼ cup (½ dL) firmly packed parsley leaves
3 medium garlic cloves, peeled
2 medium onions, peeled, cut into cubes
6 oz. (180 g) chilled butter
4 medium celery ribs, strings removed
1 lb. (450 g) fresh mushrooms, wiped clean
Salt and freshly ground pepper to taste
1 teaspoon dried thyme leaves
1 teaspoon dried sage leaves
¼ teaspoon dried savory
2 eggs

1. Place bread cubes in a bowl large enough to contain all the ingredients. Add boiling water; stir well and set aside to soften and cool, stirring occasionally.

2. Cook sausage in a large skillet over medium heat until meat turns pale and crumbly. Cool; remove from skillet with slotted spoon; add to bowl with bread. Discard fat in skillet; set skillet aside without washing.

3. Insert the *metal knife blade.* Process parsley until finely minced; add to bowl with sausage. With machine running, drop garlic cloves one at a time through food chute; scrape down sides of container. Add onions to container and process to chop with 6 to 8 half-second pulses; empty container into skillet. Add 3 tablespoons butter and cook over low heat until soft.

4. Meanwhile, change to the *medium slicing disk.* Cut celery into even lengths to fit upright in food chute and slice with a gentle push; add to skillet and cook over medium heat until celery softens; add contents of skillet to bowl. Load mushrooms in food chute with caps alternating and slice with a gentle push. Repeat with remaining mushrooms and empty container into skillet. Place a 6-tablespoon (85-g) chunk of butter in food chute and slice with a gentle push; transfer to waxed paper; wrap well and refrigerate.

5. Add remaining 3 tablespoons butter to skillet and toss mushrooms over high heat until they darken and all liquid has evaporated; add to bowl with bread. Add salt, pepper, thyme, sage, and savory to bowl. With hands or a wooden spoon, mix thoroughly and adjust seasonings to taste. Cover and refrigerate.

6. Bring stuffing to room temperature by removing from refrigerator at least 2 hours before stuffing turkey. Add reserved sliced butter and eggs to room temperature mixture; combine thoroughly; adjust seasonings to taste. Stuffing is ready to use.

Note: Store-bought pork sausage is, as a rule, more highly seasoned than homemade sausage. If you are substituting it here, omit salt and pepper from recipe. Season the stuffing to taste after all the other ingredients have been added.

ROAST STUFFED TURKEY
Makes 12 to 14 servings

I use a fast roasting method, beginning turkeys in a hot oven, because I have found it results in juicier birds.

To use this method, the turkey must be at room temperature (I leave it out in a cool dark place *unstuffed* overnight and bring it into the kitchen 3 to 4 hours before stuffing.) It also must be removed from the oven once or twice for basting, which I agree is a chore. However by removing the turkey, oven heat is kept constant, energy is saved, and the turkey cooks quickly and stays juicy.

Turkey is done when the thickest part of the thigh (away from the bone) registers 175° F (79° C) on an instant-registering thermometer and juices run clear. Remember that roasts, such as turkey, continue to cook even after they are removed from the oven, so be careful not to overcook. Turkey will stay hot, if covered loosely with aluminum foil, from 40 minutes to 1 hour.

For an extra moist turkey, cut a chilled stick (4 oz./115 g) of butter into 4 long pieces and slip those between the skin and breast meat prior to stuffing the turkey.

If desired, gravy may be thickened with a teaspoon or two of arrowroot dissolved either in cold water or in several tablespoons of Madeira.

If it is possible to obtain a fresh turkey (these may often be ordered in advance from your local butcher), I urge you to do so. While fresh turkey is slightly more costly than frozen, it has an incomparable flavor and moistness.

1 oven-ready turkey (18 to 20 lbs./9 kg), room temperature, neck, liver, and giblets reserved, stuffed with room-temperature Sausage-Sage dressing (page 73), trussed
6 cups (1½ L) cold water
1 medium onion, peeled, cut into 1-inch cubes
2 medium carrots, peeled, cut into 1-inch lengths

2 medium celery ribs, cut into 1-inch lengths
¼ teaspoon dried thyme leaves
4 tablespoons (60 g) butter
3 tablespoons olive or vegetable oil
Salt and freshly ground pepper

1. Several hours before roasting turkey, place giblets and neck in a large saucepan. Reserve liver for another use. Add 6 cups (1½ L) cold water. Heat over high heat to simmering and skim as necessary. With cover set slightly ajar, simmer slowly for 3 hours, reducing liquid to no less than 4 cups (1 L).

2. Insert *metal knife blade* in processor container. Chop onion with 4 or 5 half-second pulses; empty container into bottom of turkey roasting pan. Chop carrots and celery together with 6 to 8 one-second pulses; add to roasting pan. Add thyme and butter to roasting pan; set aside.

3. Adjust oven rack to lower position. Heat oven to 425° F (165° C). Rub turkey all over with oil; sprinkle lightly with salt and pepper. Place in roasting pan over vegetables; roast 20 minutes. Meanwhile, remove neck and giblets from saucepan. Cut meat into small pieces; discard bones; set meat aside.

4. Remove turkey from oven as quickly and carefully as possible and immediately close oven door. Baste with 1 to 1½ cups (¼ L) of the broth from the saucepan. Add cut-up neck and giblet meat to roasting pan. Return turkey to oven as quickly and carefully as possible in order to maintain oven heat. Roast 5 minutes longer and turn oven heat to 325° F (165° C). Roast 1 hour.

5. Remove turkey and close oven door immediately. Stir vegetables well. Baste turkey with an additional 1 to 1½ cups (¼ L) broth. Return turkey to oven and roast until skin is golden brown and an instant-registering thermometer inserted into the thickest part of the thigh registers 175° F (79° C) and juices run clear, about 1½ hours or slightly longer.

6. Remove turkey to carving board or platter. Cover with aluminum foil and set aside as long as 40 minutes before serving. Pour off juices and vegetables from roasting pan into a large measuring cup. Place pan on stove and heat until residue begins to sizzle. Pour in 1 cup (¼ L) turkey broth and stir well to deglaze. Strain into cup with pan juices and vegetables.

7. Skim off all fat that rises to top of liquid in cup. Transfer to a large skillet and simmer rapidly until liquid measures between 2½ to 3 cups (¾ L). Adjust seasonings to taste and keep hot. Before carving turkey, remove trussing strings. Serve pan juices (gravy) separately.

TURKEY MADRAS
Makes 4 servings

This is good for a brunch or dinner when there is leftover turkey in the house; however, a cooked turkey breast or leg and thigh meat could be substituted; you will need about ¾ pound (340 g).

Curry Sauce:

2 tablespoons (30 g) butter
2 tablespoons flour
1½ teaspoons Indian curry powder
3 cups (¾ L) hot Chicken Broth, page 40, or turkey broth
½ cup (1 dL) whipping cream
¼ teaspoon salt
Freshly ground pepper to taste
3 dashes Tabasco sauce

2 cups (½ L) boneless, cooked or leftover turkey
¼ lb. (115 g) fresh mushrooms, wiped clean
2 medium celery ribs, strings removed
2 medium carrots, peeled, cooked
6 medium green onions, roots removed
4 tablespoons (60 g) butter
¼ cup (½ dL) fresh or thawed frozen peas
4 slices warm crustless toast

1. To prepare sauce, heat butter in a high-sided medium skillet until bubbling. Add flour and stir over medium heat about 1 minute. Add curry powder and stir 1 minute longer; do not allow flour to brown. Remove skillet from heat.

Gradually whisk in hot broth. Return skillet to medium heat and slowly simmer, skimming frequently (do not stir), until liquid reduces to 1¼ cups (3 dL). Strain and discard solids. Stir in whipping cream, salt, pepper, and Tabasco. Adjust seasonings to taste; cover and set aside until ready to serve (or refrigerate overnight).

2. Insert the *medium slicing disk* in processor container. Fill food chute with turkey and slice with a gentle push; set turkey aside. Stack mushrooms in food chute with caps alternating. Slice with a gentle push; set aside. Slice celery with a gentle push; set aside. Cut cooked carrots into even lengths to fit upright in food chute and slice with a moderate push; set

aside. Dangle-slice (see page 102) white part of green onions; set aside and reserve tops for another use.

3. Heat 3 tablespoons butter in a large skillet. Toss mushrooms over high heat until liquid evaporates and mushrooms darken; transfer to waxed paper. Add celery and green onion slices and remaining butter to skillet and cook over medium heat until celery softens.

4. Add curry sauce, sliced turkey, carrots, mushrooms, and peas to skillet. Stir over low heat until very hot, but do not simmer. Adjust seasonings to taste. Spoon over warm toast and serve immediately.

11
Meat

Ground and sliced meats offer infinite creative possibilities and in these vast domains the food processor performs brilliantly. Whirl, swoosh—partially frozen meat is perfectly sliced to sauté. Whiz, zap—meat is ground to the perfect consistency for chili, tacos, meat loaf, sausage, or moussaka.

There are many advantages to grinding meat at home. First, you will always be sure of what you are getting and you can control the amount of fat. Second, you will know that ground meat is free of any additives or preservatives. You will be able to control the texture of the grind. And, finally, tasty inexpensive cuts of meat (the best ones for grinding) are often less expensive than prepared hamburger.

USING THE CONTROLLED TIMING METHOD TO GRIND MEAT

Unlike a commercial meat grinder, the food processor has no screen to trap stray pieces of fiber or gristle. Therefore, meat must be impeccably trimmed as it is cut into 1-inch (2½-cm) cubes for grinding. Unless you are on a special diet, do not remove fat; it adds flavor and moisture to ground meat mixtures.

For best results, be sure meat cubes are thoroughly chilled. Fresh pork fatback, which is tougher than meat, must be cut into ½-inch (1½-cm) cubes and partially frozen. Unless your container has an extra-large capacity, grind no more than 1½ cups (3½ dL) of meat cubes (approximately ½ pound or 225 grams) in one batch. Use the specified number of two-second on/off turns or pulses for grinding meat, to give each batch exactly the same texture; adjust as necessary for large-capacity machines (see page 10).

Providing that meat is prepared as described above, the following controlled timing guidelines may be used for grinding meat in most machines:

- Use 3 two-second on/off turns or pulses for a coarser than hamburger consistency

- Use 4 or 5 two-second on/off turns or pulses for a medium (or hamburger) grind

- Use 5 or 6 two-second on/off turns or pulses for a medium-fine grind

- Use 6 or 7 two-second on/off turns or pulses for a fine grind (not a purée)

I do not recommend grinding meat by continuous processing.

77

Quickly check over each batch of ground meat and discard any stray pieces of gristle or tendon. Check for small chunks that are not perfectly ground. (This occurs from time to time; if too many result, reduce the size of each batch of meat cubes to 1 cup/¼ L.) Include any stray meat chunks in the following batch.

Cooked meat is ground by the same methods as raw meat.

SAUSAGE MAKING

Traditional homemade sausage is nothing more than a well-seasoned mixture of about three parts ground meat and one part fat. For bulk sausage, the only equipment needed besides the food processor is a sharp knife. I much prefer the clean chop of the processor to any other sausage-making apparatus, and I have tried them all.

To make link sausages, you must fill strands of casing, either natural or synthetic, with meat mixtures; then either coil the large links, or tie or twist casings into smaller links of the desired length.

Prepare meat and fat for grinding as specified above; however, for sausage I usually place the food processor container and blade in the refrigerator to chill for 15 minutes.

Pork fatback, the dense fresh solid fat (*not* salted and *not* smoked) located above the loin, is essential to sausages. Fatback can be purchased in bulk at meat markets and in some supermarkets. It will keep in the freezer for three months. Refrigerate no longer than three days before using. There is no substitute for fatback.

Sprinkle spices and seasonings evenly over meat and fat cubes in a shallow pan and be sure to scrape all spices out of pan and into processor container when mixture is removed for grinding. If desired, spices may be sprinkled over meat and refrigerated overnight (covered) to allow flavors to penetrate.

Use a hand-stuffing nozzle (also called a horn) to stuff sausage into casings. The plain nozzle allows maximum control over stuffing and is the least expensive but most time-consuming method.

Natural sausage casings are hog or sheep intestines that have been thoroughly cleaned. Though this notion may offend the squeamish, natural casings are edible, resilient and amazingly strong. They thoroughly enclose the meat and seal in all the juices, ensuring that sausages will sputter and spurt with flavor at every bite.

Natural casings are available either packed in salt or in a vacuum-sealed "wet pack." They must always be soaked to remove salt or packing juices and then rinsed well before filling. It may require an advance order, but you usually can buy strands of casings in varying lengths from a butcher or by mail order, see page 7. Salt-packed casings may be frozen; however, they keep perfectly in the refrigerator for up to 8 months.

Fill casings firmly but not too tightly and as evenly as possible to avoid creating air pockets inside them which can hasten spoilage. Puncture the casing as necessary with a sterile needle to eliminate any large air bubbles that do form. If a casing is pierced too many times, however, it is apt to allow vital meat juices to escape during cooking.

Sausage may be cooked immediately after stuffing, but it will benefit from overnight refrigeration or "ripening," whether or not spices have been sprinkled on the meat and left overnight. Sausage may be frozen but it will suffer a slight flavor loss.

PREPARING RAW MEAT FOR SLICING

Cut meat into rectangular chunks along the grain so that, when inserted into the food chute, meat will be sliced across the grain. Size of the chunks will depend on size of the food chute. If meat, such as flank steak, is thin, it may be possible to place two chunks side by side in the food chute (see Yakitori, page 17).

Meat must be partially but not firmly frozen, or it will not pass properly through the slicing disk and damage to the disk may result. Be sure it can be easily pierced with the tip of a small sharp knife or the tip of the *metal knife blade*. A moderate push is generally used to slice partially frozen meat.

SLICING COOKED MEAT

Cooked meat slices perfectly if it is firm all the way through, generally when cooked medium-rare to well-done. Gyros meat, which is also compressed, or leftover corned beef are good examples of this, and the processor may prove handy when slicing these meats for sandwiches.

Leftover rare meat, however, must be treated like raw meat—that is, it must be partially frozen. It may be easier to slice leftover very rare cooked meats by hand.

DIANNA'S BREAKFAST SAUSAGE

Makes about 2 pounds (900 g) bulk sausage or 10 to 12 patties

These are basic American breakfast sausages. You'll find these patties to be not so highly seasoned as the commercial products, but I much prefer their milder flavor. You can use this sausage in bulk for an excellent turkey stuffing, page 73.

1 lb. (450 g) boneless pork shoulder, cut into 1-inch cubes
½ lb. (225 g) boneless beef chuck, cut into 1-inch cubes
6 oz. (180 g) fresh pork fatback, partially frozen, cut into ½-inch cubes
¾ teaspoon ground sage
½ teaspoon salt
½ teaspoon freshly ground pepper
¼ teaspoon dried marjoram leaves
¼ teaspoon sweet paprika
⅛ teaspoon ground coriander

1. Combine pork, beef and fatback in a large shallow baking dish. Mix remaining ingredients; sprinkle evenly over meat and toss well.

2. Insert the *metal knife blade*. Process meat mixture 1½ cups (3½ dL) at a time with 3 to 5 two-second pulses until meat is coarsely ground but holds together. Transfer mixture to a large bowl, adding any spices that remain in baking dish. Remove and discard any large pieces of sinew or gristle. Toss lightly with hands; do not overmix or sausage will be tough. Fry 1 tablespoon of the mixture, taste and adjust seasonings.

3. Shape sausage meat into 10 to 12 patties or leave in bowl for bulk sausage. Cover and refrigerate at least 6 hours but preferably overnight to ripen. Pan fry or broil patties, turning once, until brown on both sides and juices run clear when pierced with a fork. If desired, ripened sausage can be frozen up to 3 weeks. Wrap in plastic wrap and seal in a plastic freezer bag. Thaw in wrap.

SWEET ITALIAN SAUSAGE

Makes about 3 pounds (1,350 g)

Great in sausage and pepper sandwiches and spaghetti sauce, these fennel-seasoned sausages are also superb when simply grilled. The meat mixture may also be used in bulk for Chicago Stuffed Pizza, page 51.

2 or 3 strands natural hog casings (see page 78)
2½ lbs. (1¼ kg) boneless pork shoulder, cut into 1-inch cubes
10 oz. (285 g) fresh pork fatback, partially frozen, cut into ½-inch cubes
1½ teaspoons finely ground fennel seeds or 2 teaspoons whole fennel seeds
1½ teaspoons salt
½ to ¾ teaspoon sweet paprika
¼ teaspoon cayenne pepper
4 garlic cloves, peeled

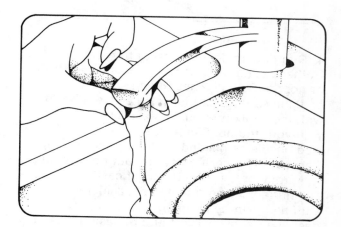

1. Soak casings in lukewarm water to cover 30 minutes. Rinse in several changes of cold water. Slip opening of casing over faucet; hold in place; run a thin stream of cold water through length of casing. Run fingers gently down length of casing to remove water. Repeat rinsing inside of casing three times. Repeat with remaining casings. Cut out and discard sections of casings with holes. Refrigerate casings covered with cold water.

2. Combine pork and fatback in a large shallow baking dish. Sprinkle fennel, salt, paprika, and cayenne evenly over meat and fat mixture. Insert the *metal knife blade*. With machine running, drop garlic cloves one at a time through food chute. Process until minced; sprinkle evenly over meat and fat mixture.

3. Process meat mixture 1½ cups (3½ dL) at a time using 4 or 5 two-second pulses until meat is ground to medium consistency but holds together. Transfer mixture to a large bowl. Remove and discard large pieces of sinew and gristle. Toss lightly; do not overmix. Fry 1 tablespoon of the mixture; taste and adjust seasonings.

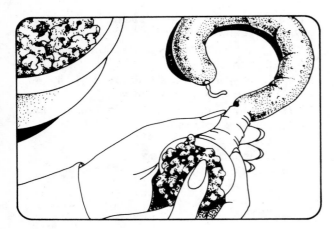

4. Run fingers down 1 casing to remove water. Gather casing onto nozzle of a sausage stuffer or nozzle. Pull 3 inches (8 cm) off stuffer; knot end. Fill sausage stuffer (also called a horn) with meat mixture; push mixture into casing with your thumb. Pierce casing with thin sterilized needle as needed to remove air pockets. Repeat, filling casings evenly but not packing too firmly or they will burst. (If casings burst, cut stuffed casing free and set aside. Begin stuffing again by knotting end of casing as described above.) Twist end of casing closed; repeat until all meat mixture is used.

5. Coil sausage; place in shallow baking dish. Refrigerate in single layer covered with plastic wrap overnight to ripen. Pan fry (adding a small amount of water after sausage browns) or broil sausage, turning once, until brown and juices run pale pink when sausage is pierced with a fork.

FRESH CHORIZO SAUSAGE
Makes about 1½ pounds (675 g)

This spicy, fresh Spanish chorizo is milder than its Mexican counterpart and contains turmeric.

I love to add it to Spanish rice mixtures such as Arroz con Pollo, page 69, or to Paella.

1 or 2 strands natural hog casings
1¼ lbs. (565 g) boneless pork shoulder, cut into 1-inch cubes.
½ lb. (225 g) pork fatback, partially frozen, cut into ½-inch cubes
1 to 1¼ teaspoons chili powder
1 to 1¼ teaspoons sweet paprika
1 teaspoon salt
½ teaspoon ground cumin
½ teaspoon ground turmeric
½ teaspoon freshly ground white pepper
⅛ to ½ teaspoon cayenne pepper
3 medium garlic cloves, peeled
½ medium onion, peeled, cut into 1-inch cubes
1 tablespoon white vinegar

1. Soak casings according to directions in Step 1 of Sweet Italian Sausage.

2. Combine pork and fatback in a large shallow baking dish. Sprinkle evenly with chili powder, paprika, salt, cumin, turmeric, pepper and cayenne. Insert the *metal knife blade.* With machine running, drop garlic cloves one at a time through food chute; process until minced. Scrape down container sides. Add onion and process to chop with 3 or 4 half-second pulses. Sprinkle onion mixture evenly over meat and fat mixture.

3. Follow Steps 3 and 4 of Sweet Italian Sausage, sprinkling vinegar over ground mixture in bowl in Step 3 before mixing. After stuffing sausage mixture into casing in Step 4, twist each filled casing into 3 or 4 even links by pressing on casing and then twisting several times. Tie open ends with string. Proceed with Step 5 to ripen and cook sausage.

MEAT LOAF
Makes 4 to 6 servings

I have saved as much as 60¢ a pound on hamburger by grinding beef chuck for meat loaf in the processor. I look for sales on bone-in chuck blade roast, trim it myself and freeze the bones for use in broth. This is Bill Kehoe's "just plain meat loaf" baked in a glass loaf pan.

Embellish as you choose, but be sure to try some cold in sandwiches.

2 lbs. (900 g) boneless beef chuck, well-trimmed, cut into 1-inch chunks
1 medium onion, peeled, cut into 1-inch cubes
1 slice day-old bread or ½ cup fresh bread crumbs
⅓ cup (¾ dL) milk
1 teaspoon salt
1 teaspoon horseradish
1 teaspoon Dijon mustard
3 tablespoons good-quality tomato paste or ketchup
1½ teaspoons Worcestershire sauce
Freshly ground pepper
2 eggs

1. Adjust oven rack to lower position. Heat oven to 400° F (205° C). Insert the *metal knife blade.* Process meat 1 cup (¼ L) at a time with 6 or 7 two-second pulses to fine hamburger consistency. Remove each batch to a large bowl.

2. Tear bread into pieces and process to fine crumbs; add to bowl. Process to chop onion with 4 or 5 half-second pulses; add to bowl; add remaining ingredients to bowl. Mix thoroughly and adjust seasonings to taste.

3. Spoon meat mixture into a 6-cup (1½-L) Pyrex loaf pan. Bake 50 to 60 minutes or until meat is just cooked through. Cover and set loaf pan aside at room temperature 15 to 20 minutes before slicing.

TACOS
Makes 10

It really is fun to make these in the processor, and the garnishes will test your skill with the disks.

Taco Filling:

1½ lbs. (675 g) boneless beef chuck, cut into 1-inch cubes, gristle removed
1 medium garlic clove, peeled
1 medium onion, peeled, cut into 1-inch cubes
1 medium tomato, peeled, seeded, quartered
1¼ teaspoons chili powder

½ teaspoon ground cumin
¼ teaspoon ground coriander seeds
¼ teaspoon dried oregano
¼ teaspoon white vinegar
6 dashes Tabasco sauce, or more to taste
2 tablespoons vegetable oil or lard
1 teaspoon salt

Garnishes:

1 chunk (4 oz./115 g) sharp Cheddar cheese, chilled
1 wedge (6 oz./180 g) iceberg lettuce, cut to fit food chute
2 medium tomatoes, halved lengthwise
10 taco shells
Sour cream, if desired

1. To prepare taco filling, insert the *metal knife blade.* Process beef cubes, 1½ cups (3½ dL) at a time to hamburger consistency, using 4 or 5 two-second on/off turns or pulses; transfer to waxed paper. With machine running, drop garlic through food chute. Process until minced; scrape down sides of container. Add onion and process to chop with 3 or 4 half-second pulses; set aside. Place tomato, chili powder, cumin, coriander, oregano, vinegar, and Tabasco in container. Process with 3 or 4 half-second pulses.

2. Heat oil or lard in a medium skillet. Add garlic and onion. Cook until onion is soft. Add tomato mixture, chopped beef, and salt. Cook over low heat, stirring frequently, until meat is thoroughly cooked, about 12 to 15 minutes. Adjust seasonings to taste. Serve immediately or cover and refrigerate up to 2 days. Heat and adjust seasonings to taste before serving.

3. Prepare garnishes as follows, placing each in a separate serving bowl. Insert the *medium shredding disk* in a dry container. Shred cheese with a gentle push. Change to the *medium slicing disk.* Insert lettuce wedge from underneath food chute; slice with a gentle push. Change to the *french-fry disk* or leave slicing disk in place. Place tomato halves upright in food chute and process with a gentle push.

4. To assemble and serve, heat oven to 250° F (120° C). Heat taco shells 5 to 6 minutes. Place ¼ cup (½ dL) filling in each; top with garnishes and sour cream. Serve immediately.

MEATBALLS
Makes 4 to 6 servings

Achieving the correct texture for these meat-balls is a two-step process: first the meat is coarsely ground; then the seasonings are added and the grinding is completed at the same time seasonings are mixed into the meat.

1 oz. (30 g) Parmesan cheese, cut into 1-inch chunks
¼ cup (½ dL) firmly packed parsley leaves
2 medium garlic cloves, peeled
1 medium onion, peeled, cut into 1-inch cubes
1 egg
¾ teaspoon salt, or more to taste
Freshly ground pepper
3 tablespoons dry bread crumbs
1 lb. (450 g) boneless beef chuck, well trimmed, cut into 1-inch cubes
¼ lb. (115 g) boneless pork shoulder, cut into 1-inch cubes

1. Insert the *metal knife blade.* Process cheese until powdery; set aside. Add parsley and process until finely minced; set aside. With machine running, drop garlic cloves one at a time through food chute; process until minced. Scrape down sides of container. Add onion and process to chop with 6 to 8 half-second pulses. Add egg, salt, pepper and bread crumbs. Process to mix with 4 half-second pulses. Scrape down sides of container.

2. Set aside half the contents of the container. Add half the meat to remaining onion mixture in container. Process to grind with 4 two-second pulses. Add half the cheese and half the parsley. Process to grind meat to a medium-fine consistency with 1 or 2 two-second pulses; transfer to bowl. Repeat to grind remaining meat, adding remaining parsley and cheese as directed. With hands, mix meat in bowl thoroughly but take care not to overwork or meatballs may become tough.

3. Adjust oven rack to lower position. Heat oven to 375° F (190° C). With wet hands, form sixteen 1½-inch (4-cm) meatballs. Place on an ungreased jelly-roll pan. Bake 20 minutes. Remove from pan and serve immediately.

TWO-DAY CHILI
Makes 8 to 10 servings

It is absolutely essential to soak the beans overnight before cooking, not only to soften them, but also to remove sugars that are difficult to digest and cause stomach and intestinal problems so often associated with beans. Milk is an odd ingredient for chili, I admit. However, I learned from making Bolognese meat sauce that a small amount of milk lends a mysterious creamy consistency—call it my secret ingredient.

1 lb. (450 g) dried kidney beans
1½ qts. (1½ L) cold water
2 lbs. (900 g) boneless beef chuck, gristle and tendon removed, cut into 1-inch cubes
5 medium garlic cloves, peeled
2 medium onions, peeled, cut into 1-inch cubes
4 tablespoons lard or vegetable oil
1 medium green bell pepper, seeded and quartered
2 cans (1 lb. 12 oz./790 g each) Italian plum tomatoes, seeded, drained, liquid strained and reserved, or 2½ to 3 lbs. (1¼ kg) fresh tomatoes, peeled, seeded, quartered
½ cup (1 dL) dry red wine
½ cup (1 dL) milk
1½ teaspoons salt
1 teaspoon ground cumin
1 teaspoon dried oregano leaves
1 teaspoon paprika
3 teaspoons chili powder, or more to taste
½ teaspoon cayenne pepper, or more to taste
2 cups (½ L) Brown Beef Broth, page 40

1. One day before making chili, place beans and cold water in a large bowl. Set aside at room temperature to soak overnight. Drain; rinse and set beans aside in a colander.

2. Insert the *metal knife blade.* Divide the meat cubes into 3 equal batches and process each portion with 4 or 5 two-second pulses to grind meat to hamburger consistency. Remove each batch of ground meat to waxed paper; set aside. With the machine running, drop garlic cloves one at a time through the food chute. Process until minced and scrape down the sides of the container. Add onions to container and process to chop with 6 to 8 half-second

pulses. Empty container into a 6-quart (6-L) soup kettle. Add lard or vegetable oil and cook over low heat until onions soften.

3. Meanwhile, change to the *medium slicing disk.* Insert each piece of green pepper from underneath food chute and slice with a gentle push. Add pepper slices to soft onion mixture and continue cooking, stirring frequently, until peppers soften. If desired, change to the *french-fry disk* or leave slicing disk in place. Load tomatoes in food chute and cut or slice with a gentle push; set aside.

4. Stir the chopped meat into the onion mixture and continue cooking over low heat until no pink remains, stirring frequently. Add red wine and milk; stir well. Simmer uncovered until none of the liquid remains, about 1½ hours. Add salt, cumin, oregano, paprika, chili powder, cayenne pepper, beef broth, beans and tomatoes with liquid. Stir well. Cover and simmer slowly 2 hours, stirring occasionally. Uncover and simmer until thickened, about 3 hours longer. Adjust seasonings to taste and serve immediately or cool and refrigerate overnight. Heat thoroughly before serving.

GYROS
Makes 8 to 10 servings

Gyros (pronounced hd-ros) are street food; the spicy Greek-American counterpart of tacos—compressed meat that is spit roasted and sliced, served in pita bread and sauced with yogurt.

To duplicate *Gyros* at home, it is necessary to make a highly seasoned loaf of meat that is compressed with weights—a technique used for pâtés. As in pâtés, fat is absolutely essential to properly bind the meat mixture and to give flavor. Be sure to check the seasoning by frying a tablespoon or two of the meat mixture as described in Step 3. Depending upon the strength of the herbs, you may wish to add a little more oregano, cumin, or fennel, as seasonings will mellow once meat has been refrigerated.

When the meat is cooked and chilled, it can be processor sliced. Then the slices are broiled until hot to simulate spit roasting.

Gyros Meat:

1½ lbs. (675 g) boneless lamb shoulder, gristle but not fat removed, cut into 1-inch cubes
½ lb. (225 g) boneless beef chuck, gristle removed, cut into 1-inch cubes
¼ lb. (115 g) fresh pork fatback, cut into ½-inch cubes, partially frozen
2 teaspoons dried oregano leaves
¼ teaspoon ground cumin
⅛ to ¼ teaspoon ground fennel seed
Pinch cinnamon
1¼ teaspoons salt, or more to taste
Freshly ground pepper
4 medium garlic cloves, peeled
2 medium onions, peeled, cut into 1-inch cubes
⅓ cup (¾ dL) dry bread crumbs
2 egg whites

Garnishes:

1 medium onion, peeled, halved lengthwise
4 medium tomatoes, cored, halved lengthwise
8 to 10 Pita Breads, page 121
1½ cups (12 oz./350 g) plain yogurt

1. For Gyros meat, adjust oven rack to lower position. Heat oven to 350° F (175° C). Mix lamb, beef, and pork fat pieces in a shallow baking dish. Sprinkle oregano, cumin, fennel, cinnamon, salt, and pepper over meat. Toss well to coat meat with spices.

2. Insert the *metal knife blade.* With machine running, drop garlic cloves one at a time through food chute. Add onions and process 20 seconds, stopping once to scrape down sides of container. Add bread crumbs and egg whites. Process 5 seconds longer or until thoroughly mixed; remove to a small bowl. Rinse and dry container and blade and return to base.

3. Process one-third of the meat and fat mixture with 4 or 5 two-second pulses. Add one-third of the onion mixture and process 20 seconds or until pasty; remove to a large bowl. Repeat to grind remaining meat mixture, combining it with onion mixture. With hands or a wooden spoon, thoroughly mix contents of bowl. Cook a small amount, taste, and adjust seasoning as needed.

4. Place ground meat mixture in a 4-cup (1-L) loaf pan. Tap pan firmly on counter to remove air bubbles. Cover with foil and place in a baking dish with enough water to come one-third of the way up the outside of the loaf pan. Do not allow pan to float. Bake 1½ hours.

5. Remove loaf pan from baking dish and place on a cake rack. Cut out a piece of cardboard to fit just inside top edges of pan and wrap cardboard with foil. Place on top of meat and top with a 5-pound (2¼-kg) weight (canned goods or a brick are good for this). Let stand 2 hours. Remove weight. Cool meat to room temperature in loaf pan. Cover and refrigerate until thoroughly chilled, about 6 hours or overnight. Meat may be frozen.

6. To slice meat and prepare garnishes, invert loaf pan over a sheet of aluminum foil. Pat meat dry with paper toweling. Cut into rectangular chunks to fit food chute, using about half the loaf; return remainder to refrigerator or to freezer if not previously frozen. Insert the *medium slicing disk*. Slice meat across the grain with a moderate push. Place on a jelly-roll pan in an even layer; set aside. Slice onion halves with a gentle push; transfer to serving bowl. Slice each tomato half with a gentle push; transfer to a serving bowl.

7. Cut 1 edge off each pita bread to make a pocket; set aside in a serving basket. Just before serving, heat broiler. Broil sliced meat close to heat source until slightly crisp and thoroughly hot, about 4 minutes. Fill each pita with hot meat, onion slices, and tomato. Generously spoon yogurt into sandwiches. Serve immediately.

SLICED STEAK SAUTE
Makes 2 servings

This is a rich steak dish akin to Steak Diane, served in small portions; it is especially good with a plain green vegetable or Potatoes Annette, page 19.

1 boneless New York cut steak (10 oz./285 g), 1-inch thick, partially frozen
⅛ cup (¼ dL) firmly packed parsley leaves
4 medium shallots or ½ medium onion, peeled,
cut into 1-inch cubes
4 teaspoons Cognac or brandy
½ teaspoon Dijon mustard
1½ teaspoons Worcestershire sauce
2 dashes Tabasco sauce
½ cup (1 dL) Brown Beef Broth, page 40
1 tablespoon whipping cream
1 tablespoon red wine vinegar
2½ tablespoons olive or vegetable oil
3 tablespoons (45 g) butter, slightly softened
Salt and freshly ground pepper to taste

1. Cut steak in half crosswise. Insert the *medium slicing disk.* Insert steak pieces upright in food chute from underneath. Slice with a moderate push; set steak aside to defrost completely.

2. Change to the *metal knife blade.* Process parsley until finely minced; set aside for garnish. With machine running, drop shallots one at a time through food chute. Process until minced; set aside.

3. In a small bowl, mix 3 teaspoons Cognac, mustard, Worcestershire and Tabasco sauces, beef broth, cream, and vinegar; set aside.

4. Heat 1½ tablespoons oil in a large skillet until sizzling. Add half the steak slices and sauté just until rare, about 1½ minutes; remove to a plate. Repeat to cook remaining steak slices. Add shallots with the remaining tablespoon oil to the skillet. Sauté until lightly browned. Pour in broth mixture. Reduce by slowly boiling until contents of skillet measure ¼ cup (½ dL).

5. Stir in butter, salt, and pepper to taste and remaining teaspoon Cognac. Whisk over low heat until butter disappears. Return the steak slices and any juices that have accumulated on the plate to the skillet. Heat just until meat is thoroughly hot. Spoon onto individual plates; garnish with parsley. Serve immediately.

LEG OF LAMB ITALIANO
Makes 8 servings

Again and again my students tell me that this is one of their favorite recipes because it is so easy to make and gains in flavor when prepared in advance. Many remark that they never would have believed lamb could be so delicious when cooked and served pink-rare!

Prosciutto-Herb Mixture:

2 medium garlic cloves, peeled
¼ cup (½ dL) firmly packed parsley leaves
½ teaspoon dried marjoram leaves or 1 teaspoon fresh marjoram
¼ teaspoon dried rosemary leaves or ½ teaspoon fresh rosemary
Freshly ground pepper
6 oz. (180 g) prosciutto, fat and rind removed, cut into 1-inch chunks

1 leg of lamb (5 to 7 lbs./2¼ to 3¼ kg)
3 tablespoons olive or vegetable oil
⅓ cup (¾ dL) dry white wine

1. Insert the *metal knife blade*. With the machine running, drop garlic through food chute and process until minced; scrape down sides of container. Add parsley, marjoram, rosemary, pepper, and prosciutto to container. Process until ground to a dry paste and mixture holds together when pinched, about 1 minute.

2. Carefully peel away the tough outer membrane, called the "fell," on the leg of lamb. Trim off any excess fat, leaving no more than a ⅛-inch (½-cm) layer overall. With a sharp paring knife, make ½-inch (1½-cm)-deep slits 1 to 1½ inches (2½ to 4 cm) apart over the entire surface of the lamb. Press the prosciutto-herb mixture into small bullet shapes and insert into slits.

3. Place lamb in roasting pan and rub with oil. Add white wine to pan and turn to coat lamb with wine. Set aside 2 to 3 hours at room temperature to marinate, turning once or twice. (Or, loosely cover and refrigerate in marinade overnight. Bring refrigerated lamb back to room temperature before roasting.)

4. Adjust oven rack to lower position. Heat oven to 425° F (220° C). Drain off marinade and reserve. Pat lamb dry with paper toweling. Return to pan and roast 20 minutes. Remove from oven and baste with reserved marinade. Return lamb to oven and reduce heat to 325° F (165° C). Roast 50 minutes longer, basting once. Remove and insert an instant-registering thermometer into the thickest part of the lamb.

It should register 125° F to 130° F (50 to 60° C) for medium-rare. If temperature is lower than 125° F, return lamb to oven and roast 5 to 8 minutes longer or until it registers at that temperature. Remove lamb from oven and cover pan tightly with aluminum foil. Set aside 15 minutes to rest before slicing.

MOUSSAKA CASSEROLE
Makes 8 servings

This is my adaptation of the classic Greek dish *moussakas.* The puffy, browned phyllo pastry dresses it up so well, that I wouldn't hesitate to put it on a buffet table or serve it as the main dish of an informal meal for company. The thing to remember here is to taste the raw eggplant after it has been rinsed to be sure all salt is removed. This casserole may be prepared one day in advance, topped with pastry and refrigerated overnight. Before baking, let casserole warm to room temperature for several hours.

3 oz. (85 g) Parmesan cheese, cut into 1-inch cubes
¼ cup (½ dL) firmly packed parsley leaves
6 medium garlic cloves, peeled
2 medium onions, peeled, cut into 1-inch cubes
1 lb. (450 g) boneless lamb shoulder, cut into 1-inch cubes, well trimmed
4 large ripe tomatoes, peeled, seeded, cored
2 eggplants (1 lb./450 g each)
2 teaspoons salt
½ teaspoon dried oregano
Scant ¼ teaspoon dried thyme
1 teaspoon cinnamon
4 tablespoons olive or vegetable oil
Béchamel Sauce, page 112
6 tablespoons (85 g) slightly softened butter
2 eggs
Pepper to taste
6 phyllo pastry leaves, see page 7

1. Insert the *metal knife blade.* Process Parmesan cheese until powdery; set aside. Process parsley until finely minced; set aside. With machine running, drop garlic cloves one at a time through food chute. Scrape down sides of container. Add onions and chop with 6 to 8 half-second pulses; set mixture aside. Grind

half the lamb to hamburger consistency with 4 or 5 two-second pulses; set aside and repeat. Cut tomatoes in quarters. Chop with 4 half-second pulses to medium consistency; set aside.

2. Quarter eggplants lengthwise. Halve crosswise or cut to fit food chute. Change to *medium slicing disk.* Insert eggplant in food chute with skin side facing cutting edge of disk. Slice with a gentle push; empty container onto 2 large platters. Sprinkle each platter of eggplant with 1 teaspoon salt. Set aside 20 minutes. Rinse well to remove salt and squeeze pieces firmly to extract bitter liquids; set aside.

3. Place lamb in large skillet. Stir over medium heat until color turns pale and meat is just cooked. Remove to a bowl with a slotted spoon, leaving 2 tablespoons pan juices in skillet. Add onion mixture to skillet and cook until onions soften. Add tomatoes. Stir over medium heat until juices evaporate. Return lamb to skillet. Add oregano, thyme, and cinnamon. Stir over medium heat until most of the liquid evaporates; return to bowl.

4. Heat 4 tablespoons oil in same skillet. Add eggplant. Sauté over medium heat, stirring frequently, until soft and no liquid remains; set aside.

5. Prepare and set aside Béchamel Sauce until ready to assemble casserole.

6. Adjust oven rack to middle position. Heat oven to 400° F (205° C). Coat a 2-quart (2-L) casserole or baking dish with 1 tablespoon butter; set aside. Mix Béchamel into cooked eggplant. To lamb mixture, add eggs, parsley, ¼ cup (½ dL) of the Parmesan cheese, and pepper to taste. Adjust seasonings and stir well. Place half the lamb mixture into the dish. Place half the eggplant mixture over meat. Sprinkle with ¼ cup (½ dL) Parmesan cheese. Repeat layering, ending with cheese.

7. Melt remaining butter. Place 1 sheet phyllo pastry on dry work surface. Brush with melted butter. Cover with another sheet of pastry; smooth if necessary. Brush with butter and repeat until all pastry is stacked. Trim stack to fit baking dish. Place pastry in dish, pressing gently to touch cheese. Bake until pastry is puffed and brown and mixture is thoroughly hot, about 45 minutes.

OSSOBUCO ALLA MILANESE
Makes 6 to 8 servings

This dish of braised veal shanks is a pillar of Milanese cooking and an indestructable classic. The beauty of the dish lies in its simplicity and in the rich taste that the unique set of flavorings brings to veal. Naturally, the flavor is best if the veal is white and milk-fed; however, it even works well with the redder grass-fed varieties.

Gremolada, the condiment stirred into the sauce at the last moment, illustrates an important food processor technique—grinding to grate citrus rind or zest. The trick is to use salt as the abrasive agent to help grind up the rind strips; in desserts sugar is used. Because there is so little salt, the strips will at first only grind to a coarse consistency. As the remaining ingredients are added, however, the rind minces, thus releasing the oils essential to the taste of this seasoning paste.

2 **medium onions, peeled, cut into 1-inch cubes**
¼ **lb. (115 g) celery ribs, strings removed, cut into 1-inch lengths**
¼ **lb. (115 g) carrots, peeled, cut into 1-inch lengths**
6 **tablespoons (85 g) butter**
1½ **lbs. (675 g) fresh tomatoes, peeled, seeded, halved lengthwise, or 1 can (1 lb. 12 oz./ 790 g) Italian plum tomatoes, seeded, drained**
2 **tablespoons olive oil**
Flour for dredging
4 to 4½ **lbs. (2 kg) hind shanks of veal, cut 1 to 1½ inches thick, patted dry**
⅔ **cup (1½ dL) dry white wine**
1½ to 2 **cups (3½ dL) Brown Beef Broth, page 40**
¾ **teaspoon crushed rosemary leaves**
1 **teaspoon dried minced sage leaves**
Freshly ground pepper

Gremolada:

Rinds of 2 small lemons, stripped off with vegetable peeler
½ **teaspoon salt, coarse (kosher) salt is best**
3 **medium garlic cloves, peeled**
⅓ **cup (¾ dL) firmly packed parsley leaves**
½ **can (1 oz./30 g) flat anchovies, rinsed, patted dry**

1. Insert the *metal knife blade*. Process to chop onions with 6 to 8 half-second pulses; transfer to a 12- to 14-inch (30- to 35-cm) skillet with lid or a 4- to 6-quart (4- to 6-L) Dutch oven; set aside. Place celery in container and repeat. Place carrots in container and chop with 4 or 5 one-second pulses; add to skillet or Dutch oven. Add 2 tablespoons butter to vegetable mixture and cook over low heat, stirring frequently, until vegetables are softened; remove from skillet and set aside.

2. Meanwhile, change to *french-fry disk* or leave blade in place. Fill food chute with tomatoes and cut with a gentle push or coarsely chop tomatoes with 3 or 4 half-second pulses; set aside.

3. Add remaining 4 tablespoons butter and the olive oil to skillet or Dutch oven; heat to bubbling. Place flour on waxed paper. Dip both sides of each veal shank piece in flour; shake off excess. Sauté veal without crowding until golden brown on both sides; turn once. Take care not to allow flour to burn or scorch; lower heat if necessary. Remove veal from skillet or Dutch oven; set aside.

4. Remove pan from heat and add wine. Scrape pan bottom with a wooden spatula to deglaze. Return vegetables to pan in an even layer. Place veal snugly over vegetables in single layer. Sprinkle chopped tomato pieces over veal and add enough broth to barely cover meat.

5. Heat liquid to a rapid simmer. Cover with aluminum foil touching top of meat. Set cover slightly ajar and slowly simmer until veal is very tender when pierced with a fork, about 1 to 1½ hours.

6. Meanwhile prepare Gremolada. Insert *metal knife blade* in clean dry container. Process lemon rind with salt until coarsely chopped, about 30 seconds, scraping down container sides several times. With machine running, drop garlic cloves through food chute. Scrape down container sides and process 10 to 20 seconds longer so that lemon rind breaks up into smaller pieces. Add parsley and process until finely minced; scrape down container sides. Add anchovies and process about 10 seconds longer or until mixture is pasty; set aside.

7. When veal is tender, use a slotted spoon to remove it to a warm serving plate. Stir in rosemary and sage leaves. Rapidly simmer the contents of the skillet until mixture measures 3 to 3½ cups (¾ L). Stir in the Gremolada and freshly ground pepper. Adjust seasonings to taste and spoon sauce around veal pieces. Serve immediately.

HUNAN-STYLE ORANGE BEEF
Makes 2 to 4 servings

One of my favorite Hunanese dishes is stir-fried orange beef, which I have adapted for the food processor because it illustrates so many slicing techniques.

Partially frozen beef is sliced across the grain into strips. Green onions are dangle-sliced into thin rings. The peel of an orange slices into julienne strips best when partially frozen. The orange lends its pungent oils to the flavoring of this dish, but this same julienne could be blanched and used in a sauce for *Caneton à l'Orange* or blanched and candied for the garniture of desserts. Garlic may be slivered for Chinese cooking by passing it through the slicing disk, an interesting but offbeat method (the thinner the disk, the thinner the slivers).

½ **medium navel orange, peel removed in 2 equal pieces**

Sauce Mixture:
1 **teaspoon all-purpose soy sauce**
½ **teaspoon rice or white vinegar**
1 **teaspoon sesame oil**
1 **tablespoon dry sherry**
1 **teaspoon ketchup**

Marinade:
1 **egg white**
1 **teaspoon cornstarch**
½ **teaspoon all-purpose soy sauce**
2 **teaspoons Grand Marnier or orange liqueur**

1 **chunk (½ lb./225 g) boneless sirloin steak, or flank steak, well trimmed, cut to fit food chute, partially frozen**
½-**inch length (½ oz./15 g) fresh ginger root, peeled**

3 whole green onions, roots removed
1 medium garlic clove, peeled
2 cups (½ L) peanut oil
¼ teaspooon crushed red pepper flakes, or
  more to taste

1. Cut the orange peel pieces lengthwise in half and place in freezer. Juice the orange and set the juice aside. Insert the *metal knife blade.* To prepare the sauce mixture, place soy sauce, vinegar, sesame oil, sherry, ketchup, and 2 tablespoons of the orange juice in the container. Process 10 seconds and transfer to a cup. Set cup aside near stove.

2. Wipe container and blade dry and return them to processor base. To prepare marinade, place egg white, cornstarch, soy sauce, Grand Marnier, and 1 teaspoon of the orange juice in container. Process 10 seconds; remove the blade.

3. Insert the *medium slicing disk.* Slice the steak with a moderate push. Toss with marinade; transfer to a bowl until ready to cook. Replace disk and slice ginger root with a firm push; remove to waxed paper. Dangle-slice (page 102) white parts of green onions and cut green parts by hand into 1-inch (2½-cm) lengths; set all onion aside on waxed paper. Change to *thin slicing disk* or leave medium disk in place. Stack orange peel and press into a U-shape. Insert sideways from underneath

food chute and position so open ends of U face the direction of the oncoming disk. Slice peel with a moderate push; remove to waxed paper. With machine running, drop garlic clove through food chute and insert pusher quickly to be sure it passes through disk; remove to waxed paper.

4. Set a large strainer over a medium heat-proof bowl. Place bowl next to stove. Heat oil in wok using highest heat setting until it gently bubbles around dry chopstick when inserted. Add beef to oil and stir to separate pieces. Cook, stirring to keep pieces separate, until meat turns pale, about 1 minute. Carefully pour beef and oil into strainer; drain.

5. Return 3 tablespoons oil to wok and reheat. Add sliced ginger and cook until lightly browned, about 1½ minutes; discard. Add orange rind slices and cook until crisp, about 1 minute; set aside with beef. Add garlic and cook 30 seconds. Add onions and red pepper flakes; stir-fry 30 seconds longer. Stir in sauce mixture, beef, and orange peel. Stir-fry vigorously until thoroughly hot, about 1 minute. Serve immediately.

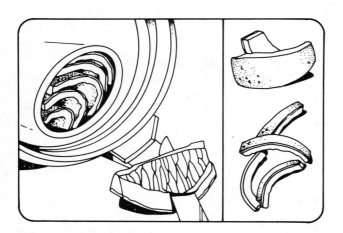

12
Vegetables

I can date my discovery of vegetables by my first trip to Europe. They seemed better, fresher, and tastier there and I shall never forget fried artichokes in Rome, wild mushrooms in Florence, and sliced tomatoes with fresh herbs in Paris.

It wasn't always that way, however. For years I was "allergic" to asparagus. Zucchini made me gag and I never would touch a green pepper. Spinach was OK, "it makes you strong," and I especially liked it mixed with mashed potatoes. I ate my carrots because they were "good for your eyes" and I always ate my rice because I felt sorry for "all the starving children in China."

It was under the influence of Italian cooking—where vegetables constitute a separate course of their own—that my menus became more vegetable intensive. By using them for appetizers, main courses, and salads rather than side dishes or accompaniments, I have come to fully understand their lightness, simplicity, and importance to those of us concerned with good health.

You will find techniques for using the food processor to prepare vegetables in many guises throughout this book. Most are to be found in the section on Basic Techniques; the litany will not be repeated here. Consider the Hot Vegetable Terrine, page 29, where vegetable purées bound with hollandaise bake into a feather-light pâté, or the Ligurian Vegetable Soup, page 39, which is created by literally sweating the flavors out of the minced vegetables—these are the high-powered performances.

The following recipes fall into two groups. Some, like the Zucchini Soufflé, Tomato Quiche with Three Cheeses, or Stir-fried Cabbage with Pork, may be used as main courses. Those based on potatoes and rice belong to the traditional category of accompaniments.

There are many cooking methods for vegetables and all are equally valid. Lately I have been steaming because I find that it gives less flavor loss than other methods. Blanching or plunging vegetables into a large quantity of lightly salted rapidly boiling water, is also excellent because the rapid movement of the water causes vegetables to move freely and cook evenly and quickly. Cooking vegetables by microwave is yet another practical and fast method.

VEGETABLE PUREES AND BABY FOOD

I am not especially fond of vegetable purées, and so I have only included one—the spinach purée which I use as a filling for the Layered Omelette Cake, on page 94. However, purées (or baby food) are easy to make.

First remove fiber, peels, or strings from vegetables. Cook until tender, then cut hot vegetables into 1-inch (2½-cm) chunks. Place in 1½ (3½ dL) batches into processor container fitted with *metal knife blade.* Chop finely, processing about 30 to 40 seconds, then scrape down the container sides. Process, drizzling a small amount of liquid (milk, water, cream, melted butter, broth, vegetable steaming liquid, or even baby formula or yogurt) through the food chute slowly. Stop and check consistency after 30 seconds of processing. Amount of liquid to add depends on quantity and consistency of the vegetable. Flavorings such as cooked shallots, onion, or garlic may be processed with vegetable to heighten flavor, unless purées are used as baby foods.

POTATOES

Look for firm skins, free of sprouts, bruises, soft spots, and green tinge and store potatoes in a cool, dry place. Russet burbank or Idaho potatoes are my first choice because they have a great taste and firm texture. I soak raw potatoes in cold water for a short time to remove excess starch because I believe it makes them taste better.

When deep-frying potatoes, always use fresh vegetable oil or oil which has been used only to fry potatoes. Raw potatoes absorb any flavor that has previously been introduced into the oil.

I have never been satisfied with processor-made mashed potatoes although I have used them occasionally for croquettes. If you must "processor-mash," try this method: shred the cooked (Idaho or russet) potatoes with a very gentle push, then change to the *metal knife blade.* To the cooked shredded potatoes, add either cream or softened butter and process to mix with 6 to 8 half-second on/off turns or pulses.

TOMATO QUICHE WITH THREE CHEESES
Makes 8 servings

Use this basic quiche recipe as is, or vary filling (omitting tomatoes) to include cooked ingredients such as ham, sausage, leeks, spinach or mushrooms.

Vegetables and quiche dough may be prepared in advance; however quiche will be best if freshly baked and set aside at room temperature (as long as all day) until ready to serve.

All-Purpose Tart and Quiche Variation Crust, page 150
1 chunk (2 oz./60 g) mozzarella cheese, chilled
1 chunk (2 oz./60 g) Gruyère or Swiss cheese, chilled
4 medium green onions
1 oz. (30 g) Parmesan cheese, cut into 1-inch chunks
1 egg
1 egg yolk
1 cup (¼ L) whipping cream
Salt and pepper to taste
2 dashes nutmeg
1 tablespoon olive or vegetable oil
3 ripe medium tomatoes, sliced ¼-inch thick
2 teaspoons Dijon mustard
¾ to 1 teaspoon dried oregano or 2 teaspoons chopped fresh oregano
1 teaspoon dried basil leaves or 8 leaves freshly chopped basil

1. Prepare and partially bake quiche crust, as directed. Adjust oven rack to middle position. Heat oven to 375° F (190° C).

2. Insert the *medium shredding disk.* Shred mozzarella with a gentle push; set aside. Shred Gruyère with a gentle push and set aside. Change to the *medium slicing disk.* Dangle-slice (page 102) white part of green onions; set aside. Reserve or discard green tops for another use. Wipe out container and change to *metal knife blade.* With machine running, drop Parmesan cheese chunks through food chute. Grind until powdery, about 1 minute; set aside. Add egg, egg yolk, cream, salt, pepper, and nutmeg to container. Process to mix with 3 half-second pulses; correct seasonings. Leave mixture in container.

3. Place oil and green onions in a large skillet. Cook until soft but not brown. Remove from skillet with a slotted spoon and set aside. Add tomato slices to skillet and cook over medium heat until skin loosens. Transfer to paper toweling and lift off skins.

4. Brush mustard onto cooled crust. Add mozzarella in an even layer. Place tomato slices, green onions, oregano, and basil over mozzarella. Salt and pepper lightly. Top with Gruyère shreds. Slowly pour in egg mixture. Sprinkle with Parmesan cheese.

5. Bake 25 to 30 minutes or until puffy and browned. Cool on a cake rack to lukewarm. To remove quiche from pan, center pan bottom on a can or jar and let ring fall away. Serve lukewarm or at room temperature.

Variation:

Bacon-Cheese Quiche
Omit tomatoes, oregano, and basil. Proceed with Steps 1 and 2. In Step 3, cook green onions as directed; then cook ½ pound (225 g) bacon until crisp; drain well on paper toweling; break into pieces. Proceed with Step 4; spread bacon and green onions evenly over mozzarella cheese; *do not add salt*. Proceed with recipe as directed.

ZUCCHINI SOUFFLE
Makes 4 appetizer servings; 2 main course servings

A classic vegetable soufflé may be served as an appetizer or a main course, for brunch, lunch or dinner. The processor makes short work of shredding zucchini, which must be salted and squeezed to remove excess moisture. If desired, these may be baked as small individual soufflés and served with Marinara Sauce, page 109.

1 chunk (1 oz./30 g) chilled Gruyère or Swiss cheese
1¼ lbs. (565 g) zucchini, stem ends removed
1 teaspoon salt
Béchamel Sauce, page 112, made with ⅔ cup (1½ dL) milk
½ slice day-old white or whole wheat bread or
¼ cup (½ dL) dry bread crumbs
4 medium shallots, peeled, or ½ medium onion, peeled, cut into 1-inch cubes
1½ tablespoons olive, vegetable or safflower oil
1 tablespoon (15 g) softened butter
2 eggs, separated, room temperature
Salt and freshly ground pepper
4 egg whites, room temperature
¼ teaspoon cream of tartar

1. Insert the *medium shredding disk.* Shred cheese with a gentle push; set aside. Shred zucchini with a firm push. Empty container as necessary on a large platter and sprinkle with 1 teaspoon salt. Set aside 30 minutes. Squeeze to remove bitter liquid. Rinse thoroughly and taste to be sure all the salt is removed; squeeze dry.

2. Meanwhile, prepare Béchamel Sauce, using ⅔ cup (1½ dL) milk; cover with plastic wrap touching top of sauce and set aside at room temperature (or refrigerate overnight).

3. Wipe container and lid dry. Insert the *metal knife blade.* Tear bread in pieces and process to fine crumbs; set aside. With machine running, drop shallots one at a time through food chute. Process until minced. Transfer to a medium skillet; add oil. Cook over low heat until soft. Add zucchini to skillet and increase heat to medium. Continue cooking, tossing frequently, until all liquid has evaporated. Remove from heat; set aside.

4. Adjust oven rack to lower position. Heat oven to 400° F (205° C). Generously butter a 1½-quart (1½-L) soufflé dish; dust with bread crumbs and tap out excess. Set dish aside.

5. Stir egg yolks, shredded cheese, and cooled zucchini mixture thoroughly into Béchamel. Season to taste slightly salty and peppery, otherwise soufflé will be bland as egg whites dilute taste.

6. Beat the 6 whites and cream of tartar with a whisk or electric beater in a clean dry bowl until whites just form firm peaks. Fold about 1 cup (¼ L) of the whites thoroughly into the zucchini mixture; then fold lightened zucchini mixture into whites only until no large streaks remain. Spoon into soufflé dish; smooth top; make a deep X with a knife. Place dish in oven

and immediately reduce heat to 375° F (190° C). Bake 30 to 35 minutes, until puffy and browned. Soufflés rise most during last several minutes of baking; take care not to bang oven door. Serve immediately.

Variation:

Mushroom Soufflé

In Step 1, substitute ¾ pound (340 g) fresh mushrooms, wiped clean, for zucchini and omit the 1 teaspoon salt. Do not salt, squeeze, or rinse shredded mushrooms; simply shred and proceed with recipe.

EGGPLANT PARMESAN
Makes 6 to 8 servings

Mozzarella cheese can be deceptively difficult to shred. Be sure it is well chilled and use very gentle pressure—just enough to hold the cheese against the disk.

Beer Batter, page 67
3 oz. (85 g) Parmesan cheese, cut into 1-inch cubes
¼ cup (½ dL) firmly packed parsley leaves
10 oz. (285 g) mozzarella cheese, chilled and cut in chunks to fit food chute
1 eggplant (1½ to 1¾ lbs./675 to 800 g), stem removed
2 qts. (2 L) vegetable oil
1 qt. (1 L) Marinara Sauce, page 109
Salt and pepper to taste

1. An hour or more in advance, prepare Beer Batter; set aside.

2. Insert the *metal knife blade* in container. Process Parmesan cheese until powdery; set aside. Process parsley until finely minced; set aside. Change to the *medium shredding disk.* Shred mozzarella with a gentle push; set aside. Peel eggplant and slice by hand into ¼-inch (¾-cm)-thick rounds.

3. Place oil in a 6-quart (6-L) kettle or large skillet deep enough to hold 2 inches (5 cm) of oil. Heat oil to 375° F (190° C) on a deep-fry thermometer. Dip eggplant rounds into batter; shake off excess. Fry 3 or 4 at a time, turning

once, until golden brown, about 3 to 5 minutes. Place fried eggplant on paper toweling; drain.

4. Adjust oven rack to lower position. Heat oven to 400°F (205° C). Spread 1 cup (¼ L) Marinara Sauce on bottom of an 11¾- × 7- × 1½-inch (30- × 18- × 4-cm) glass or porcelain baking dish. Place eggplant in an even layer over Marinara Sauce; sprinkle lightly with salt and pepper. Sprinkle a third of the mozzarella cheese over eggplant. Top with a third of the Parmesan. Repeat layering two more times using 2 cups (½ L) Marinara Sauce for the middle layer. Bake 40 minutes, until cheese is well browned. Garnish with parsley.

STIR-FRIED CABBAGE WITH PORK
Makes 2 to 4 servings

A quickly made, delicious and economical stir-fried vegetable cooked in a wok.

1 medium garlic clove, peeled
½ lb. (225 g) lean boneless pork shoulder, cut into 1-inch cubes
2 tablespoons all-purpose soy sauce
1 teaspoon dry sherry
¼ teaspoon cornstarch
1 teaspoon cold water
1 lb. (450 g) curly (Savoy) or green cabbage, cored
2 tablespoons peanut or vegetable oil
2 tablespoons water
1 teaspoon sesame oil
Salt

1. Insert the *metal knife blade.* With machine running, drop garlic clove through food chute. Process until minced; scrape down the sides of the container and add pork. Process to chop with 6 one-second pulses; transfer to a small bowl. To bowl add ½ tablespoon soy sauce, sherry, cornstarch, and 1 teaspoon water. Stir well. Cover and refrigerate 2 hours.

2. Remove tough outer leaves from cabbage. Cut cabbage into wedges to fit food chute. Insert the *medium slicing disk* and slice each wedge with a firm push; empty container as necessary.

3. Heat 1 tablespoon oil in wok until very hot. Add pork and stir-fry only until it changes color, 1½ to 2 minutes; remove to a plate. Heat remaining oil in wok about 30 seconds. Stir-fry cabbage until coated with oil; add remaining soy sauce and 2 tablespoons water. Cover, lower heat, and cook until cabbage softens, about 2 minutes longer.

4. Uncover, increase the heat to high, and stir-fry until liquid has evaporated. Stir in cooked pork and sesame oil. Toss until thoroughly hot; taste and add salt if necessary. Serve immediately.

FRITTATE
Makes batter and filling for 2 omelettes

Flat, or pancake, omelettes with the filling mixed into the batter are called *frittate* (*frittata* is the singular) in Italian. These may be cut into wedges or squares and eaten warm or tepid as appetizers, for lunch or a light dinner. The fillings can be made from almost any vegetable (or sausage); feel free to substitute whatever is available.

The variation is called "plain omelette," and it has nothing whatever to do with Italian cooking. I use it to garnish the Ceylonese Chicken Curry (page 70). The golden strands of egg represent the real gold and silver threads that once were used to adorn *Pilaf.* When cold, this omelette slices surprisingly well in the processor to make julienne strips.

Mushroom, or Olive, or Sausage Filling, see below
1½ oz. (45 g) Parmesan cheese, cut into 1-inch chunks
4 eggs
2 egg yolks
2 tablespoons whipping cream
Freshly ground pepper
2 tablespoons olive or vegetable oil

1. Prepare filling as directed and set it aside near stove.

2. Clean and dry container and insert *metal knife blade.* Process Parmesan cheese until powdery; remove cheese to waxed paper. Place eggs, egg yolks, whipping cream, and pepper in a large measuring cup; mix with a fork.

3. Heat broiler on high setting. Place oil in omelette pan and set over medium heat. Swirl to coat pan with oil. When oil is very hot, lower heat and pour in ⅔ cup (1½ dL) egg mixture. Swirl eggs gently until edges begin to set and continue swirling so that omelette slides freely in pan. When omelette is cooked enough so that only the center is still liquid, remove pan from heat; sprinkle over half the Parmesan cheese and half the filling.

4. Immediately place pan under broiler until edges puff and top browns. Carefully slide omelette off onto warm plate; cover loosely with foil to keep warm. Wipe out pan with paper toweling and repeat with remaining egg mixture, cheese, and filling. Serve immediately.

Mushroom Filling:

2 oz. (60 g) fresh mushrooms, wiped clean (about 7 medium)

Insert the *medium slicing disk.* Load mushrooms in food chute with caps alternating and slice with a gentle push; set aside until ready to use.

Olive Filling:

3 oz. (90 g) black pitted olives, rinsed and drained

Pat olives dry on paper toweling. Insert the *metal knife blade.* Process to chop olives with 4 one-second pulses; set aside until ready to use.

Sausage Filling:

6 oz. (180 g) Sweet Italian Sausage, page 79, cooked and drained, casing removed

Insert the *metal knife blade.* Process to chop drained cooked sausage with 3 one-second pulses, to fine but not pasty consistency.

Variation:

Plain Omelette
Omit filling and Parmesan cheese. Mix 2 eggs, 1 egg yolk, 1 tablespoon whipping cream, and freshly ground pepper in a cup or bowl. Pro-

ceed with Step 3 of recipe, cooking under the broiler until top of omelette is set but not browned.

LAYERED OMELETTE CAKE WITH SPINACH FILLING
Makes 4 servings

Rustic is the word for this exuberant omelette "cake" which marries a French vegetable purée to Italian omelettes and sauce. It is an arrangement that works, however, especially as a brunch or supper dish.

5 qts. (5 L) boiling water
1½ lbs. (675 g) fresh spinach, rinsed, stemmed, drained
⅓ cup (¾ dL) whipping cream
1 teaspoon lemon juice
Salt and freshly ground pepper to taste
Dash nutmeg
1 cup (¼ L) hot Marinara Sauce, page 109
Frittate, page 93

1. Heat water to boiling in an 8-quart (8-L) soup kettle or Dutch oven. Add spinach and push it down with a spoon. When water returns to a rolling boil, remove from heat; drain spinach and immediately rinse with cold water. Press to extract liquid. Place spinach in a dry cloth towel and twist to wring out as much liquid as possible.

2. Insert the *metal knife blade*. Place spinach, cream, lemon juice, a pinch of salt, pepper and nutmeg in container. Process to purée 40 seconds, until smooth. Adjust seasonings to taste. Set aside until ready to assemble the omelette cake.

3. To assemble omelette cake, heat sauce and spinach purée. Prepare or place 1 prepared omelette on a heated seving plate. Spread spinach purée over omelette; top with second omelette. Spoon Marinara Sauce over top of omelettes to make an X design; then spoon remainder around edge of omelettes or pass separately. Serve immediately.

POTATO PANCAKES
Makes 4 servings

Garnish with homemade applesauce, sour cream, or yogurt.

1½ lbs. (675 g) medium potatoes, peeled
Cold water
½ medium onion, peeled, cut into 1-inch cubes
2 eggs
2 tablespoons flour
1 teaspoon salt
Pepper to taste
⅓ to ½ cup (¾ to 1 dL) vegetable oil

1. Attach *medium* or *fine shredding disk*. Insert potatoes from underneath food chute (trim if necessary) and shred with a firm push. Transfer shredded potatoes to a large bowl and fill with cold water to cover. Set aside 15 minutes.

2. Change to the *metal knife blade*. With machine running, drop onion pieces one at a time through food chute. Process until minced. Add eggs; process 10 seconds. Mix in flour, salt, and pepper by processing 5 seconds.

3. Drain potatoes and pat dry between 2 cloth towels. Dry the bowl; add the potato shreds and egg mixture. Stir well.

4. Heat 2 tablespoons oil in a medium skillet until very hot. Spoon ¼ cup (½ dL) batter into skillet for each pancake. Spread to a 3½-inch (9-cm) circle. Fry pancakes 3 at a time on medium heat until undersides are well browned. Turn and fry 3 to 4 minutes longer, until well browned. Remove to paper toweling and repeat to fry remaining pancakes, adding more oil if necessary. Blot tops of pancakes with paper towels to remove excess oil. Keep hot; serve immediately.

POTATO GRATIN
Makes 4 to 6 servings

A rich, classic French potato dish to which a sliced onion has been added. It is especially good when potatoes are thinly sliced.

2 medium garlic cloves, peeled, crushed (use pusher if desired)

1 cup (¼ L) whipping cream or half-and-half
1½ lbs. (675 g) russet potatoes, peeled, ends
    cut blunt
Cold water
1 medium onion, peeled, halved lengthwise
3 tablespoons (45 g) butter
3 oz. (90 g) Gruyère or Swiss cheese, chilled
Salt and freshly ground pepper to taste
Dash each: ground nutmeg and cayenne
    pepper

1. Place garlic and cream in a small saucepan. Simmer slowly 10 minutes.

2. Meanwhile, insert the *medium* or *thin slicing disk*. Trim potatoes as necessary to fit food chute. Insert each upright from underneath and slice with a moderate push. Empty container into a large bowl and add cold water to cover. Set aside until ready to assemble gratin. Slice onion halves with a gentle push. Empty container into a medium skillet. Add 2 tablespoons butter and cook until onions soften; set aside to cool. Change to the *medium shredding disk*. Shred cheese with a gentle push; set aside.

3. Adjust oven rack to middle position. Heat oven to 350° F (175° C). Coat a 4-cup (1-L) baking dish with 1 tablespoon of the butter. Place half the onions in the baking dish; sprinkle lightly with salt and pepper. Drain potato slices in a colander and pat dry on paper toweling. Add half the potatoes to the baking dish. Cover with half the cheese. Repeat layering, ending with cheese.

4. Remove garlic from cream with a slotted spoon; discard garlic. Stir a generous pinch of salt, freshly ground pepper, nutmeg, and cayenne pepper into cream. Pour cream over potatoes. Bake 1 hour 20 minutes, or until potatoes are easily pierced with the tip of a knife and cheese is browned.

POTATO NESTS
Makes 8 servings

Shredded potatoes packed into a special basket mold and deep fried result in beautiful little brown nests used to hold vegetables or other types of potatoes. The temperature of the oil and the type of potato used are critical to the success of the recipe, which should be carefully followed.

2 lbs. russet potatoes, peeled, placed in a bowl
    of cold water
3 to 4 qts. (3 to 4 L) vegetable oil
Salt to taste

1. Trim potatoes as necessary to fit food chute. Insert the *medium shredding disk*. Insert each potato from underneath food chute and shred with a firm push. Empty container as necessary into a bowl of fresh cold water. Set aside 10 minutes.

2. Drain potatoes and pat dry between 2 cloth towels. Roll up and refrigerate until ready to cook, as long as 6 hours.

3. Heat oven to 250° F (120° C). Place oil in a 10-inch diameter (25-cm) deep fryer or in a soup kettle that can hold at least 4 inches (10 cm) of oil. Heat to 375° F (190° C). Tightly pack ⅔ cup (1½ dL) potatoes in bottom of a wire bird's-nest maker. Insert top basket; secure clamps.

4. Immerse basket in hot oil until potatoes are golden brown, about 2 minutes. Remove and hold upside down over paper toweling. Remove clamps and bottom basket. Cool a minute or two. Meanwhile skim off any potato shreds from oil.

5. To remove potatoes from basket, loosen edges and, cupping the hot potatoes gently with a towel, ease the potatoes off the wire basket. Cook remaining baskets as directed above and repeat to remove. Salt lightly and keep warm in oven until ready to serve. Fill finished nests with vegetables such as peas, baby carrots, or classicly "turned" fried potatoes.

FRENCH-FRIED POTATOES
Makes 4 servings

These illustrate only one of the many uses for the *french-fry disk*.

1½ lbs. (675 g) russet potatoes, peeled, placed in a bowl of cold water
2 qts. (2 L) vegetable oil
Salt to taste

1. Heat oven to 250° F (120° C). Place a cake rack on a baking sheet; set aside. Trim potatoes to fit sideways in food chute and pat dry. Insert *french-fry disk*. Place potatoes in food chute from underneath and cut each with a firm push. Discard any small pieces. Place cut potatoes between 2 dry cloth towels.

2. Heat oil in a 6-quart (6-L) soup kettle or in a skillet large and deep enough to hold 2 inches (5 cm) of oil. Heat oil to 375° F (190° C) on a deep-fry thermometer. Deep fry potatoes, a handful at a time, 1 minute or until golden brown. Do not crowd potatoes in oil. Remove with a slotted spoon. Drain on paper toweling 2 to 3 minutes. Transfer to cake rack and place in oven to keep hot and crisp until ready to serve. Before serving, sprinkle potatoes lightly with salt.

Note: If you wish to process potatoes and fry them several hours later, place the processed potatoes in a large bowl and cover them with cold water. Before frying, drain thoroughly and pat very dry in cloth towels so that excess water on surface of potatoes does not cause oil to pop when frying.

PILAF WITH VEGETABLES
Makes 4 servings

This method for cooking rice produces the fluffy, slightly dry, separate grains that mix easily with assorted cooked vegetables. More robust rice dishes might include bits of chopped meat such as sausage.

The best Pilaf, also called *pilaw* or *pilau*, is made with Basmati rice, an unpolished, long-grain Indian variety with an especially nutty flavor, frequently found in stores specializing in Indian or Middle Eastern products.

The carrot and cabbage vegetable variation was created for use with the Ceylonese Chicken Curry on page 70.

Basic Pilaf:

1 medium onion, peeled, cubed
1 tablespoon (15 g) butter
1 cup (230 g) long-grain rice, preferably Basmati
2 cups (½ L) chicken broth or water
Salt to taste

Vegetables:

½ cup (1 dL) firmly packed parsley leaves
1 medium green pepper, cored, cut into 1-inch strips
½ lb. (225 g) mushrooms, wiped clean
6 tablespoons (85 g) butter, softened
Freshly ground pepper to taste
2 dashes cayenne pepper

1. To prepare pilaf, insert the *metal knife blade*. Process to chop onion with 4 to 6 half-second pulses. Empty container into medium saucepan; add 1 tablespoon butter. Stir over low heat until onion softens; add rice and stir until grains turn milky white, about 3 minutes. Stir in broth; add salt and cover. Heat liquid to boiling. Stir well; then cover and simmer until all liquid is absorbed by rice, about 20 to 25 minutes. Set aside off heat but covered to keep rice hot.

2. While rice is cooking, prepare vegetables. Wipe container and blade dry. Process parsley until finely minced; transfer to waxed paper. Change to the *medium slicing disk*. Turn lid over, pull pusher back and wedge pepper strips upright in food chute from underneath. Slice with a gentle push; set aside separately from parsley. Stack mushrooms in food chute with caps alternating; slice with a gentle push; repeat as necessary; empty container into a medium skillet.

3. Add 4 tablespoons butter and sauté mushrooms until they darken in color and all liquid evaporates; set aside. Add an additional tablespoon of butter, and green peppers to skillet. Sauté until peppers are just cooked through.

4. When rice is cooked, stir in mushrooms, green peppers, parsley, remaining 2 tablespoons butter, pepper, and cayenne pepper. Mix gently but thoroughly. Taste and adjust

seasonings, adding salt if necessary. Serve immediately.

Variation:

Pilaf with Carrots and Cabbage
1. Omit parsley, green peppers, and mushrooms from vegetables. Substitute ¼ pound (115 g) carrots, peeled, 3 whole medium green onions, and 1 green cabbage wedge (¼ lb./115 g). Substitute the following for Steps 2 and 3.

2. Insert *medium shredding disk.* Load carrots sideways in food chute; shred with a firm push; empty container into a medium skillet. Cut green onions to fit food chute. Change to *medium slicing disk* and slice with a gentle push; slice cabbage wedge with a firm push.

3. Add 4 tablespoons butter to skillet and cook carrots over low heat until crisp-tender, about 8 minutes. Stir in green onion and cabbage; toss to coat with butter. Cook over low heat until cabbage is crisp-tender, about 10 minutes longer. Proceed with Step 4.

13
Salads

Salads are so often dismissed as rabbit food that I feel a special need to defend their integrity. These lovely mélanges of lettuces, vegetables, herbs, eggs, fish, seafood, and meat seasoned with various dressings are the brightly colored quick-change artists of the table.

Anything goes when it comes to salad making. Their assembly is governed by no strict rules with regard to ingredients, presentation, or their role in the meal. Salads need no longer take a walk-on part. They now can become stars in their own right whether served as hors d'oeuvres, appetizers, main courses, vegetables, salads, or desserts.

While a crisp green salad of tasty lettuces tossed with a properly tart vinaigrette is a rare and wondrous thing, its use is limited largely to a palate cleanser of a type envisioned by the French gastronome Brillat-Savarin when he wrote that salad "freshens without enfeebling and fortifies without irritating."

Salads of a different type—the French call them *salades composées* or composed salads—offer a practical dimension that corresponds with the trend towards lighter meals and are especially well suited to preparation in the food processor. I prefer to call these "assembled salads," however, because most of mine are informal, non-French, and lack the structure and high drama of the true *salade composée*.

Underlying my notion of "assembled salads" is the idea of serving three or four at a time, European style, as the first course for informal entertaining or as the main course of a luncheon. This approach works especially well for buffets. It has the added strength of allowing advance preparation and easing the serving duty of the host or hostess as well.

The key to salad making in the food processor is using the slicing disks effectively; the *french-fry disk* plays a secondary role, as it does for vegetables. The beauty of the salad will depend to a large extent on your skill with the disks because each food requires a different push or pressure, according to its texture. Consult the Basic Techniques, beginning on page 9, or the Conversion Chart, page 164.

A NOTE ABOUT PROCESSING BELL PEPPERS

There are three ways in which bell peppers may be sliced for use in salads:

1. Into 1-inch (2½-cm)-long slivers (see Cuban Black Bean Soup, page 37)
2. Into half-round strips (see Sweet and Sour Chicken, page 68)
3. Into julienne strips when roasted peppers are rolled (see Mediterranean Vegetable Salad, page 101)

EGG SALAD
Makes 6 servings

Chop medium-firm celery and gherkins with one-second on/off turns or pulses; chop eggs (a soft food) with half-second pulses.

¼ **cup (½ dL) firmly packed parsley leaves**
4 **medium shallots, peeled, or ½ medium onion, peeled, cut into 1-inch cubes**
2 **medium sweet gherkins, halved**
1 **medium celery rib, cut into 1-inch lengths**
1 **teaspoon Dijon mustard, or more to taste**
½ **cup (1 dL) Mayonnaise, page 114**
8 **large hard-boiled eggs, cooled, peeled, halved**
¼ **teaspoon salt**
Freshly ground pepper to taste

1. Insert the *metal knife blade*. Process parsley until finely minced; set aside. With machine running, drop shallots through food chute. Process until minced and scrape down sides of container. Add gherkins and celery to container. Chop with 3 one-second on/off turns or pulses; set mixture aside with parsley.

2. Place mustard and mayonnaise in container and process 3 seconds. Add eggs, parsley, gherkins, shallots, celery, salt, and pepper. Process with 7 or 8 half-second pulses, or until thoroughly mixed and eggs are broken into coarse chunks. Adjust seasonings to taste; transfer mixture to a bowl; cover and refrigerate until ready to serve.

COLE SLAW
Makes 4 to 6 servings

Cabbage is shredded by slicing it across the grain; cut ends of cabbage wedges blunt for best results.

1 **lb. (450 g) curly (Savoy) cabbage, or plain green cabbage, core removed**
½ **medium onion, peeled, cut into 1-inch cubes**
1 **tablespoon white vinegar, or more to taste**
1 **tablespoon vegetable oil**
2 **teaspoons sugar**
¼ **teaspoon salt**
Freshly ground pepper to taste
½ **cup (1 dL) Mayonnaise, page 114**

1 **tablespoon white horseradish**
2 **tablespoons plain yogurt or whipping cream**
1 **teaspoon caraway seeds (optional)**

1. Cut cabbage into wedges to fit food chute and attach the *medium slicing disk*. If necessary, insert cabbage wedges from underneath food chute; slice each with a gentle push. Empty container as necessary into large bowl.

2. Change to the *metal knife blade*. Process to chop onion with 4 half-second pulses. Add vinegar, oil, sugar, salt, pepper, mayonnaise, horseradish, and yogurt to container; process to mix with 5 half-second pulses. Pour contents of container over cabbage and toss well to coat. If desired, stir in caraway seeds. Cover and refrigerate until ready to serve.

POTATO SALAD WITH BACON AND DILL
Makes 4 to 6 servings

Potatoes slice best for salad when thoroughly chilled.

2 **lbs. (900 g) russet potatoes, unpeeled**
4 **qts. (4L) lightly salted water**
3 **whole green onions**
½ **lb. (225 g) bacon, preferably without preservatives, cooked crisp, well drained**
¼ **cup (½ dL) milk**
½ **cup (1 dL) plain yogurt or sour cream**
½ **cup (1 dL) Mayonnaise, page 114**
2 **teaspoons Dijon mustard**
1 **tablespoon lemon juice, or more to taste**
½ **teaspoon salt**
Freshly ground pepper to taste
3 **tablespoons snipped fresh dill weed or 1½ teaspoons dried dill weed**

1. Boil potatoes, covered, in lightly salted water until tender when pierced with a knife, about 30 minutes. Drain and rinse with cold water. Refrigerate until chilled; then peel. If large, halve or quarter lengthwise to fit food chute and cut ends blunt so potatoes will slice evenly. Insert the *medium slicing disk* and slice each potato with a very gentle push; transfer to a bowl. Dangle-slice (page 102) white part of green onions; add to potatoes (reserve tops of onions for another use).

2. Change to the *metal knife blade* and wipe out container. Break up bacon and chop by processing for 7 seconds; add to bowl with potatoes and replace blade. Place milk, yogurt, mayonnaise, mustard, lemon juice, salt, pepper, and dill in container. Process 6 seconds; scrape down container sides; process to mix 4 seconds longer. Pour contents of container into bowl; toss well. Cover and refrigerate. Adjust seasonings to taste before serving.

CUCUMBER SALAD WITH YOGURT
Makes 4 servings

Select tall, slim cucumbers that will fit easily in food chute.

2 medium cucumbers (1 lb./450 g), scored, ends cut blunt
2 medium garlic cloves, peeled
2 tablespoons fresh mint leaves or ¾ teaspoon dried crushed mint
1½ cups (12 oz./340 g) plain yogurt
1 tablespoon fresh lemon juice
1 teaspoon honey
¼ teaspoon salt, or more to taste
Pepper to taste

1. Cut cucumbers into even lengths to fit upright in food chute. Insert *thin or medium slicing disk.* Slice cucumbers with a gentle push; transfer to a bowl. Change to the *metal knife blade.* With machine running, drop garlic cloves one at a time through food chute; process until minced. Scrape down side of container. If fresh, add mint leaves and process to mince 20 seconds. If not, add dried mint leaves with yogurt, lemon juice, honey, salt, and pepper to container. Process 20 seconds to mix.

2. Pour contents of container over cucumbers. Toss well. Chill. Before serving, adjust seasonings to taste.

Variation:

Dilled Cucumber Salad
Omit honey and 1 garlic clove. Substitute 3 tablespoons fresh snipped dill weed or 1 teaspoon dried dill weed for fresh or dried mint.

CAPONATA
Makes 8 to 10 appetizer servings

The tart vinegar-sugar mixture, called *agro-dolce* in Italian, gives the very characteristic piquancy to this Sicilian vegetable appetizer.

4 lbs. (1,800 g) medium eggplants, rinsed, ends cut blunt
2 tablespoons salt
½ cup (1 dL) firmly packed parsley leaves
6 medium celery ribs, cut into 1½-inch lengths
1 medium onion, peeled, cut into 1-inch cubes
1 cup (¼ L) olive or vegetable oil
2 lbs. (900 g) tomatoes, cored and peeled
1 can (2 oz./60 g) flat anchovies, drained
2 tablespoons sugar
⅓ cup (¾ dL) white wine vinegar
Freshly ground pepper to taste
6 oz. (180 g) black pitted olives, well drained

1. Cut eggplants into wedges to fit food chute. Insert the *medium slicing disk.* Place eggplant in food chute with skin facing the cutting edge of the disk to avoid twisting and slice with a moderate push. Empty container as necessary onto large platters or jelly-roll pans. Sprinkle eggplant evenly with salt; set aside 45 minutes. Rinse slices well and taste to be sure all salt is removed. Rinse again if necessary. Squeeze dry; set aside.

2. Insert the *metal knife blade.* Process parsley until finely minced; set aside. Chop celery with 4 or 5 one-second pulses; transfer to a large skillet. Place onion in container and chop with 3 or 4 half-second pulses; add to skillet. Add oil to skillet and cook vegetables over medium heat until lightly colored. Add eggplant; stir constantly over high heat until eggplant colors lightly.

3. Meanwhile, quarter tomatoes and chop in 1 cup (¼ L) batches with 3 or 4 half-second pulses; set aside. Place anchovies, sugar, and vinegar in container and process to purée 10 seconds. When eggplant is colored lightly, stir in tomatoes and anchovy mixture. Stir frequently over medium heat until mixture is pasty and liquid has evaporated, usually about 30 minutes. Cool to room temperature. Stir in parsley and adjust seasonings to taste with salt and pepper. Serve at room temperature and garnish with whole olives.

MEDITERRANEAN VEGETABLE SALAD
Makes 6 to 8 servings

The mild sweet taste of roasted bell peppers distinguishes this salad. Baked onions add another interesting flavor and surprisingly few calories.

2 large yellow onions, unpeeled
3 red bell peppers
¾ lb. (340 g) fresh broccoli, stems peeled, rinsed
½ lb. (225 g) fresh mushrooms, wiped clean
½ lb. (225 g) small zucchini, ends cut blunt
Vinaigrette Dressing, page 113

1. Heat oven to 350° F (175° C). Wrap onions in aluminum foil and place on a baking sheet. Bake 1 to 1¼ hours, until onions pierce easily with a knife; unwrap and cool. Place peppers on a gas stove burner or under the broiler. Turn over high flame until skins are completely charred and blackened. Transfer to a bowl; cover and set aside 15 minutes. Uncover and scrape off charred skin with a knife. Slit open peppers, remove and discard core and seeds; set peppers aside.

2. Place broccoli in a vegetable steamer basket. Insert basket in a large saucepan with enough water to barely touch the bottom. Cover and steam over high heat until crisp-tender, about 8 to 9 minutes. Remove; rinse with cold water; drain well. Remove flowerets and transfer to a serving bowl.

3. Meanwhile, insert the *medium slicing disk*. Peel and quarter onions, adding any juices to bowl with broccoli flowerets. Insert each piece sideways in food chute and slice with a gentle push; add to bowl. Roll up each pepper tightly. Insert two rolls upright and side by side from underneath food chute; slice with a gentle push. Cut the third pepper in half crosswise; insert as before and repeat to slice peppers into julienne strips; add to bowl. Place broccoli stems upright in food chute; slice with a gentle push. Stack mushrooms with caps alternating in food chute; slice with a gentle push; add contents of container to bowl. Load zucchini upright in food chute; slice with a firm push; add to bowl.

4. Pour Vinaigrette over vegetables; toss well.

Cover and set aside at room temperature to marinate for 2 hours before serving. Adjust seasonings to taste; serve salad at room temperature.

CAESAR SALAD
Makes 4 to 6 servings

The pusher may be used to crush the garlic cloves that flavor the croutons.

Garlic Croutons:
¼ lb. (115 g) dry bread, cut into ½-inch cubes
¼ lb. (115 g) butter
2 medium garlic cloves, crushed

1½ oz. (45 g) Parmesan cheese, cut into 1-inch chunks
1 large garlic clove, peeled, or more to taste
3 flat anchovy fillets
½ teaspoon Dijon mustard
Dash Worcestershire sauce
Freshly ground pepper to taste
1 egg
⅓ cup (¾ dL) olive or vegetable oil
1 medium head (¾ lb./340 g) romaine lettuce

1. To prepare croutons, heat oven to 375° F (190° C). Toast bread on baking sheet 20 minutes or until completely dried, turning as necessary. Melt butter in a large skillet. Add 2 cloves garlic and simmer 3 to 4 minutes; remove and discard garlic. Add bread; cook over medium heat, turning frequently to coat with butter, until lightly browned. Drain and cool croutons on paper toweling. If prepared in advance, store in an airtight container until ready to use.

2. Insert *metal knife blade*. With machine running, drop Parmesan cheese one piece at a time through food chute. Process until powdery; set aside. With machine running, drop 1 garlic clove and anchovies through food chute. Process until minced; scrape down sides of container. Add mustard, Worcestershire sauce, pepper, and egg; process 5 seconds. With machine running, pour oil through food chute within 15 seconds; process 5 seconds longer. Refrigerate contents of container until ready to serve salad.

3. Rinse, core, and dry lettuce. Line a large salad bowl with large leaves. Tear up enough remaining leaves to fill bowl; chill until ready to serve.

4. To serve, add croutons, dressing, and cheese to salad bowl. Grind fresh pepper over salad to taste. Toss and serve immediately.

EPICUREAN SALAD
Makes 4 to 6 servings

This salad is adapted from the Cobb Salad I often ate as a child at the original Brown Derby Restaurant in Los Angeles. After lunch, we would be taken to the movies at Grauman's Chinese Theatre where our greatest thrill was to find a movie star's footprints that matched our own. Then my father would take us up the street (Hollywood Boulevard) to Brown's for hot fudge sundaes.

If a *french-fry disk* is not available, quarter the beets lengthwise, place them upright in the food chute and slice into wedge shapes with the *medium slicing disk.*

½ lb. (225 g) bacon, preferably without
   preservatives, cooked crisp, well drained
2 hard-boiled eggs, peeled
½ lb. (225 g) fresh mushrooms, wiped clean
3 cups (¾ L) firmly packed stemmed spinach
   leaves, rinsed, well drained
2 medium bunches whole green onions, roots
   removed
3 medium tomatoes, halved lengthwise, ends
   cut blunt
1 lb. (450 g) fresh cooked beets, peeled, or 1
   jar (1 lb./450 g) whole pickled beets, drained
Vinaigrette Dressing, page 113

1. Insert the *metal knife blade.* Break bacon strips into pieces and process 5 to 8 seconds to chop; remove to waxed paper. Halve eggs and process to mince with 6 to 8 half-second pulses; set eggs aside separately.

2. Wipe out container and change to the *medium slicing disk.* Stack mushrooms with caps alternating in food chute; slice with a gentle push; set aside. Divide spinach leaves into 6 batches and stack. Roll up stacks tightly. Insert rolls, two at a time, upright from underneath

food chute (see page 13, upper right illustration); slice with a gentle push; empty container as necessary into a bowl. Dangle-slice (see below) white parts of green onions; set aside (reserve tops for another use). Insert tomato halves from underneath food chute and slice with a gentle push; set aside.

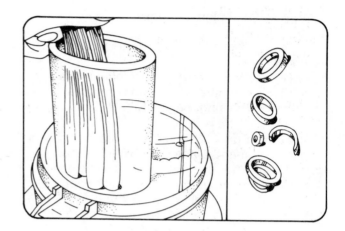

3. Change to the *french-fry disk.* Pat beets dry. Load in food chute and cut with a gentle push. Using a large salad bowl or a round serving platter, arrange ingredients with colors and textures in stripes, bunches, or concentric circles. For example, spinach could be placed around outside of salad bowl, tomatoes placed in a ring next, then mushrooms, beets, chopped egg, bacon, and green onion in the center. Cover and refrigerate. Before serving, pour dressing over evenly but do not toss.

SESAME CHICKEN SALAD
Makes 4 servings

Cooked chicken breasts slice best when chilled and when food chute is snugly packed. Leftover cooked chicken (including dark meat) or turkey may be substituted. Sesame paste *(tahini)* and chili oil are available at stores specializing in Chinese or Middle Eastern foods.

3 split, skinned, boned chicken breasts (½
   lb./225 g each)
2 thin slices fresh ginger root or ½ teaspoon
   powdered ginger

3 **cups (¾ dL) Chicken Broth, page 40**
2 **medium garlic cloves, peeled**
2 **tablespoons sugar**
¼ **cup (½ dL) sesame paste (*tahini*) or plain peanut butter**
2 **tablespoons sesame oil**
1 **teaspoon chili oil**
2 **tablespoons rice or cider vinegar**
3 **tablespoons all-purpose soy sauce**
6 **medium green onions**
½ **medium cucumber, scored**
Lettuce or bok choy leaves
½ **cup (3 oz./85 g) toasted slivered almonds**

1. Place chicken breasts, ginger, and broth in a large deep skillet. Heat to simmering. Cover and poach at a bare simmer just until chicken is cooked through, about 4 to 6 minutes. Uncover and let cool to room temperature (this will finish the cooking) in the hot cooking liquid. Remove chicken and pat dry. Refrigerate. Discard ginger; reserve broth for another use.

2. Halve chilled chicken breasts crosswise. Insert *french-fry disk* or *thick slicing disk*. Insert chicken pieces, blunt ends down, from underneath food chute. Slice 2 pieces at a time, or enough to fill food chute, with a gentle push. Repeat until all chicken is sliced; do not worry if chicken becomes slightly shredded. Remove chicken to a mixing bowl; set aside.

3. Change to the *metal knife blade*. With machine running, drop garlic cloves through food chute. Process until minced. Add sugar, sesame paste, sesame oil, and red hot oil to container. With machine running, drizzle in rice vinegar and soy sauce. Mix 10 seconds longer. If mixture is very thick, drizzle in enough reserved broth to thin mixture to a consistency where it will easily coat chicken. Pour contents of container over chicken; toss to coat. Set aside until ready to serve.

4. Just before serving, insert *medium* or *thin slicing disk* in clean container. Dangle-slice (page 102) white parts of green onions; set aside. Cut cucumber to fit upright in food chute and insert from underneath if necessary. Slice with a gentle push; set aside. Arrange chicken salad on lettuce or bok choy leaves. Garnish with cucumber, green onion, and slivered almonds.

PANZANELLA
Makes 6 to 8 servings

My first encounter with this bread salad occurred in Florence at a little *trattoria* near the *Ponte Vecchio;* the recipe is my happy souvenir. Only the Florentines could transform chopped vegetables and old bread into such a divine and wickedly addictive dish. Prepare the salad a day in advance to allow flavors to mingle, and use the full amount of oil specified in the recipe or it will be dry.

½ **cup (1 dL) firmly packed parsley leaves**
2 **medium garlic cloves, peeled**
1 **medium onion, peeled, cut into 1-inch cubes**
½ **cup (1 dL) red wine vinegar**
½ **teaspoon salt**
Freshly ground pepper
1½ **cups (3½ dL) olive, vegetable, or safflower oil**
3 **medium celery ribs, strings removed, cut into 1-inch lengths**
3 **medium tomatoes, halved lengthwise, cored**
½ **lb. (225 g) three-day-old French or Italian bread, cut by hand into ½-inch cubes**

1. Insert the *metal knife blade*. Process parsley until finely minced; place in a large bowl. With the machine running, drop garlic cloves through food chute. Process until minced and scrape down the container sides. Add onion, vinegar, salt, and pepper to the container. With the machine running, pour half the oil through food chute within 30 seconds; add mixture and remaining oil to bowl with parsley. Place half the celery in container and process to chop with 4 to 5 one-second pulses; add celery to bowl; repeat.

2. Change to the *french-fry disk* or *medium slicing disk*. Insert tomatoes in food chute from underneath and cut with a moderate push; add to bowl. Toss contents of bowl to mix thoroughly and adjust seasonings to taste salty and peppery.

3. Add bread to bowl. With hands or two large spoons, toss thoroughly to distribute oil and vinegar mixture evenly over bread cubes, so that bread will soften and absorb it evenly. Cover and refrigerate overnight.

4. Remove salad from refrigerator several hours before serving to warm to room temperature.

Toss well and adjust seasonings to taste. Serve at room temperature.

TOMATO ASPIC LOBSTER
Makes 10 to 12 servings

It almost looks real. The idea for this delicious creature began to take shape the moment I tasted my friend Eve Acheson's tomato aspic—a sweet-sour tomato taste spiked with the pungency of pickling spice.

To achieve the full effect, a 14-inch (35-cm) copper mold in the shape of a lobster is essential. Arrange the filling *only* over those sections that normally would contain lobster meat—arms, claws, body, and tail, and pile it high. When unmolded, the filling will be a surprise, and the "lobster" will be a sensation.

Tomato Aspic:

3 **medium onions, peeled, cut into 1-inch cubes**
2 **cans (1 lb. 12 oz./790 g each) Italian plum tomatoes, drained, seeded, liquid reserved, or 3 lbs. (1,350 g) fresh tomatoes, peeled, seeded, juice reserved**
1¼ **teaspoons pickling spice**
4 **tablespoons (packages) unflavored gelatin**
1 **cup white wine vinegar**
¾ **cup (145 g) sugar**

Filling:

¼ **cup (½ dL) firmly packed parsley leaves**
½ **medium green bell pepper, cored, seeded, cut into 1-inch pieces**
1 **small onion, peeled, cut into 1-inch cubes**
1 **small celery rib, cut into 1-inch lengths**
1 **tablespoon (package) unflavored gelatin**
¼ **cup (½ dL) cold water**
⅓ **cup (¾ dL) plain yogurt or sour cream**
⅓ **cup (¾ dL) Mayonnaise, page 114**
¼ **teaspoon salt, or more to taste**
Freshly ground pepper
¼ **lb. (115 g) cooked salad (small) shrimp, rinsed, drained, patted dry**
Anchovy Dressing, page 114, or Green Goddess Dressing, page 115

1. To prepare the aspic, insert the *metal knife blade*. Process onions until smooth, about 30 seconds. Transfer puréed onions to a large nonreactive saucepan. Strain tomato liquid into saucepan and set it aside. Process half the tomatoes until smoothly puréed; add to saucepan. Repeat to purée remaining tomatoes and add to saucepan. Stir in pickling spice. Heat mixture to boiling; cover and simmer 25 minutes. Pour hot mixture into a bowl; rinse and dry saucepan.

2. In the clean saucepan, mix gelatin with vinegar and stir to dissolve. Place a large medium-fine mesh strainer over pan. Strain tomato liquid from bowl into saucepan, pressing solids firmly to extract all liquid. Discard solids. Stir in sugar. Heat to boiling; cover and simmer 5 minutes, stirring occasionally. Uncover and cool to room temperature. Aspic is ready to mold.

3. Rinse lobster mold with water. Add 4 cups (1 L) tomato aspic and refrigerate until firm, about 1 to 1½ hours. Clean and dry container and reinsert the *metal knife blade*. To prepare the filling, process parsley until finely minced; set aside in a medium bowl. Process to chop green pepper with 3 one-second pulses; add to bowl with parsley. Place onion and celery together in container. Process to mince with 5 one-second pulses; add to bowl. Return blade to container.

4. Mix gelatin and water in a small saucepan. Place pan over very low heat and stir until gelatin is dissolved. Pour hot gelatin into container. Add yogurt, mayonnaise, salt, and pepper. Process 4 seconds; add to bowl with vegetables. Add shrimp to bowl and stir well. Adjust seasonings to taste; set aside in a cool place (do not refrigerate).

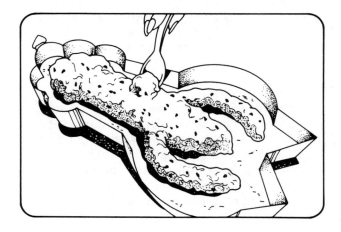

5. Remove lobster mold from refrigerator and brush the surface of the set aspic lightly with cold water. Spoon shrimp mixture into mold, carefully placing it over tail and body sections and over tips and curved parts of claws, so that when it is unmolded, the lobster will look real. Pile shrimp mixture about ¾ inch (2 cm) high and do not allow it to touch edges of mold or filling will show. Refrigerate until filling is firmly set.

6. Remove lobster mold from refrigerator. Again, brush exposed surface of tomato aspic lightly with cold water, working around filling. Pour in remaining room temperature aspic. Cover and refrigerate 6 hours or as long as overnight.

7. To unmold, run the tip of a knife around inside edge. Dip mold carefully in warm water. Place a serving dish over mold, invert and lift off mold. Serve chilled. Pass dressing separately.

FRUIT SALAD WITH KIWI
Makes 6 to 8 servings

Kiwi fruit, named after the shaggy little New Zealand bird it resembles, is actually a Chinese gooseberry. High in vitamin C and low in calories (about 30 per fruit), they make a beautiful and delicious addition to this salad. If purchased when firm, kiwis keep well in the refrigerator for several weeks. To ripen, place at room temperature until slightly soft to the touch; chill before slicing.

½ **medium orange**
2 **tablespoons sugar**
1 **pineapple (2 to 2½ lbs./1¼ kg), peeled, top and core removed**
2 **firm ripe bananas, peeled, ends cut blunt**
2 **medium kiwi fruit, peeled, ends cut blunt**
½ **pt. (¼ L) ripe strawberries, hulled, rinsed, well drained**

1. Insert the *metal knife blade*. Strip off the orange rind with a vegetable peeler, allowing rind to fall into container. Add sugar. Process until rind strips are finely minced. Squeeze orange and add 3 tablespoons of the juice to container. Process 10 seconds; place in a serving bowl.

2. Cut pineapple in rectangular chunks to fit food chute. Change to *thick* or *medium slicing disk*. Blunt ends of pineapple chunks and slice with a firm push. Place slices in bowl and toss with orange mixture. Halve bananas crosswise and insert pieces side by side in food chute. Slice with a gentle push. Add bananas to bowl and spoon some liquid from the dish over the bananas to prevent discoloring. Slice each kiwi with a gentle push; add to bowl. Place several strawberries, hulled ends down, directly on slicing disk (see page 22). Place lid on container so food chute encloses berries. Fill chute from top, stacking berries hulled ends down, and slice with a gentle push. Repeat with remaining berries or quarter berries by hand. Add berries to bowl and toss well. Cover and refrigerate no longer than 2 hours. Serve cold.

14

Sauces and Salad Dressings

"Yes, it is true, one judges a cook by his sauces."

—Roger Vergé

Sauces are liquid seasonings and salad dressings are simply sauces for salads—even the words are related. Both derive from the Latin *salsus,* which means salted, since salt was the original seasoning.

Fine sauces traditionally have been an intimidating area of the cooking repertory. Perfection has always been demanded, and many cooks believed that to create wonderful sauces one was required to be part chemist and part alchemist.

The food processor has transformed the making of sauces and salad dressings to such an extent, however, that professional quality sauces are now within the reach of any cook. Moreover, the methods for preparing three important French sauces—hollandaise, béarnaise, and *beurre blanc*—have been changed here by new methods adapted for use in the processor.

This breakthrough in the preparation of hollandaise, béarnaise, and *beurre blanc* is possible because the food processor emulsifies (suspends one liquid in another) so perfectly and so rapidly. As a result, these are no longer unstable mixtures that require last-moment preparation. Using my methods, hollandaise, béarnaise, and *beurre blanc* have become dependable and can be made as long as an hour in advance and reheated.

PROCESSOR HOLLANDAISE AND BEARNAISE BY THE MODIFIED *SABAYON* METHOD

These sauces are so light and foamy that you barely realize you are eating something that is also wonderfully rich—a definite improvement over the traditional heavy sauces.

The new light texture and durability that is created by the modified *sabayon* base is nothing more than egg yolks processed with warm water (or the béarnaise reduction) for 1 minute. The yolks become pale and fluffy because a small amount of air has been incorporated. The warm water also begins the cooking process, thus the air is trapped. This base prevents the sauces from separating and permits them also to be reheated. There is no on-the-stove cooking and both sauces are quickly made.

The modified *sabayon* base will absorb more than the usual quantity of butter. Hot clarified butter is used and the optimum temperature is 160 to 180° F (71 to 82° C). As the butter is added, the cooking is finished and the sauce perfectly emulsified. All that remains is to season the sauce to taste, and it is ready to serve (or to be set aside for several hours before reheating).

If either sauce were to be made on top of the stove, the egg yolks and water would be beaten for the *sabayon* in a skillet or double boiler until very thick and foamy. Because the yolks are not beaten on the stove, however, I call the processor version a "modified" method.

The airy consistency of Processor Hollandaise gives a lift to old favorites like Eggs Benedict and poached asparagus; it transforms a simple piece of poached or grilled fish into an exquisite main course.

Béarnaise, long a standard partner of red meat, also is superb with poached or steamed chicken or vegetables such as artichokes. Béarnaise further serves as a base for such sauces as *Choron* when tomato purée is added, *Arlésienne* when tomato and anchovy paste are added, or *Paloise* when mint replaces tarragon in the reduction.

BEURRE BLANC BY THE "HOT BUTTER" METHOD

Beurre blanc is the darling of the new French cooking; a tart sauce of such character and versatility, it has quickly become a classic. This sauce hails from France's Loire River valley and was originally served with fish from those waters and made with local wine such as Muscadet.

Beurre blanc translates literally as "white butter" and is always made in two basic steps. First, shallots are slowly cooked with an acid such as wine until the liquid is radically reduced; this is called the reduction. Then cold butter is whisked into the reduction, either over low or high heat, to produce a sauce which is delicious, foamy, and light.

My new hot butter method eliminates the cooking by using hot (but not bubbling) melted butter (between 160 and 180° F/71 and 82° C), rather than cold butter. It is foolproof. The advantages are no on-the-stove cooking and speed—the sauce is made in less than a minute. It may be kept warm in the processor container (provided the pusher is left in the food chute and the lid is in place) as long as 15 minutes before serving or set aside at room temperature as long as 1 hour before reheating.

Beurre blanc is the perfect partner for fish dishes of all types, especially when broiled, poached, or grilled. It may accompany fish or

vegetable mousses or vegetables such as asparagus or leeks. Flavorings such as watercress, puréed red bell pepper, tomato, basil, and saffron may be added.

Beurre Blanc Mousseux, or the foamy Beurre Blanc variation, is a hybrid. An egg yolk and cream are added to thicken and enrich the basic sauce. Use Beurre Blanc Mousseux when a sauce with more body is required (see Coquilles St. Jacques Nouvelles, page 55).

Beurre Rouge, or red wine and butter sauce, is made by substituting a red wine (with a high alcoholic content and deep color) for white wine. It is a traditional accompaniment to beef but also may be paired with grilled or sautéed veal or lamb. Marrow, meat glaze, or wild mushrooms may be added to deepen the taste.

MAYONNAISE AND VINAIGRETTE

Mayonnaise is the base of so many cold sauces that it is essential in the repertory of every cook. Watching it take on a pale yellow color and luscious creamy consistency is fascinating when you realize that each egg is absorbing so many times its own weight in oil.

Mayonnaise usually takes no longer than 2 minutes to make and its virtues are many. It has a fresher, better taste than mayonnaise that is store bought. It is free of additives and preservatives and more economical to make than to purchase. Mayonnaise or salad dressings may be prepared ahead and kept on hand in the refrigerator. See page 6 for information about oil to be used in salad dressings.

Vinaigrette, or oil and vinegar dressing, is a kitchen basic. I have used my recipe for years. The character of vinaigrettes may be changed by either the vinegar or the oil used. Often, when I want a strong taste, I substitute sherry wine vinegar in a vinaigrette for cold green vegetables like broccoli or green beans. Fruit vinegars—raspberry, strawberry, or blueberry—also provide interesting flavors. For the majority of salads I blend these vinegars with the rich taste of Italian olive oil.

Note: For best results with emulsified sauces, add butter or oil within time specified by recipe. If butter or oil is added too rapidly, sauce will be thin; if added too slowly sauce will be thicker than recipe specifies.

FIVE SAUCES FOR PASTA

Special note should be made of the five

simple sauces for homemade pasta or spaghetti, because none require lengthy cooking. All are designed to be served Italian style, that is, tossed with pasta or spaghetti until they coat or cling to noodles rather than form a puddle in which the noodles sit. When just coated with sauces, noodles retain their firm texture and never become squishy soft.

The Marinara Sauce doubles as an all-purpose tomato sauce used on the Layered Omelette Cake, with Eggplant Parmesan, or to set off the Zucchini Soufflé. During the summer I make quarts of Marinara from our ripe garden tomatoes and freeze it in 1-quart (1-L) and 1-cup (¼-L) containers to have convenient amounts on hand. When that supply is exhausted or when tomatoes are out of season, I prefer good quality canned Italian plum tomatoes to cottony, tasteless fresh tomatoes.

PROCESSOR HOLLANDAISE
Makes 1¼ cups (about 3 dL) or 4 to 5 servings

The clarified butter may be prepared well in advance and stored in an airtight container in the refrigerator (see page 4), but it takes only minutes to make.

2 large egg yolks, at room temperature
2 tablespoons warm water
Generous pinch salt
¾ cup (180 g) hot clarified butter (180° F/82° C)
Freshly ground white pepper
1 teaspoon fresh lemon juice, or more to taste
2 dashes Tabasco sauce

1. Insert the *metal knife blade*. Place egg yolks, warm water, and salt in container. Process until frothy, at least 1 minute. With machine running, pour hot clarified butter through food chute within 30 seconds. Process 5 seconds after all butter is added.

2. Add pepper, lemon juice, and Tabasco. Process to mix 5 seconds; then adjust seasonings to taste. Sauce is ready to serve. If desired, cover with lid (be sure pusher is inserted in food chute) and sauce will stay warm about 15 minutes; process 5 seconds before serving.

3. Or transfer sauce to a small heavy-duty

saucepan and place plastic wrap touching the top. Set aside at room temperature as long as 2 hours (do not refrigerate). To reheat, remove plastic, place saucepan over low heat and whisk vigorously until sauce is hot to the touch—it will thicken slightly. *Note:* A small amount of hot water may be added to restore light consistency. Do not allow sauce to approach a simmer.

Variation:

Mustard Hollandaise
Add 2 to 3 tablespoons Dijon mustard to sauce after butter has been added in Step 1. Process 5 seconds and continue with Step 2.

Sauce Béarnaise
Omit 1 tablespoon of the water and the lemon juice. Before beginning recipe, peel 4 medium shallots (1 oz./30 g). Insert the *metal knife blade*. With machine running, drop shallots one at a time through food chute; process until minced. Scrape shallots into a small (non-aluminum) saucepan. Add ¼ cup (½ dL) dry white wine, ¼ cup (½ dL) white wine vinegar, and 1 teaspoon dried tarragon leaves. Boil slowly until liquid is reduced to a glaze that just coats bottom of saucepan; take care shallots do not burn. Meanwhile rinse and dry container and blade and return them to base (clarify butter if not already prepared). Begin Step 1, placing egg yolks and 1 tablespoon water in container. Strain contents of saucepan into container, pressing firmly to extract all liquid from shallots; discard solids. Proceed with recipe for Processor Hollandaise.

BEURRE BLANC
Makes 1¼ cups (3 dL) or 4 servings

Use a good-quality dry white French or California wine, but I do not recommend using a jug wine.

The temperature of the butter may be measured with an instant-registering thermometer or judged by eye when the milk solids foam and rise to the top (like foam on a glass of beer) and steam also rises.

½ medium garlic clove, peeled
4 medium shallots (1 oz./30 g), peeled

1 cup (¼ L) dry white wine, such as Muscadet
   or Pinot Chardonnay
1 tablespoon white wine vinegar, or slightly
   more to taste
¼ teaspoon salt, or more to taste
1 cup (225 g) hot melted butter (160 to
   180° F/71 to 82° C)

1. Insert the *metal knife blade*. With machine
running, drop garlic and shallots one at a time
through food chute. Process until minced.
Transfer mixture to a small (nonaluminum)
saucepan. Add wine; simmer uncovered at a
slow steady rate until liquid is radically reduced
and together liquid and shallots measure ¼ cup
(½ dL). Stir in 1 tablespoon vinegar and the
salt. If desired, reduction may be cooled and
refrigerated as long as overnight. Heat mixture
to a rapid simmer—it must be hot—before
continuing with recipe.

2. Meanwhile, clean and dry food processor
container and blade and return them to base.
Strain the reduction into the container, pressing very firmly to extract all possible liquid
from shallot mixture; discard shallots.

3. With machine running, slowly pour hot
melted butter through food chute within 35 seconds; process 10 seconds longer. Taste; adjust
seasonings, adding additional vinegar and salt
if desired. Sauce may now be left in container,
covered, and with pusher inserted in food
chute. It will stay warm as long as 15 minutes.
Process 5 seconds before serving.

Or sauce may be set aside at room temperature
as long as 1 hour. Reheat over low heat, whisk-
ing vigorously, until just hot to the touch; do
not allow sauce to simmer when reheating;
serve immediately.

Variations:

Beurre Blanc Mousseux
Follow directions through end of Step 2. Mix 1
egg yolk and 2 tablespoons whipping cream
together in a cup. With machine running, pour
egg mixture through food chute within 5 seconds. Proceed with Step 3.

Beurre Rouge
Substitute a red wine such as Côtes du Rhône,
a Médoc, Pauillac or a red California table wine
(but not a jug wine), for white wine. Substitute
red wine vinegar for white wine vinegar.

MARINARA SAUCE
Makes 2½ qts (2½ L)

A mild, thick, and wonderfully vegetable-rich
sauce with a light tomato flavor. There is no
cause for alarm about the quantity of garlic
which takes on a surprisingly gentle flavor
when cooked.

Prepared tomato sauce is not a recommended substitute for the sweet, plump, whole
tomatoes called for here.

10 medium garlic cloves, peeled
1 lb. (450 g) medium onions, peeled, cut into
   1-inch cubes
½ lb. (225 g) carrots, peeled, cut into 1-inch
   lengths
6 medium celery ribs, strings removed, cut into
   1-inch lengths
¼ cup (½ dL) olive or vegetable oil
4 cans (1 lb. 12 oz./790 g each) Italian plum
   tomatoes, drained, seeded, liquid reserved, or
   fresh tomatoes (see Variation)
2 teaspoons salt
¼ cup (½ dL) firmly packed fresh basil leaves
   or 2 tablespoons dried basil leaves
4 tablespoons (60 g) butter
½ cup (1 dL) milk
Freshly ground pepper
2 teaspoons Mixed Herbs, page 6

1. Insert the *metal knife blade*. With machine
running, drop garlic cloves one at a time
through food chute. Transfer minced garlic to a
6-quart (6-L) soup kettle; set aside. Chop onions in 2 batches, each with 6 to 8 half-second
pulses; add to kettle. Chop carrots with 7 or 8
one-second pulses; add to kettle. Chop celery
with 4 to 6 one-second pulses; add to kettle.

2. Add olive oil to kettle and stir well to coat
vegetables. Cook vegetables over medium heat
until liquid begins to evaporate, about 10 to 15
minutes. Add tomatoes and 4 cups (1 L)
strained juice. Heat to boiling. Stir in salt.
Simmer uncovered for 25 minutes.

3. With the *metal knife blade* in place, purée 2
cups (½ L) tomato mixture at a time 20 seconds; transfer to a large bowl. Add fresh basil
to container after last batch of sauce, and
process 20 seconds or until minced.

4. Return all the puréed tomato mixture to the
soup kettle. Stir in basil, butter, milk, pepper,

and herbs. Set cover slightly ajar and simmer 30 minutes. Adjust seasonings to taste. Use immediately or cool thoroughly and refrigerate overnight. Sauce also may be frozen.

Variation:

Summer Marinara Sauce
Substitute 6 pounds (2¾ kg) round or Italian plum tomatoes, cored, peeled, quartered, juice reserved, for canned tomatoes and liquid. Use all tomato liquid from fresh tomatoes.

MEAT SAUCE
Makes 3 quarts (3 L)

This is a good all-purpose meat sauce that may be prepared with fresh tomatoes and herbs during summer months (see Variation). When cooked, the sauce should taste slightly over-seasoned since its flavor will be dulled slightly when tossed with pasta. If made a day in advance, the flavor will only improve.

½ cup (1 dL) firmly packed parsley leaves
6 medium garlic cloves, peeled
2 medium onions, peeled, cut into 1-inch cubes
6 tablespoons (¾ dL) olive or vegetable oil
½ lb. (225 g) boneless pork shoulder, cut into 1-inch cubes
1 lb. (450 g) boneless beef chuck or neck, cut into 1-inch cubes
3 tablespoons flour
3 cans (1 lb. 12 oz./790 g each) Italian plum tomatoes, drained, seeded, liquid reserved
1 tablespoon dried oregano leaves
1½ teaspoons dried thyme leaves
1 teaspoon salt, or more to taste
1 teaspoon dried basil leaves
½ teaspoon ground fennel seed
Pinch ground coriander
Pepper to taste

1. Insert the *metal knife blade*. Process parsley until finely minced; set aside. With machine running, drop garlic cloves one at a time through food chute. Process until minced. Add onions to container. Chop with 6 to 8 half-second pulses. Transfer contents of container to a 6-quart (6-L) soup kettle. Add oil. Cook over low heat until onions soften.

2. Dry container and blade and return them to base. Process beef and pork in 1½ cup (3½ dL) batches to medium hamburger consistency with 4 to 5 two-second pulses; set meat aside.

3. Sprinkle flour over onions. Stir over medium heat until thick and pasty, about 3 minutes. Add pork and beef. Stir over medium heat only until meat turns pale.

4. Purée 2 cups (½ L) tomatoes at a time in processor container 30 seconds; add to soup kettle. Strain and add 4 cups (1 L) drained tomato juice to kettle. Reserve remainder for another use such as tomato paste (see page 7).

5. Add parsley, oregano, thyme, salt, basil, fennel, and coriander to kettle. Heat to a rapid simmer. Cover and slowly simmer 10 minutes, stirring once or twice. Uncover and simmer until sauce is thickened, 1 to 1½ hours or longer. Add pepper to taste and adjust seasonings. Use immediately, or cool thoroughly and refrigerate overnight. (Or place sauce in airtight containers, and freeze up to 3 months. Thaw in refrigerator 24 hours or uncovered at room temperature.)

PESTO
Makes 1½ cups (3½ dL) or enough for ½ to ¾ pound (225 to 340 g) cooked pasta

What an absolute sensation a cold salad of macaroni or shells with pesto will bring to a midsummer picnic! No matter how much you make there is never any left over. We live on pesto all summer long because basil grows so quickly in the garden. We love it pungent, garlicky and made with olive oil. But the garlic may be reduced to one clove, and the sauce may be lightened by using safflower oil and yogurt—especially for dips.

2 oz. (60 g) Parmesan cheese, cut into 1-inch chunks
1 oz. (30 g) Romano cheese, cut into 1-inch chunks

2 medium garlic cloves, peeled
3 tablespoons pine nuts (*pignolas*)
¼ teaspoon salt, or more to taste
½ cup (1 dL) olive oil or safflower oil
2 cups (½ L) firmly packed basil leaves, rinsed, patted dry
¼ cup (½ dL) whipping cream or plain yogurt

1. Insert the *metal knife blade*. Process Parmesan and Romano cheese chunks together until powdery; set aside. With machine running, drop garlic through food chute. Scrape down sides of container. Add pine nuts and salt. With machine running, pour oil through food chute within 15 seconds. Scrape down sides of container.

2. Add basil leaves to container; push down as necessary to fit. Purée 30 seconds or until a fine paste forms. Mix in whipping cream by processing 5 seconds. Use within 4 hours by tossing with hot or room temperature pasta, or as a dip for Crudités, page 18.

Variation:

Freezer Pesto
If pesto is to be frozen, prepare but omit salt, cheeses, and cream. Freeze in an airtight container. Defrost overnight in refrigerator. Add grated cheese, cream, salt, and adjust seasonings.

CREAM SAUCE WITH VEGETABLES
Makes about 2 cups (½ L) or enough for ½ to ¾ pound (225 to 340 g) pasta

A light, spirited cream sauce with a mild mushroom flavor and crisp-tender bits of broccoli. It is especially delicious and beautiful when tossed with whole wheat or carrot noodles.
   Virtually any cooked vegetable may be substituted (including green or yellow bell peppers, julienned carrots, peas, or wild mushrooms). Prosciutto, seafood such as scallops, or chicken also may be combined with vegetables.

¾ lb. (340 g) fresh broccoli, well rinsed, drained
¼ lb. (115 g) fresh mushrooms, wiped clean
4 whole green onions

1 oz. (30 g) Parmesan cheese, cut into 1-inch chunks
3 tablespoons olive or vegetable oil
2 tablespoons (30 g) butter
½ cup (1 dL) dry white wine or dry vermouth
1½ cups (3½ dL) whipping cream
Salt and freshly ground pepper

1. Remove broccoli flowerets and set aside. Peel stems with a sharp knife or vegetable peeler and cut to fit upright in food chute. Insert the *medium slicing disk*. Slice stems with a gentle push; set aside with flowerets. Load mushrooms with caps alternating in food chute; slice with a gentle push; set aside. Dangle-slice white part of green onions; set aside; set tops aside for another use. Wipe container dry. Change to the *metal knife blade*. Process Parmesan cheese until powdery; set aside.

2. Place oil and butter in a large skillet. Add broccoli flowerets and stems and wine. Stir over medium heat until broccoli is partially cooked and wine is reduced by half.

3. Add cream to skillet and simmer until flowerets are just tender when pierced with the tip of a knife. Add mushrooms and green onions. Continue simmering, stirring frequently, until cream turns a fragrant light beige and thickens slightly. Add salt and pepper to taste slightly overseasoned. Add half the cheese and hot cooked pasta. Toss well and serve immediately with remaining cheese.

FRESH CLAM SAUCE
Makes about 1½ cups (3½ dL) sauce or enough for ¾ to 1 pound (340 to 450 g) fresh pasta, linguine, or spaghettini

Fresh clam sauce, made with tiny, quarter-size Adriatic clams, is an Italian national treasure. Littleneck clams are the closest in size and texture; although their taste is quite different, they work well for this sauce. The recipe suggests shucking and chopping all the clams. However, I often set aside two unshucked clams per person, cook them at the last moment and nestle them into the pasta or linguine for garnish.

36 littleneck clams or 18 cherrystone clams, depending on size
3 cups (¾ L) cold water
¼ cup (½ dL) firmly packed parsley leaves
1 teaspoon dried basil leaves or 12 chopped fresh basil leaves
3 to 4 medium garlic cloves, peeled
6 medium shallots, peeled, or 1 medium onion, cut into 1-inch cubes
½ cup (115 g) melted butter
½ cup (1 dL) dry white wine or dry vermouth
Salt and freshly ground pepper to taste

1. To clean clam shells, brush vigorously under cold running water. Place in a basin with enough cold lightly salted water to cover. Set aside 30 minutes; drain. Transfer clams to a 6-quart (6-L) soup kettle. Add 3 cups (¾ L) cold water. Cover and cook over medium-high heat, shaking pot once or twice, until clams are nearly wide open. Check after 8 minutes and take care to remove clams as soon as they open or they will be tough.

2. Place open clams in a colander and immediately rinse with cold running water. Cover and cook any unopened clams until they open. Pull clam meat out of shells, discard shells. Strain clam liquid through a cheesecloth-lined strainer or a fine sieve. Reserve 1 cup (¼ L) clam juice; use remainder for another purpose (it may be frozen and eventually added to fish stock).

3. Insert the *metal knife blade.* Process parsley and basil until finely minced; set aside. With machine runing, drop garlic and shallots one at a time through food chute and process until minced. (Or process to chop onion with 4 half-second on/off turns or pulses.) Remove garlic mixture to a medium skillet; set aside. Process to chop clam meat coarsely with 6 one-second pulses; refrigerate until ready to use. Return blade to container.

4. Add 3 tablespoons butter to skillet with garlic mixture. Cook over medium heat until soft. Add wine and strained clam liquid. Simmer rapidly to reduce liquid to 1 cup (¼ L). Place reduction in a container and purée 5 seconds. With machine running, pour remaining melted butter through food chute within 15 seconds. Add parsley mixture and process to combine with 2 one-second pulses. Set sauce aside until ready to serve, as long as 4 hours.

5. Before serving, stir sauce in a large skillet or heat-proof serving dish over low heat, but do not allow sauce to simmer. Add chopped clams and stir well. Heat clams thoroughly. Adjust seasonings to taste slightly salty and peppery. Add cooked pasta and toss thoroughly. Serve immediately.

COLD TOMATO SAUCE
Makes about 1¼ cups (3 dL)

The quality of the sauce will vary with the ripeness of the tomatoes. Use as an accompaniment to cold poached fish, vegetable or fish pâtés, pasta salads, chicken, or as a low-calorie "dip" for vegetables.

1¼ lbs. (565 g) top quality vine-ripened tomatoes, cored, peeled, seeded, and quartered
1 tablespoon olive oil
1½ tablespoons sherry wine vinegar or more to taste
Salt and freshly ground pepper
Several dashes of Tabasco sauce
Dash Worcestershire sauce (optional)

1. Insert the *metal knife blade.* Process tomatoes 2 at a time to a coarse but even consistency using 6 to 10 half-second on/off turns or pulses depending upon ripeness. Empty container into a medium nonaluminum skillet.

2. Add olive oil and simmer rapidly, stirring frequently until all liquid evaporates and a loose paste forms, usually about 15 minutes. Mixture will measure about 1¼ cups (3 dL). Stir in sherry wine vinegar, salt, pepper, Tabasco, and Worcestershire sauces, if desired. Cool to room temperature and sauce is ready to serve. If served chilled, adjust seasoning to taste once sauce is refrigerator cold.

BECHAMEL SAUCE
Makes about 1½ cups (3½ dL)

Although it is not made in the processor, Béchamel Sauce is an important ingredient of several recipes. When made thick with cream and used to give body to a pâté, see page 27, French chefs call it a *fondante*.

2 tablespoons (30 g) butter
2 tablespoons flour
1 cup (¼ L) milk, scalded, or specified amount
  hot, but not scalded, whipping cream
Salt and pepper to taste
Dash nutmeg

1. Melt 2 tablespoons butter in a 2-quart (2-L) saucepan. Add flour and stir over medium heat until cooked but not colored, about 2 minutes. Remove from heat and slowly whisk in hot milk or cream.

2. Return saucepan to low heat and stir until sauce thickens to the consistency of a very light pudding. Add salt, pepper, and nutmeg to taste. Cover with plastic wrap touching top of sauce to prevent a skin from forming. Set aside at room temperature until ready to use.

VINAIGRETTE DRESSING
Makes ¾ cup (1¾ dL)

"Four persons are wanted to make a salad. A spendthrift for oil, a miser for vinegar, a counselor for salt, and a madman to stir it all up," wrote Sydney Smith, a 19th-century Scottish literary critic and gastronome. This rule still holds true.

1 small garlic clove, peeled
¼ cup white or red wine vinegar
2 teaspoons Dijon mustard
¼ teaspoon salt
Freshly ground pepper
½ cup (1 dL) olive, vegetable, or safflower oil

Insert the *metal knife blade*. With machine running, drop garlic clove through food chute; scrape down sides of container. Add vinegar, mustard, salt, and pepper. With machine running, pour oil through food chute within 20 seconds. Process 5 seconds longer. Serve at room temperature.

Variation:

Sherry Wine Vinaigrette

Substitute 2 tablespoons dry sherry for the mustard.

SUMMER HERB DRESSING
Makes about 1 cup (¼ L)

The basic vinaigrette mixture acts as a carrier for the fresh herbs. This dressing is equally good on lettuce, cooked vegetables, spaghetti, and even cold cooked seafood.

1 medium bunch watercress, stems removed
1 small garlic clove, peeled
2 tablespoons white wine vinegar
¼ teaspoon salt, or more to taste
1 teaspoon Dijon mustard
½ cup (1 dL) olive, vegetable, or safflower oil

1. Rinse and thoroughly towel dry watercress leaves. Insert the *metal knife blade*. Add leaves to container and process to chop with 3 one-second pulses; remove to waxed paper.

2. With machine running, drop garlic through food chute. Scrape down sides of container. Add vinegar, salt, and mustard. With machine running, add oil through food chute within 30 seconds. Return watercress to container and process together with oil mixture for 10 seconds. Adjust seasonings to taste. Use at room temperature and stir well. Best if used within 8 hours.

Variations:

Dill or Basil Herb Dressing
Substitute ½ cup (1 dL) firmly packed fresh dill weed sprigs or stemmed basil leaves for the watercress. Makes about ¾ cup (1¾ dL).

HERB BUTTER
Makes ¾ pound (340 g)

Keep herb butters on hand in the freezer to use on canapés, hot vegetables, steaks or chops. If desired, butter may be molded in a plastic-lined *pain de mie* pan, and when chilled (but not frozen), sliced with the medium disk.

¼ cup (½ dL) firmly packed parsley leaves
¾ lb. (340 g) softened butter, cut into 1-inch
   chunks
2 teaspoons lemon juice

Insert the *metal knife blade* in dry container. Process parsley until finely minced. Add butter and lemon juice. Process until smooth, scraping down sides of container from time to time. Place in a dish or shape as desired. Cover with plastic and refrigerate or freeze.

Variations:

Basil Butter
Substitute ½ cup (1 dL) firmly packed fresh basil leaves for the parsley.

Shallot Butter
Substitute 6 peeled medium shallots for the parsley. Process, dropping shallots through food chute one at a time; scrape down sides of container before adding butter.

Dill Butter
Substitute 1½ tablespoons dried dill weed for the parsley.

MAYONNAISE
Makes 1¾ cups (4 dL)

It is important to add oil to eggs very slowly at first, until mixture "takes" or begins to thicken—listen for the change in sound. Thereafter oil may be poured in more quickly, but if added too quickly, the mayonnaise may be thin.

1 egg, room temperature
2 egg yolks, room temperature
½ teaspoon salt, or more to taste
Dash each: Tabasco sauce, freshly ground
   white pepper
2 tablespoons fresh lemon juice
1¼ cups (3 dL) olive, vegetable, or safflower oil

1. Insert *metal knife blade.* Add egg, egg yolks, salt, Tabasco, pepper, and lemon juice. Process

30 seconds until slightly fluffy. With machine running, very slowly drizzle oil through food chute until mixture begins to thicken, then oil may be poured in a slow steady stream; add all oil within 1 minute.

2. Adjust seasoning to taste, adding salt and pepper as necessary. Mix with 2 two-second on/off turns or pulses. Refrigerate covered, or store in an airtight container as long as 4 or 5 days.

Variations:

Mustard Mayonnaise
Mix in 4 tablespoons Dijon mustard after oil is added in Step 1. Proceed with recipe.

Garlic Mayonnaise (Aioli)
Before beginning Step 1, turn on the empty machine and toss 2 peeled medium garlic cloves through food chute. Process until minced and continue with recipe.

Curried Mayonnaise
Add 1 tablespoon curry powder to container after lemon juice in Step 1. Continue as directed.

Green Mayonnaise
Before beginning Step 1, place ⅓ cup (¾ dL) stemmed, firmly packed spinach leaves in container. Process 15 seconds. Continue with recipe. Thin if desired with cream or plain yogurt.

ANCHOVY DRESSING
Makes 1½ cups (3½ dL)

Surprisingly good with fruit, vegetable, or cold seafood salads.

¼ cup (½ dL) firmly packed parsley leaves
1 small garlic clove, peeled
2 shallots, peeled, or 2 cubes (1 inch each) of
   onion
1 can (2 oz./60 g) flat anchovy fillets, drained,
   rinsed, patted dry
1 egg
1½ tablespoons fresh lemon juice
2 tablespoons plain yogurt, sour cream or
   whipping cream

Freshly ground pepper to taste
¾ cup (1¾ dL) vegetable or safflower oil

1. Insert the *metal knife blade.* Process parsley until finely minced; remove to waxed paper. With machine running, drop garlic and shallots through food chute. Process until minced; scrape down sides of container. Add anchovies, egg, lemon juice, yogurt, and pepper. Process 15 seconds to purée anchovies; scrape down sides of container.

2. With machine running, pour oil through food chute within 20 seconds, starting slowly at first. Process 5 seconds longer. Add parsley and process 7 seconds, until mixed. Refrigerate in an airtight container up to 4 days. Serve chilled.

Variations:

Green Goddess Dressing
Peel, pit, and quarter 1 medium ripe avocado; set aside. Proceed with recipe. In Step 2, after oil is added, add avocado to container. Purée 30 seconds before adding remaining ingredients. Proceed with recipe. Makes about 2½ cups (6 dL).

Bleu Cheese Dressing
Omit horseradish and parsley. Remove rind from 3 ounces (85 g) bleu cheese; cut into 1-inch chunks. Proceed with recipe. After yogurt is added, add bleu cheese to container and process with 4 half-second pulses to chop and combine simultaneously.

CREAM DRESSING

Makes about 2 cups (½ L)

A good basic dressing with especially fine variations.

¼ cup (½ dL) firmly packed parsley leaves
1 small garlic clove, peeled
2 or 3 whole green onions, cut into 1-inch lengths
1 egg
1 tablespoon white wine vinegar
1 tablespoon fresh lemon juice
1 teaspoon white horseradish (optional)
¼ teaspoon salt
Freshly ground pepper
½ cup (1 dL) vegetable or safflower oil
1 cup (¼ L) plain yogurt or sour cream

1. Insert the *metal knife blade.* Process parsley leaves until finely minced; set aside. With machine running, drop garlic clove through food chute; scrape down container sides. Add green onions to container. Process to chop with 4 to 6 half-second pulses; set aside with parsley.

2. Place egg, vinegar, lemon juice, horseradish (if desired), salt, and pepper in container. With machine running, add oil through food chute within 20 seconds. Add parsley, green onions, and yogurt to container. Process to mix 3 or 4 seconds. Cover and refrigerate up to 5 days.

TARTAR SAUCE

Makes 2 cups (½ L)

Before serving tartar sauce that has been made and refrigerated more than 24 hours, taste and, if necessary, adjust seasonings.

3 medium sweet gherkins, quartered
2 cubes (1 inch each) peeled onion
6 green pitted olives
1 hard-boiled egg yolk
1 raw egg
1 raw egg yolk
1 tablespoon white vinegar, or more to taste
2 teaspoons Dijon mustard
1¼ cups (3 dL) vegetable or safflower oil
¼ teaspoon salt
Freshly ground pepper to taste (optional)

1. Insert the *metal knife blade.* Place gherkins, onion cubes, olives, and hard-boiled egg yolk in container. Process to chop with 4 to 6 half-second pulses, scraping down container sides as necessary; remove to waxed paper.

2. Add raw egg, raw egg yolk, vinegar and mustard to container. With machine running, pour oil through food chute within 30 seconds, starting very slowly. Mix in salt, pepper, and gherkin mixture with 2 to 4 half-second pulses, scraping down container sides as necessary. Refrigerate covered or store in an airtight container up to 4 or 5 days.

15

Yeast Breads

We could smell the bread baking that first night, as we returned to our hotel. But it was not until the third day of our stay in Haut-de-Cagnes, an ancient village nestled in the hills of the French Riviera between Antibes and Nice, that we found the door to the town bakery.

Like the walls and streets of the old town, the bakery was made of stone. The baker, a small Niçois clad in the traditional leather shorts and skull cap, was just beginning his work. It was midnight; the start of his day. By 8 o'clock that morning, the bread for the entire town was baked, and we had learned, firsthand, the myriad secrets of the baker's art.

It was a surprise to see how little of the work was still done by hand. Only the weighing of the dough, the shaping of the round country loaves, the slashing of the dough to allow it to expand during baking, and the glazing of croissants had escaped mechanization—even in this small corner of France.

The pages of my notebook filled rapidly as the baker and his apprentice recited weights, sizes, and proportions of each of the various breads. The rise would be slow, they told me, because they used a very small amount of

yeast in the dough. They instructed me in the art of slashing the *baguettes* and indicated that these and several other breads were to be sprayed with steam so that, in contact with the heat radiated from the stone floor of the oven, the crusts would become extra crisp. I remarked at the ferociously hot ovens—breads were baked at 230° C or about 600° F. "The faster the better," they said.

After my return home, I reworked all my breads to incorporate the starter or sponging method and adapted other French bakery techniques as well. As a result, my breads are made differently than others you may encounter. However, I strongly believe that once you become accustomed to making them this way, you will find bread to be faster and easier to prepare than ever before.

ABOUT YEAST

Yeast is generally available in two forms: compressed cakes and packages of granules called dry active yeast. The granules are easy to use and packages are stamped with an expiration date to ensure freshness. Before buying, check the date on the package and avoid those which have expired.

In these recipes you will find that I use less than a package of yeast. Always measure amount as directed. Tape packages closed, or transfer leftover granules to a jar, close tightly, and keep refrigerated.

USING A BREAD STARTER OR SPONGE

If you were to look at yeast under a microscope, you would find that it is composed of cells. When kept dry and cool, the cells remain dormant. In contact with moisture, warmth, and a food such as flour, the cells activate and begin to consume the natural sugars in the flour. During this activity, yeast gives off harmless carbon dioxide, which forms bubbles and makes dough rise.

Bread doughs made with batterlike starters or sponges that contain yeast, flour, and warm liquid begin to bubble immediately after mixing. If your starter does not have bubbles on the surface within 10 minutes, the yeast probably is not alive. Discard the starter and the yeast and begin with a new package.

There are several advantages to using the starter or sponging method. The first is taste. Breads made by sponging have a better taste because acids that naturally produce good taste have extra time to develop. Sponging provides the same benefits as the third rise that many professional bakers consider necessary for good bread. Starters eliminate the need to add sugar to bread dough. While sugaring has become standard practice, it is a bad and unnecessary one, I believe. Also, starters are convenient. They can be made as long as 3 to 5 days in advance and refrigerated, thus reducing the overall preparation time on the day that the bread is to be made. Bread doughs made with starters added while the machine is running are less likely than other doughs to clog or slow the kneading action of the food processor because, in effect, the machine has a "running start."

I do not mix or leave starter to rise in the processor because it is the last ingredient to be added to the dough. Normally, I mix it in a plastic bowl with a pouring spout so that I can scrape the starter directly into the food chute with a spatula. Do not be concerned about small lumps of flour left in the starter; they will dissolve as the yeast activates.

YEAST DOUGHS MIXED BY THE "RUNNING START" METHOD

Stir starter well before measuring and bring it to room temperature (75 to 80° F/25° C). Some will be thick and may from time to time be troublesome to pour. The funnel attachment fitted onto the food chute will facilitate the pouring until you become accustomed to working with the starters. Or you may transfer the starter to a glass measuring cup first rinsed with cold water. If you have kept a starter longer than recommended, it may be used as long as it is thick and elastic. When it becomes thin with a creamlike consistency, it has lost its effectiveness.

IMPORTANT INFORMATION ABOUT FLOUR USED IN BREAD BAKING

Flour used in bread dough is very important to good taste and easy handling. I have found it best to blend two types of flour: unbleached all-purpose flour or bread flour with 12 to 14 grams of protein per 4 ounces and cake flour with 8 grams of protein per 4 ounces in a 60% to 40% blend. Both flours are widely available in supermarkets, and the average protein content is listed on the side of every package. Flour differs from region to region, however, and in some parts of the country, all-purpose flour is equivalent in protein to cake flour. Check the package carefully (see page 5 for further information).

RAPID-SIFTING

Dry ingredients are processed with 2 five-second pulses to "rapid-sift" so no hand sifting is required. Before processing dry ingredients, make sure the pusher has been inserted in the food chute.

KNEADING BREAD IN THE FOOD PROCESSOR

Begin to time kneading the moment all the starter has been added to the dough. Most processors will knead these bread doughs within 20 to 30 seconds. Kneading time affects the texture of bread—do not overprocess and never allow dough to become hot as a result of overkneading.

Several of these doughs are very wet and sticky, particularly French Bread and Country

Sourdough. The consistency is taffylike and may be totally unlike other bread doughs you may have encountered. The soft wet consistency is intentional; bread doughs in France often have the consistency of wet plaster. Add as little additional flour as possible to the container when kneading doughs. Begin recipes with smallest flour amounts listed, and add 2 tablespoons at a time only if doughs are runny or pourable or if machine bogs down. Wet sticky doughs give light texture to bread and are easier to knead and shape than heavy, flour-bound doughs.

Some bread doughs will not form a ball in the container. This is not important. The consistency of the dough, however, is very important. Dough must be soft all the way through to be fully kneaded—pinch and prod carefully to be sure. If the dough has a hard center core after 30 seconds of kneading, cut it in half with a knife and knead an additional 10 seconds; check again. If necessary, remove half the dough and knead halves separately for 10 seconds longer.

THE SLOW RISE

These bread doughs will rise more slowly than others because they contain less yeast. Wetter doughs also tend to take longer to rise than stiff doughs. Slow rising to triple the original volume will improve the texture and flavor of bread.

Dough will rise according to time indicated in recipes if placed in a draft-free place where temperature is a constant 75 to 80° F (25° C). I do not recommend rising bread above 80° F, nor do I recommend placing it in warm ovens to rise. To slow the rise (this is sometimes convenient), place bowl in a cool spot where temperature is between 50° F (10° C) and 70° F (21° C). The rise will be significantly slower than indicated in the recipe. All breads except the sourdough loaf may be pressed down and refrigerated overnight after the first rise and before shaping.

In addition to temperature, the humidity or season can and will affect rising time. In general, bread rises faster on humid days and during the summer.

To be sure dough is fully risen, test by poking gently with your finger. If indentation immediately disappears, bread usually needs

more rising. If indentation disappears very slowly, bread is usually ready. You will learn to gauge this from experience.

SHAPING DOUGHS

Most doughs are shaped on a generously floured work surface, coated with 2 to 3 tablespoons flour. Before folding or sealing shaped dough, always remove excess flour with a soft, dry pastry brush.

THE FINAL RISE

The final rise of doughs that are not baked in pans or molds takes place on a thin bed of flour (this replaces the French baker's cloth). The bottom of the bread will absorb some of the flour, however, the flour prevents the bread from sticking to the cooking surface (cookie sheet or oven stone) and ensures that the bottom of the loaf does not have a fried texture. Cornmeal is used only with the egg bread. If desired, excess flour may be scraped from the bottom of the cooled baked loaves.

SLASHING THE RISEN SHAPED LOAVES

Dough is slashed to allow for even expansion during the first 15 minutes of baking when it continues to swell and rise. Slashing is especially important for French and sourdough loaves. It is not as simple as it appears and will take considerable practice before your breads have a professional look. Slashes must be made firmly but gently. They must cut the dough ¼ inch (¾ cm) deep to be effective. Hold the razor blade or razor-sharp knife at a deep angle, almost parallel to the top of the dough, and make diagonal cuts. A firm dough, like Cinnamon Raisin Bread (page 122), may be slashed with the *metal knife blade* of the processor.

COOLING AND STORING BAKED BREAD

Cool bread to room temperature before slicing. Store breads well wrapped in aluminum foil at room temperature for as long as 3 days. Refrigeration will change the texture of the bread. They will stay fresh up to 5 days, but slightly stale bread makes delicious toast or excellent bread crumbs.

USING THE OVEN STONE

Oven stones are porous rectangular or round stone plates that both absorb and radiate heat. Place them directly onto the oven rack to approximate the stone floor of a pizzeria or French bakery oven. The intense heat of the stone promotes even cooking and browning and gives a superb crisp crust. Pizza baked on an oven stone tastes like the professional product. I acquired my first oven stone in 1976 and have been using it ever since to bake certain breads and pizzas.

The layer of flour on which the bread doughs rise, permits them to be loosened from the cookie sheet (or wooden baker's paddle or peel that comes with the stone). I use a thin flexible-bladed knife or a long cake-icing spatula to loosen the doughs. Sliding dough off the sheet or paddle and into the oven does require practice. I suggest you become familiar with the doughs by making them several times on baking sheets before attempting to use the oven-stone method. In the process of placing bread on the stone, flour will also be transferred. It will brown as the breads bake and can be scraped off the stone with a pastry scraper when cool.

Caution: The oven stone remains very hot even after the oven cools. Handle it with extreme care. If you must remove it from the oven while still hot, protect your hands and place it on a heat-proof surface well out of the reach of children.

SPRAYING BREAD TO PRODUCE STEAM

Steam gives bread an extra-crisp crust, so it pays to keep a plant mister or plastic spray bottle filled with cold water on hand for spraying the oven before, during, and after baking. Be sure, however, to avoid spraying the oven light with the cold water.

ALL-PURPOSE STARTER
Makes 1 cup (¼ L)

If desired, this recipe may be doubled.

¾ cup (105 g) unbleached all-purpose flour or bread flour

1¼ teaspoons dry active yeast
⅔ cup (1½ dL) warm water (110° F/45° C)

1. Place flour and yeast in a medium bowl. Stir in warm water until mixture is thick and batter-like. Cover bowl tightly with plastic. Set aside to rise until starter is bubbly, thickened, and approximately doubled in bulk, about 2 to 2½ hours.

2. Before using, stir starter well. It must be thick and viscous. Use immediately or refrigerate, if desired, in an airtight 4-cup (1-L) container or jar.

Variations:

Milk Starter
Substitute ¾ cup (1¾ dL) warm milk (110° F/45° C) for water.

Special Starter
Use 1 cup (150 g) unbleached all-purpose flour or bread flour, 1¼ teaspoons dry active yeast, and 1 cup (¼ L) warm water (110° F/45° C).

FRENCH BREAD
Makes 2 ½-pound (225-g) loaves

This is my staple bread. The light airy crumb and thin crisp crust are as close as I have found to the real thing in France. I always felt that this combination of unbleached flour or bread flour and cake flour was very close to French flour. And when my sister returned from France, we tested the flour she brought, and the recipe did indeed work perfectly. The consistency of the kneaded dough is very important. It must be sticky and taffylike when pulled from the container, and it will appear to need more flour. However, unless the dough is actually runny, keep to the minimum amount of unbleached flour or bread flour indicated below. Be sure to allow the shaped loaves to rise until tripled before slashing. I also suggest baking them on the baking sheet until you have made the bread several times. Then try your hand at sliding the loaves off the sheet and onto the hot oven stone—it requires confidence.

All-Purpose Starter, page 119
1½ to 1¾ cups (225 to 255 g) unbleached all-purpose flour (see page 5) or bread flour
1 cup (120 g) cake flour
1½ teaspoons salt
⅔ cup (1½ dL) warm water (110° F/45° C)
About 2 tablespoons unbleached all-purpose flour or bread flour
1 egg white

1. Begin starter 2 or more hours in advance or bring refrigerated starter to room temperature; stir well.

2. Insert the *metal knife blade.* Place 1½ cups (225 g) unbleached flour, cake flour, and salt in container. Process to rapid-sift with 2 five-second pulses. With machine running, pour water through food chute within 8 seconds; scrape down sides of container. With machine running, pour starter through food chute as quickly as possible; as soon as it is added, process 20 to 30 seconds longer, until dough is

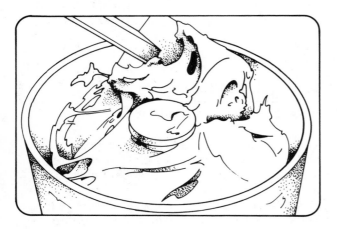

soft all the way through, very sticky and taffy-like. It will not form a ball. If dough is runny, add up to ¼ cup (30 g) additional unbleached flour 2 tablespoons at a time and process 5 seconds after each addition.

3. Rinse a large bowl with warm water; drain but do not dry. Place dough in bowl, cover with plastic and set aside to rise until dough is slightly more than triple in bulk. Timing will depend on room temperature, but normal rise takes 2½ to 3 hours.

4. Sift the 2 tablespoons unbleached flour evenly over an ungreased cookie sheet; set aside. Generously flour a work surface. Remove

dough from bowl without kneading and work it as little as possible. Cut in half. With floured hands, pat or roll one piece into a 12- × 8-inch (30- × 20-cm) rectangle. Brush off excess flour with a pastry brush. Fold lengthwise into thirds; brush off excess flour. Flatten dough with the heel of your hand. Fold in half lengthwise; then bring 2 long edges up. Center and pinch 2

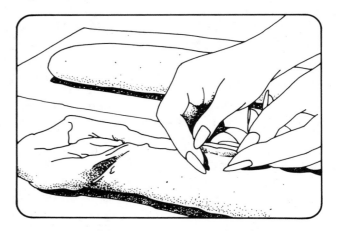

edges together firmly to form a cigar-shaped loaf. Turn dough seam down and carefully transfer to floured baking sheet. Repeat to shape other half of dough, and place it parallel to first loaf on baking sheet. When baked, breads will approximate those called *bâtards.* If desired, the entire batch of dough may be shaped into 1 large loaf by kneading into a rough, long oval shape. Cover loaves loosely with a dry cloth towel and set aside to rise until tripled in bulk, usually 2 to 2½ hours.

5. Adjust oven rack to lower position. Heat oven to 450° F (230° C). If using oven stone, place it on oven rack and heat 30 minutes in

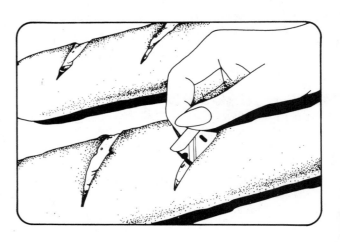

advance. Using a razor blade or sharp knife, make 3 or 4 evenly spaced, diagonal slashes about ⅝ inch (1½ cm) deep in top of each risen loaf. Work carefully when slashing and be sure not to be too rough with loaves or they will deflate. Dampen a small, soft pastry brush with water. Dip in egg white and brush egg white on tops and sides of risen slashed loaves.

6. Place baking sheet on oven rack.* Immediately spray loaves 3 or 4 times using a plant mister filled with cool water. Close oven door immediately; bake 15 minutes; spray; bake 10 to 15 minutes longer, until loaves are crisp and golden brown. Remove from oven, place on cake rack and spray 2 or 3 times again. Cool to room temperature before slicing; scrape excess flour off bottom of loaves, if desired.

*If using oven stone, slide a metal spatula under each risen loaf to loosen it from baking sheet and take care not to stretch loaves. Gently shake to be sure loaves move freely; if not, loosen again. With one swift motion, slide loaves off baking sheet and onto stone. Spray and bake as described above. *Do not place a baking sheet on oven stone.*

Variation:

Whole Wheat French Bread
Substitute 1⅓ cups (207 g) whole wheat flour for 1½ cups unbleached flour. If desired, substitute cake flour for unbleached or bread flour on the baking sheet.

PITA BREAD
Makes 10 to 11 loaves

Pita breads are those flat round loaves with hollow centers that may be split into 2 thin disks or trimmed to form a pouch into which ground or sliced meats, vegetables, or grains may be placed. Breads of this type are found throughout the Mediterranean world—in Israel, Syria, Lebanon, and Greece; however, their origin is probably Egyptian where the art of baking leavened bread, called *ta*, was developed around the 12th century B.C. In their shape and use, pita loaves are related to Mexican *tortillas*, Indian *chapatti*, Neopolitan pizza and even to Chinese pancakes, *pao ping*. They are delicious as well as easy to make and great for sandwiches such as Gyros, page 83, or snacks such as Pita Oreganata, page 16.

All-Purpose Starter, page 119
1¼ to 1½ cups (180 to 225 g) unbleached all-purpose flour (see page 5) or bread flour
1 cup (120 g) cake flour
1½ teaspoons salt
¼ cup (½ dL) warm water (110° F/45° C)
¼ cup (½ dL) olive or vegetable oil

1. Begin starter 2 or more hours in advance or bring refrigerated starter to room temperature; stir well.

2. Insert the *metal knife blade.* Place 1¼ cups (180 g) unbleached flour, cake flour, and salt in container. Process to rapid-sift with 2 five-second pulses. With machine running, pour water through food chute within 5 seconds and oil within 5 seconds; scrape down sides of container. With machine running, quickly pour starter through food chute; process 20 to 30 seconds longer, until dough is spongy, slightly sticky, and soft all the way through. If runny, add up to ¼ cup (30 g) additional unbleached flour 2 tablespoons at a time and process 5 seconds after each addition.

3. Rinse a large bowl with warm water; drain but do not dry. Place dough in bowl, cover with plastic and set aside to rise until dough is slightly more than triple in bulk. Timing will depend on room temperature, but normal rise takes 2 to 2½ hours.

4. Adjust oven rack to middle position. Heat oven to 450° F (230° C). If using oven stone, place it on oven rack and heat 30 minutes in advance. Generously flour a baker's paddle (peel) or 2 ungreased baking sheets; set aside.

5. Generously flour work surface. Pull dough from bowl without kneading and work it as little as possible. With floured hands, roll dough into a thick sausage about 20 inches (50 cm) long and 2 inches (5 cm) thick. Cut into 10 pieces. Place dough pieces flat on work surface. Press thumb firmly down into the center of each to make a small well. Pull sides of dough up and over well; pinch tightly to seal. Turn dough pinched side down and press into a 3-inch (8-cm) circle. Cover with a towel and set aside.

6. Reflour work surface if necessary to keep dough from sticking. Working quickly, roll out 3 dough circles to 7 to 8 inches (18 to 20 cm) by rolling, flipping dough over and giving each a one-quarter turn to keep dough round and even on both sides. Place the 3 rolled out pieces on baker's paddle or baking sheet.

7. Immediately slide dough off paddle and onto oven stone or place baking sheet on oven rack. Bake until breads puff up completely, about 4 minutes. Remove from oven and immediately place between 2 damp towels. Repeat to roll out and bake all dough, working 3 pieces at a time. Cool breads to room temperature between damp towels. Refrigerate or freeze in plastic bags.

Variation:

Whole Wheat Pita Bread
Substitute 1 cup (155 g) whole wheat flour for the cake flour.

WHITE BREAD
Makes 1 loaf (1½ to 1¾ pounds/675 to 800 g)

A classic white loaf that keeps well. The dense, even texture makes it especially good for sandwiches or toast.

Milk Starter, page 119
1½ to 1¾ cups (225 to 255 g) unbleached all-
**   purpose flour (see page 5) or bread flour**
¾ cup (85 g) cake flour
1¼ teaspoons salt
½ cup (1 dL) warm water (110° F/45° C)
3 tablespoons warm melted butter
**   (110° F/45° C)**
Egg Glaze, page 5

1. Begin starter 2 or more hours in advance or bring refrigerated starter to room temperature; stir well.

2. Fit the food processor container with the *metal knife blade.* Add 1½ cups (225 g) unbleached flour, cake flour, and salt. Process to rapid-sift with 2 five-second pulses. With machine running, pour water and butter through

food chute within 10 seconds; stop and scrape down container sides.

3. Attach funnel if desired. With machine running, pour starter through food chute as quickly as possible. After starter is added, process 20 to 30 seconds longer, until dough is sticky, elastic, and soft all the way through. This dough should form a ball; so if runny or loose, add up to ¼ cup (30 g) additional unbleached flour 2 tablespoons at a time and process 5 seconds after each addition.

4. Rinse a large bowl with warm water; drain but do not dry. Place dough in bowl, cover with plastic and set aside to rise until dough is slightly more than tripled in bulk. Time will depend on room temperature, but normal rise takes 2½ hours.

5. Lightly oil a 6-cup (1½-L) loaf pan; preferably black; set aside. Generously flour a work surface. Pull risen dough from bowl but do not knead. With floured hands, pat dough into a 10- × 8-inch (25- × 20-cm) rectangle. Fold in half to measure 5 × 8 inches (13 × 20 cm). Flatten dough vigorously. Fold lengthwise in thirds; then fold lengthwise in half, matching the 2 long edges and pinching them together to form a seam with no gaps. Pinch ends closed. Place dough in pan seam side down and press firmly into pan to make an even loaf.

6. Cover pan loosely with a dry cloth towel. Set aside to rise until fully tripled in bulk and dough is mounded over rim of pan 1 to 1¼ inches (2½ cm). Adjust oven rack to lower position. Heat oven to 400° F (205° C). Just before baking, brush top of loaf with Egg Glaze. Bake 30 to 35 minutes, until golden brown. Cool pan on cake rack 5 minutes. Turn loaf out of pan and cool on cake rack to room temperature before slicing. Refrigerate or freeze in plastic bag.

CINNAMON RAISIN BREAD
Makes 1 loaf (2 pounds/900 g)

This delicious variation on the white bread theme makes delicious toast that disappears all too quickly.

Milk Starter, page 119
White Bread dough (preceding recipe)
⅓ **cup (65 g) sugar**
3 **tablespoons dark brown sugar**
1 **teaspoon cinnamon**
2 **dashes nutmeg**
2 **teaspoons cold water**
1 **tablespoon cold milk**
½ **cup (3 oz./85 g) black seedless raisins**
Egg Glaze, page 5

1. Begin starter 2 or more hours in advance or
bring refrigerated starter to room temperature;
stir well.

2. Prepare White Bread dough as directed
through Step 4.

3. Lightly oil a 6-cup (1½-L) loaf pan, preferably black; set aside. Insert *metal knife blade* in
a clean container. Process sugar, brown sugar,
cinnamon, nutmeg, and water until mixed,
about 5 seconds. Generously flour work surface. Pull risen dough from bowl but do not
knead. Pat or roll dough into a 14- × 9-inch
(35- × 23-cm) rectangle; brush with milk. Leaving a 1-inch (2½-cm) border on one short end,
spread all but 1 tablespoon cinnamon mixture
over dough. Sprinkle raisins evenly over and
press them gently into the dough.

4. Tightly roll up dough beginning with the
blank short end. Seal by firmly pinching edge
of dough onto roll. Pinch ends firmly too, so no
filling shows through. Place dough seam side
down in loaf pan. Press firmly into pan to make
an even loaf.

5. Cover pan loosely with a dry cloth towel. Set
aside to rise until fully tripled in bulk and
mounded 1 to 1¼ inches over rim of pan.
Adjust oven rack to lower position. Heat oven
to 400° F (205° C). Just before baking bread,
use the *metal knife blade* or a sharp knife, to
make a 7-inch (18-cm)-long and ¼-inch (¾-
cm)-deep cut down the center of the risen loaf.
Brush top with Egg Glaze and press reserved
cinnamon mixture onto top of bread. Bake until
golden brown, about 35 minutes. Cool pan on
cake rack 5 minutes. Turn loaf out of pan and
cool on cake rack to room temperature before
slicing. Store at room temperature in plastic
bag or freeze.

ROUND PAIN DE MIE
Makes 1 loaf (½ pound/225 g)

Pain de Mie is French sandwich bread with a
tight even crumb. During baking, the dough is
held prisoner in a closed pan, either rectangular, round, or oval. The resulting loaf takes the
shape of the mold. This recipe was developed
for the small round pan because the diminutive
bread fits beautifully into the food chute of
most processors, and the little disks of bread
are ideal for canapés or Melba Toast.

Pain de Mie slices best when first refrigerated
24 hours. The oval loaf fits only wide food
chutes of standard- and large-capacity machines.

½ **cup (1 dL) Milk Starter, page 119**
¾ **cup (105 g) unbleached all-purpose flour**
   (see page 5) or bread flour
2 **tablespoons cake flour**
¼ **teaspoon salt**
1 **tablespoon warm melted butter (110° F/45° C)**
2 **tablespoons warm water (110° F/45° C)**
Vegetable shortening

1. Begin starter 2 or more hours in advance or
bring refrigerated starter to room temperature;
stir well.

2. Fit the *metal knife blade* in the processor
container. Process unbleached flour, cake flour,
and salt to rapid-sift with 2 five-second pulses.
With machine running, pour butter and water
through food chute; scrape down sides of
container. Turn on machine and quickly pour
starter through food chute. After starter is
added, process 20 to 30 seconds longer, until
smooth, slightly sticky and soft all the way
through; dough should form a small ball.

3. Rinse a medium bowl with warm water; drain
but do not dry. Place dough in bowl, cover
tightly with plastic and set aside to rise until
dough is slightly more than tripled in bulk.
Time depends on room temperature, but normal rise takes 2 hours.

4. Remove the metal post from a 1-cup (¼-L)
round *pain de mie* pan. Coat inside of pan,
including hinge, with vegetable shortening. Set
pan aside. Lightly flour work surface. Pull
dough from bowl but do not knead. Place on

floured surface. Pat or roll into a 12- × 3-inch (30- × 8-cm) rectangle. Fold in thirds to make a 12- × 1-inch (30- × 2½-cm) strip. Flatten folded dough with the heel of your hand. Fold lengthwise in half. Pinch long edges together to form a seam with no gaps. Turn dough seam side down. Tuck ends under and pinch as necessary to make dough fit in pan. Place in 1 side of pan and press down firmly.

5. Cover pan loosely with a cloth towel and set aside to rise until dough has risen enough to form a gentle mound in pan. This rise usually takes 30 to 35 minutes.

6. Adjust oven rack to lower position. Heat oven to 400° F (205° C). Close lid of pan over risen dough. Insert metal post. Bake 30 minutes. Cool pan on cake rack 8 minutes. Remove post and carefully open pan. Turn out bread onto cake rack and cool to room temperature. Wrap in double layers of plastic and refrigerate overnight or as long as 2 days before slicing.

Variation:

Oval Pain de Mie
Makes a ¾-pound (340-g) loaf in the 3-cup (¾-L) oval *pain de mie* pan. Increase Milk Starter to ¾ cup (1¾ dL). Increase unbleached flour to 1 cup plus 2 tablespoons (155 g), cake flour to ¼ cup (25 g), and warm melted butter to 2 tablespoons (30 g).

MELBA TOAST
Makes about 100 slices, depending upon thickness and accuracy of slicing disk

These crisp, golden toast rounds are perfect accompaniments to Steak Tartare, page 25, and Salmon Tartare with Scallops, pages 24–25. If you have never before sliced a *pain de mie* loaf, practice with a 1-inch (2½-cm) length, then check to see how well your slicing disk has performed.

1 round Pain de Mie (½ lb./225 g), page 123, refrigerated
About ½ cup (225 g) warm melted butter

1. Heat oven to 325° F (165° C). Cut Pain de

Mie into lengths long enough to fit food chute. Cut off and discard baked ends. Attach the *medium slicing disk.* Place each piece in food chute from underneath, resting it against the side of the food chute opposite the direction of the oncoming disk. If properly inserted, the force of the disk will hold the bread in place against the side of the chute and eliminate twisting and uneven slices. Slice each piece with a firm, but not hard, push.

2. Place slices on baking sheets and brush liberally with butter. Bake 20 minutes, until bread rounds are crisp and evenly browned. Serve warm or at room temperature. If made in advance, cover loosely with aluminum foil and let stand at room temperature. This recipe may be halved or quartered.
   Note: Oval Pain de Mie is sliced exactly as round loaves, but a somewhat larger than normal food chute, generally found on large-capacity machines, or an expanded food chute attachment, usually is required.

CHEDDAR CHEESE ROLLS
Makes 8 pan rolls; 16 cloverleaf rolls

These are appropriate for a breakfast, brunch, or luncheon when interesting rolls, plain or cloverleaf, are desired. While they are too rich to be used as dinner rolls, they should go well with a light, late-night supper and are one of the few types of bread that improve when served warm.

All-Purpose Starter, page 119
1 wedge (5 oz./145 g) sharp cheddar cheese, chilled
2 cups (300 g) unbleached all-purpose flour (see page 5) or bread flour
½ teaspoon salt
⅓ cup (¾ dL) large-curd cottage cheese, room temperature
Butter
Egg Glaze, page 5

1. Begin starter 2 or more hours in advance or bring refrigerated starter to room temperature; stir well.

2. Insert the *medium shredding disk.* Shred

cheese with a gentle push; remove to waxed paper. Change to the *metal knife blade.* Place flour, salt, shredded cheese, and cottage cheese in the container. Process to mix 7 seconds. With machine running, quickly pour starter through food chute. Process to knead dough 20 to 30 seconds longer, until a smooth ball forms and dough is soft all the way through.

3. Rinse a large bowl with warm water; drain but do not dry. Place dough in bowl, cover tightly with plastic wrap and let rise in a warm place until slightly more than tripled in bulk. Time will depend on kitchen temperature, but normal rise takes 2½ hours.

4. For pan rolls, heavily coat a 9-inch (23-cm) oven-proof skillet with butter; set aside. Lightly flour a work surface. Pull risen dough from bowl without kneading. Place on work surface and roll into a 16-inch (40-cm)-long sausage. Cut crosswise into 8 pieces. Knead each piece into a ball and place in skillet, making a ring of dough balls around edge and placing 1 in the center. Flatten dough so edges touch. Cover with a dry cloth towel and set aside in a warm place to rise until skillet is three-fourths filled.

5. For cloverleaf rolls, generously butter 16 muffin cups (⅓ cup/¾ dL each). Cut dough into 16 pieces as indicated in Step 4. Then cut each of the 16 pieces into thirds. Roll each little dough piece into a ball and place 3 balls into each muffin cup; press down. Cover with a dry cloth towel and set aside to rise until dough mounds slightly over edge of muffin cups.

6. Adjust oven rack to middle position. Heat oven to 350° F (175° C). Just before baking, brush top of rolls with Egg Glaze. Bake 30 to 35 minutes, until rolls are golden brown. Cool on cake rack 5 minutes. Turn rolls out of skillet or muffin tins. Cool to room temperature or serve warm.

MUSHROOM BREAD
Makes 1 loaf (1½ pounds/675 g) or 2 loaves (10 to 12 ounces/285 g each)

Duxelles, that savory classic French mushroom jam (also used for fillings, sauces, and soups)

freckles and flavors this mushroom-shaped loaf. The recipe made its debut in 1977, when it appeared in a series of cooking lessons in the *Chicago Sun-Times.* Originally, the mushrooms were minced, but I later discovered that shredded mushrooms for *duxelles* exuded more liquid and absorbed more butter.

This bread makes wonderful toast, sensational canapés and, if any is leftover, incredible stuffing for turkey. If desired, it also may be baked in loaf pans or made into rolls.

All-Purpose Starter, page 119

Duxelles:

½ **medium garlic clove, peeled**
4 **medium shallots (1 oz./30 g), peeled**
6 **tablespoons (85 g) butter**
¾ **lb. (340 g) fresh mushrooms, wiped clean**
Salt and freshly ground pepper to taste

2¼ to 2½ **cups (300 to 375 g) unbleached all-purpose flour (see page 5) or bread flour**
¼ **teaspoon baking soda**
¼ **teaspoon salt**
⅔ **cup (1½ dL) large-curd cottage cheese**
Vegetable oil
Egg Glaze, page 5

1. Prepare starter 2 or more hours in advance or bring refrigerated starter to room temperature.

2. To prepare *duxelles,* insert the *metal knife blade.* With machine running, drop garlic clove and shallots one at a time through food chute. Empty container into a medium skillet. Add butter to skillet and cook shallot mixture over low heat until soft; remove from heat.

3. Meanwhile, change to the *medium shredding disk.* Load mushrooms in food chute and shred with a gentle push. Remove in large handfuls and place in a dry cloth towel. Twist towel firmly to wring out excess moisture from mushrooms, adding each squeezed batch of mushrooms to the skillet.

4. Toss to coat mushrooms with excess butter. Place over high heat and stir frequently until all additional liquid has evaporated. Reduce heat to medium-low; cook, stirring occasionally, until mushrooms are dark, dry, and have given up

all of their excess moisture, about 20 to 25 minutes longer. Remove from heat and cool to lukewarm.

5. Return the *metal knife blade* to the processor container. Add 2¼ cups (300 g) flour, baking soda, and salt. Process to rapid-sift with 2 five-second pulses. Add cottage cheese and *duxelles* to container. With machine running, quickly pour starter through food chute. Process to knead dough 20 to 30 seconds, until dough is smooth, sticky, and soft all the way through. If dough is extremely sticky, add up to ¼ cup (30 g) additional flour and process 5 seconds.

6. Lightly coat a large bowl with oil. Add dough, cover tightly with plastic and set aside to rise until dough is slightly more than doubled in bulk, usually 2 to 2½ hours, depending on room temperature.

7. Meanwhile, oil a #12 *brioche mousseline* mold or coat two 1-pound coffee cans with oil (a 1-quart [1-L] aluminum measuring cup with lip is also useful). Pull dough from bowl without kneading. On a lightly floured surface, flatten dough into a 12- × 8-inch (30- × 20-cm) rectangle. Roll dough into a ball; then work it into a 4-inch (10-cm) diameter cylinder (about 8 inches high) with 1 smooth end and 1 end pinched to bring all edges of dough together. Press dough into mold pinched end down or cut in half it it is to be baked in coffee cans and place in cans with cut ends up. Cover mold or cans loosely with a cloth towel and set aside to rise until dough has risen even with rim, usually about 1 hour.

8. Adjust oven rack to lower position. Heat oven to 375° F (190° C). Brush top of dough evenly with Egg Glaze. Place in oven and bake 35 to 40 minutes until top is rounded into the shape of a mushroom cap and golden brown. Remove mold or cans from oven and place on a cake rack; cool 15 minutes. Loosen bread from mold with a small knife and turn bread out onto rack. Cool to room temperature before serving.

Note: Brioche mousseline molds are available in specialty cookware stores.

EGG STARTER
Makes 1¼ cups (3 dL)

The egg yolk enriches the starter and gives the bread dough a light yellow tint.

1 cup (150 g) unbleached all-purpose flour (see page 5) or bread flour
1½ teaspoons dry active yeast
1 egg
¾ cup (1¾ dL) warm water (110° F/45° C)

1. Place flour, yeast, and egg in a medium bowl. Slowly add water, stirring until mixture is a thick batter. Cover bowl tightly with plastic wrap and set starter aside to rise in a warm place for 2 to 2½ hours, until spongy and doubled in bulk.

2. Stir well. Starter is ready to use or refrigerate in an airtight 4-cup (1-L) container overnight. Bring chilled starter to room temperature and stir well before using.

BRAIDED EGG BREAD
Makes 1 loaf (1½ pounds/675 g)

The dough for this lovely rich bread, also known as *challah,* may be braided in four strands rather than three, or rolled into a single long rope and coiled into a turban shape. Day-old egg bread makes superb French toast.

This is a soft, very sticky dough. If it clogs the processor, slowing the motor, stop and remove dough from around blade with a spatula; add 2 tablespoons flour and continue processing to knead.

Egg Starter (see above)
1½ cups (225 g) unbleached all-purpose flour (see page 5) or bread flour
¾ cup (85 g) cake flour
1½ teaspoons salt
⅓ cup (80 g) warm melted butter
¼ cup (½ dL) warm water (110° F/45° C)
2 egg yolks
2 tablespoons cornmeal
Egg Glaze, page 5
1½ teaspoons poppy seeds

1. Begin starter 2 or more hours in advance or bring refrigerated starter to room temperature; stir well.

2. Insert the *metal knife blade.* Place unbleached flour, cake flour, and salt in container and process to rapid sift with 2 five-second pulses. With machine running, pour butter and water through food chute within 10 seconds; scrape down sides of container. Add egg yolks and with machine running, quickly pour starter through food chute. Process to knead 20 to 30 seconds after all starter is added, until dough is smooth, sticky, and soft all the way through.

3. Lightly coat a large bowl with oil; wipe out excess. Place dough in bowl and cover tightly with plastic wrap. Set aside in a warm place to rise until dough is slightly more than tripled in bulk. Time will depend on temperature, but normal rise takes about 2½ hours.

4. Generously flour a work surface. Pull dough from bowl but do not knead. Place on work surface and cut into 3 equal pieces. Add flour to work surface if necessary to prevent dough from sticking. Roll out each piece of dough to an 18-by-1- to 1½-inch (45- × 2½-cm) rope. Place ropes of dough side by side. Press all 3 together at 1 end to seal. Brush off all excess flour with a dry pastry brush. Loosely braid dough to make a 16-inch (40-cm)-long braided loaf. Gather loose ends together and press to seal. Tuck both ends underneath the braid, flattening them as necessary, so they do not show. Brush off any excess flour.

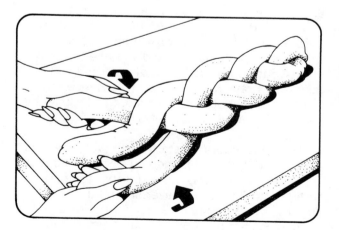

5. Sprinkle a baking sheet with cornmeal. Place dough braid diagonally on baking sheet and cover loosely with a dry cloth towel. Set aside to rise in a warm place until slightly more than doubled in bulk, about 1½ hours.

6. Adjust oven rack to middle position. Heat oven to 400° F (205° C). Just before baking, brush bread with Egg Glaze and sprinkle evenly with poppy seeds. Bake 30 to 35 minutes, until golden brown. Remove from baking sheet to a cake rack and cool to room temperature before slicing.

FRUIT AND NUT LOAF
Makes 1 loaf (1¾ pounds/800 g)

Consider this to be an expedient all-purpose "festive" loaf that may be used at Easter, Christmas, or even at the Jewish New Year. The addition of sugar, fruits, and nuts to an egg-bread dough is common to many cuisines including Austrian, French, German, Polish, Russian, Jewish, and Italian. The bread may be baked in the shape of a mound as suggested here, twisted into a turban, braided in a ring, or divided and baked in coffee cans. Coarse-crystal sugar may be sprinkled on top of bread after glazing.

1 medium lemon
½ medium orange
3 tablespoons sugar
Pinch cinnamon
Braided Egg Bread dough (preceding page)
¾ cup (4 oz./115 g) white sultana raisins
⅓ cup (2 oz./60 g) shelled pine nuts (pignolas)
Vegetable oil
Butter
Egg Glaze, page 5

1. Begin starter 2 or more hours in advance or bring refrigerated starter to room temperature; stir well.

2. Strip off rinds of lemon and orange with a vegetable peeler; reserve fruit for another use. Insert the *metal knife blade.* Process rind strips,

sugar and cinnamon until fine. Leave mixture in container and prepare Braided Egg Bread dough through Step 2, so that sugar and rind are incorporated into dough. Add raisins and pine nuts to the dough and process until mixed about 5 to 10 seconds longer.

3. Lightly coat a large bowl with oil; wipe out excess. Cover bowl tightly with plastic wrap and let rise in a warm place until slightly more than tripled in bulk.

4. Butter an 8-cup (2-qt./2-L) soufflé dish; set aside. Generously flour a work surface. Pull dough from bowl and place on work surface. With floured hands, flatten dough and fold it in half; repeat. Knead dough into a cushion-shaped ball about 10 inches (25 cm) in diameter or to same size as soufflé dish; press dough into dish. Cover loosely with a dry cloth towel. Set aside to rise in a warm place until dough is barely mounded over top of dish.

5. Adjust oven rack to lower position. Heat oven to 400° F (205° C). Just before baking, brush top of dough with Egg Glaze. Bake 30 to 35 minutes, until golden brown. Cool soufflé dish on cake rack 10 minutes; turn bread out of dish and cool to room temperature before slicing. (This bread can be frozen wrapped in a plastic bag; defrost in refrigerator.)

SOURDOUGH STARTER
Makes about 2 cups (½ L)

Although sourdough bread is most often associated with the American pioneers and the city of San Francisco, it has been made for thousands of years, probably first by the ancient Greeks. Souring, or fermentation, a process that creates gas, was used initially as a means of getting bread dough to rise. Most often a chunk of the soured, day-old dough was added to the new batch.

The French call the sour mixture a *levain* or "leavener" from the French verb *lever,* meaning to lift or rise. While there are many theories about the origins of San Francisco sourdough, a popular one suggests that it was introduced by French settlers migrating to California from Canada and Mexico.

There are many methods for producing sourdough bread, and starters are available by mail or passed down through families for generations. One of the simplest ways to produce good sourdough bread with a light sour taste and a miraculously chewy crust is to use this starter. In theory, it need be prepared only once, since it can be replenished indefinitely, and, as it ages, the flavor and aroma become more pronounced. Not all sourdough starters contain yeast. They can be made by "spontaneous fermentation" of flour and water. However, this yeast-based starter is reliable, as well as practical, for cooks in urban areas who are not likely to have wild yeast spores flying "spontaneously" through open windows.

1½ cups (225 g) unbleached all-purpose flour (see page 5) or bread flour
1 package dry active yeast
1½ cups (3½ dL) warm water (110° F/45° C)

1. Five days before making bread, place flour and yeast in a medium bowl. Slowly add water, stirring until mixture is a thick batter. Cover bowl tightly with plastic wrap. Set starter aside in a warm place to sour. Stir well once each day and keep bowl tightly covered to avoid evaporation. After 5 days, starter is ready to use; stir well; use at room temperature.

2. After using starter, replenish by adding ¾ cup (105 g) unbleached all-purpose flour or bread flour and ¾ cup (1¾ dL) warm water to leftover starter. Cover bowl tightly with plastic wrap and set aside in a warm place to ripen overnight.

3. Transfer starter to an airtight 4-cup (1-L) container, date and refrigerate at least 2 days before using again. Flavor will become more pronounced with age. Liquid will rise to top of starter during refrigeration; often liquid will take on a greyish tinge. This is no cause for concern and should be ignored. Starter may be kept refrigerated indefinitely.

4. To use refrigerated starter, stir well; then stir in ¼ cup (30 g) unbleached all-purpose flour to reactivate. Cover and bring to room temperature (about 2 hours); starter should thicken slightly. Stir again before measuring for use. Replenish as described in Step 2; do not add additional yeast.

COUNTRY SOURDOUGH BREAD

Makes 1 loaf (1½ pounds/675 g)

This is my favorite bread. The chewy, gently speckled sourdough crust and the heavy crumb with its coarse weblike texture and faintly sour taste make it a real treat. The trick here is to bring the dough to the perfect consistency—an elastic mess that just holds its shape. If the dough is too wet and runny, the bread will flatten; if too much flour is added, the lovely texture can be lost.

The rising time for this loaf varies according to the age of the starter (the older it is, the slower the rise), as well as room temperature. In general, it rises far more slowly than the other breads, and may take from 3 to 8 hours on the first rise. As with French Bread, bake this one on the baking sheet several times before advancing to the more complex oven stone method.

1 cup Sourdough Starter
2½ to 2¾ cups (375 to 405 g) unbleached all-purpose flour (see page 5) or bread flour
1½ teaspoons dry active yeast
1½ teaspoons salt
⅔ cup (1½ dL) warm water (110° F/45° C)
Vegetable oil
2 to 3 tablespoons unbleached all-purpose flour or bread flour
1 egg white

1. Stir starter well. Insert the *metal knife blade.* Place 2½ cups (375 g) flour, yeast, and salt in container. Process to rapid-sift with 2 five-second pulses. With machine running, pour water through food chute within 10 seconds; scrape down container sides. Attach funnel, if desired. With machine running, pour starter through food chute as quickly as possible. Process 20 to 30 seconds longer, until dough is gooey, taffylike, and soft all the way through. If machine clogs, stop and scrape down away from blade; process until kneaded. Dough does not usually form a ball but it must hold its own shape and not ooze. If necessary, add additional ¼ cup (30 g) flour 2 tablespoons at a time, processing 5 seconds after each addition.

2. Rinse a large bowl with warm water. Place dough in bowl, cover tightly with plastic wrap and set aside to rise until dough is slightly more than doubled in bulk. Timing will depend on room temperature and sometimes on the age of the starter; rise can vary from 3 to 8 hours.

3. Sift 2 to 3 tablespoons unbleached flour evenly over a baking sheet or baker's paddle (peel); set aside. Generously flour work surface. Pull dough from bowl and roll in flour on work surface if dough sticks to hands. Then gently knead into a round, cushion-shaped loaf. Place loaf mounded side up on baking sheet or paddle. Cover with a dry cloth towel and set aside to rise until slightly more than doubled in bulk. Rising time will vary from 2½ to 4½ hours.

4. Adjust oven rack to lower position. Heat oven to 450° F (230° C). Heat oven stone 30 minutes. Use a razor blade or sharp knife to make a tic-tac-toe pattern on top of the loaf, making each slash ⅛ inch (½ cm) deep. Slash carefully so loaf does not deflate. Brush top and sides of loaf with egg white, using a damp pastry brush.

5. With a plant mister, spray inside of oven several times. Place baking sheet on oven rack;* do not remove excess flour. Or carefully loosen dough from paddle with a metal spatula; shake to be sure it slides freely and slide onto oven stone. Bake 25 to 30 minutes, spraying bread once after 15 minutes. Remove bread from oven to cake rack. Spray once or twice with water. Cool to room temperature before slicing.
   *Do not place baking sheet on oven stone.

PIZZA DOUGH

Makes dough for a 14-inch (35-cm) thin-crust pizza

The additional overnight rise (if dough is prepared in advance and refrigerated) improves, rather than harms, the flavor of the dough.

½ cup (1 dL) All-Purpose Starter, page 119
⅔ to ¾ cup (90 to 105 g) unbleached all-purpose flour (see page 5) or bread flour
½ cup (60 g) cake flour
½ teaspoon salt
2 tablespoons warm water (110° F/43° C)
2 tablespoons olive or vegetable oil

1. Prepare starter 2 or more hours in advance or bring refrigerated starter to room temperature.

2. Fit processor container with the *metal knife blade.* Add ⅔ cup (90 g) unbleached flour, cake flour, and salt, and process to rapid-sift with 2 five-second pulses. With machine running, pour water and oil through food chute within 5 seconds. Scrape down sides of container. Turn on machine and quickly pour starter through food chute. Process to knead dough 20 to 30 seconds longer, until dough is smooth, sticky, and soft all the way through. If dough is very liquid, add up to ¼ cup (30 g) additional flour and process 5 seconds longer.

3. Rinse a large bowl with warm water. Place dough in bowl, cover tightly with plastic and set aside to rise until dough is slightly more than triple in volume. Timing will depend on room temperature, but normal rise takes 2 to 2½ hours. When risen, dough is ready to press down and roll for pizza; keep covered until ready to use. If desired, pressed-down dough may be returned to a bowl, covered and refrigerated overnight (it will rise again) or until ready to roll for pizza.

STUFFED PIZZA DOUGH
Makes enough dough for 14-inch (35-cm) stuffed pizza

A firm, silky dough that stretches beautifully.

Special Starter variation recipe, page 119
2¼ cups (330 g) unbleached all-purpose flour (see page 5) or bread flour
1 cup (120 g) cake flour
1½ teaspoons salt
¼ cup (½ dL) olive or vegetable oil
⅓ cup (¾ dL) warm water (110° F/45° C)

1. Prepare starter 2 or more hours in advance or bring refrigerated starter to room temperature.

2. Fit processor container with the *metal knife blade.* Process to rapid-sift unbleached flour, cake flour, and salt with 2 five-second pulses. With machine running, pour olive oil and warm water through food chute within 15 seconds. Continue processing, pouring starter through food chute as quickly as possible. When all starter is added, process 30 to 40 seconds longer, until dough forms a smooth ball that is the same consistency all the way through.

3. Rinse a large bowl with warm water; drain but do not dry. Add dough. Cover with plastic and set aside to rise until dough is slightly more than tripled in bulk, approximately 2½ hours, depending on room temperature. When risen, dough is ready to press down, divide, and roll for pizza. Keep dough covered until ready to use. If desired, pressed-down dough may be returned to a bowl, covered, and refrigerated overnight (it will rise again) or until ready to roll for pizza.

16

Batter Breads, Loaf Cakes, and Cookies

One of the bulwarks of my youth was the marble pound cake brought for family brunch each Sunday by my grandparents. What a cake it was—tart with the tang of sour cream, heavy of crumb and shot through with chocolate. Baked in a plain brown wrapper that we folded around the loaf as it shrank, that cake still lives in my mind as a symbol of simple goodness that "real" flavors bring to baking.

My efforts to recreate that pound cake without fuss led me to work with the batters on which these quick breads and coffee cakes are based. It also led me to develop streamlined baking methods and several new techniques that make from-scratch baking faster, easier and more fun in the food processor than ever before. Gone are the traditional chores like presifting dry ingredients or the messy melting of chocolate. Chopping fruits and nuts has now become effortless, and the tedious creaming of butter with sugar takes less than a minute with the food processor.

If you follow the directions exactly—without changing procedures, the order, or timing—you will have perfect results. Also, it will not be necessary to clean the processor container between processing tasks unless the recipe specifically states to do so.

THE BASIC BATTER

Quick breads and coffee cakes are fast and easy to make because they contain no yeast, so no time is spent waiting for the dough to rise. The basic batter consists of eggs, sugar, flour, shortening, liquid, flavorings, leavening, such as baking soda or powder, and frequently fruits or nuts.

Mixing batters in the food processor requires only seconds because the blade works so quickly. At this rapid speed, mixing times are dramatically shorter than those of traditional preparation methods.

MEASURING AND RAPID-SIFTING DRY INGREDIENTS

To rapid-sift dry ingredients, first measure with a dry measure cup by scooping and leveling off flour with the edge of a metal spatula or knife. Before starting the machine, be sure to replace pusher in the food chute, as flour tends to fly up the chute. To rapid-sift dry ingredients (unless a large quantity of seeds or nuts is ground at the same time), use 2 five-second on/off turns or pulses. For easy handling and clean up, empty the sifted contents of the processor container onto waxed paper. No other sifting is required for these recipes. For best results, always use the type of flour indicated in the recipe (see page 5 for further information), otherwise dry, heavy cakes can result.

A NEW PROCESSOR CREAMING METHOD CALLED FOAMING

The secret of light, fine-textured cakes is creaming—beating air into butter and sugar until the sugar dissolves and the mixture becomes light and fluffy. Because the food processor does not cream in the conventional manner, another method must be used. I have discovered that foaming, or beating, eggs to a fluffy texture is a good alternative. This method produces greater aeration than any other processor creaming method; thus cakes and quick breads are higher.

I have developed two variations on foaming for these recipes: "warm foaming" when hot melted butter is used in the recipe and "cool foaming" when oil is used. Foaming takes about 20 to 35 seconds in the processor.

Warm foaming is not entirely new. The French have used a similar process to make *génoise,* the extra-rich sponge cake, for years. What is new is that hot but not bubbling melted butter (about 180° F/82° C) is added directly to room-temperature whole eggs in a method similar to the one used to make Processor Hollandaise.

Warm Foaming with Hot Melted Butter

For warm foaming, always use hot but not bubbling melted butter. An instant-registering thermometer is extremely helpful in verifying the temperature. However, it is useful to know that melted butter separates between 160 and 180° F (71 and 82° C) when the white milk solids rise to the top like foam on beer. Whether butter is melted on the stove or in the microwave, look for the white foam, check to be sure all butter is melted, and do not allow butter to become so hot that it boils. It will be at the correct temperature for warm foaming.

Always add butter to the eggs in a thin steady stream, pouring it through the food chute while the machine is running. (I use a 2-cup [½-L] glass measure with pouring spout and find it easy to melt the butter in the microwave in the same cup.) Then slowly pour the sugar into the warm mixture (a glass measure or funnel attachment facilitates this), and process as specified to allow the sugar to begin to dissolve.

Cool Foaming with Vegetable Oil

The cool-foaming method simply substitutes room temperature vegetable oil for melted butter and is related to making mayonnaise rather than hollandaise. Do not, however, substitute butter for oil in recipes.

PROCESSING NUTS AND DRIED FRUITS

Here are some general guidelines for processing nuts and dried fruits for use in these recipes as well as for future baking:

- Oily nuts, such as walnuts, peanuts, and Brazil nuts, must be chopped with a small amount of flour to absorb excess oils, otherwise they soften and can turn to nut butter.

- If whole nuts are used, prechop, adding flour as necessary, unless recipe directs otherwise. However, if nut pieces are used, they may be added to the batter and simultaneously chopped while they are mixed.

- Always place nut pieces, as directed, on top of dry ingredients so they will be lightly coated with flour during chopping and mixing. Coated nuts will remain suspended (rather than sink) in the batter.

- Nonoily nuts, such as almonds or hazelnuts (filberts), may be finely ground in the processor and used as a dry ingredient. Once ground, nuts should be sifted directly into the remaining dry ingredients.

- Soft fresh fruit, such as pitted cherries, need not be prechopped. Like nut pieces, they may be chopped and mixed into the batter at the same time.

- Firm dried fruit, such as dried apricots, requires prechopping. If sticky, add a small amount of flour (2 to 4 tablespoons).

- Sticky candied fruit or soft dried sticky fruit, such as dates or figs, should always be chopped with flour.

- Fresh vegetables and fruits, such as carrots,

zucchini, apples, or bananas, should be processed by shredding, puréeing, chopping, or julienne before being added to the batter. This does require an extra step, but these fresh ingredients add a wonderful moistness and natural sugar to baking goods.

QUICK-MELTING METHOD FOR SEMISWEET CHOCOLATE

Semisweet (or sweet) chocolate may be melted in the food processor container by the "quick-melting" method. First, the room-temperature chocolate should be broken into ½-inch (1½-cm) chunks. The *metal knife blade* is used to grind the chocolate (most machines which will grind hard cheese will also handle chocolate) to various consistencies, depending upon processing time. The method is most efficient when chocolate is finely ground to the consistency of small, irregular beads or pebbles, which may glisten slightly as the chocolate is heated by friction.

The ground chocolate then may be melted with as little as ¼ cup (½ dL) hot liquid such as melted butter, milk, or water. For best results, liquid should be no hotter than 180° F (82° C) because semisweet chocolate has a low melting point—about 100° F (38° C). Temperature of hot liquid can be verified with an instant-registering thermometer.

BAKING SODA AND BAKING POWDER

Baking soda and baking powder are the traditional leavening agents for batters. Both begin their activity upon contact with moisture and do their jobs by producing harmless carbon dioxide, which causes the batter to rise and become light when baked.

Baking soda is the faster and more volatile of the two, swinging into action so quickly that the batter must be baked the moment it is mixed lest the soda expend itself on the kitchen counter. Baking soda is traditionally used in high-acid batters containing buttermilk or large amounts of sour cream, heavy ingredients like molasses, or large amounts of pungent spices such as cloves and nutmeg. Soda is often used in conjunction with baking powder.

Baking powder is the most commonly used leavening agent since it provides longer-lasting action. My recipes call for double-action baking powder, which begins to work on contact with

moisture and then provides another boost in contact with oven heat. Baking powder loses potency with age. Most cans are date stamped—check carefully. When in doubt, a quick test will determine whether or not the powder is active: In a cup, combine a teaspoon baking powder with ⅓ cup (¾ dL) warm water. If powder fizzes immediately, it is active; if not, a new can is required.

CHECKLIST FOR BAKING

- Always be sure all ingredients are on hand before beginning these recipes—quick breads and coffee cakes won't wait.

- Be sure the oven is clean and free of dark patches or baked-on foods, which can cause burning or uneven baking.

- Verify capacity of baking pans before using. A pan that is too small will produce breads and cakes with large unsightly mounds in the center; too large a pan yields flat or swayback loaves and cakes. To measure capacity, fill pans to the brim with water poured from a measuring cup. If possible, mark capacity on bottom of each pan with an indelible marker (I also do this on soufflé dish bottoms) for easy reference.

- It is normal and desirable for loaf cakes to rise well above the pan rim and crack majestically. If your quick breads and cakes are flat, barely cracked or swayback, but the pan has the correct capacity, you may wish to change to a longer, narrower pan of the same capacity, which will give a more pleasing shape. I prefer long narrow loaf pans with black finish. My favorite 8-cup (2-L) pan measures 11¾ × 3½ × 3 inches (30 × 9 × 8 cm). I have been able to find a good selection of pans in specialty cookware stores.

- I strongly recommend using an oven thermometer (the mercury type is best). Always adjust oven heat according to the thermometer after 10 minutes of preheating; do not rely on the oven gauge. Self-cleaning ovens are especially susceptible to changes in calibration after cleaning cycles; I have found as much as a 50° variance in mine.

TESTING FOR DONENESS

Baking times are never hard and fast, they

are always estimates. Before assuming any cake or quick bread is done, always test as follows:

- Gently remove pan from oven to cake rack.

- Close oven door immediately to keep temperature constant.

- Use a cake tester, trussing needle, or long thin toothpick to pierce the cake in the center. Insert the tester as far down as possible. Be gentle—do not stab—and withdraw the tester gently.

- When tester is withdrawn clean, cake is done.

- If tester is not clean, return pan to oven and bake as recipe directs; retest. If necessary, continue baking and testing at 10-minute intervals until done. Allow breads and cakes to come to room temperature before slicing.

ZUCCHINI-PECAN BREAD
Makes 1 loaf, 10 to 12 servings

Cake flour is used in combination with unbleached flour to keep this bread tender. Pecans are chopped and mixed into batter simultaneously.

1½ cups (225 g) unbleached all-purpose flour
½ cup (60 g) cake flour
1½ teaspoons baking powder
½ teaspoon baking soda
½ teaspoon ground cinnamon
¼ teaspoon salt
1 zucchini (6 oz./180 g), ends trimmed
2 eggs, room temperature
½ cup (1 dL) vegetable oil
1 cup plus 2 tablespoons (214 g) sugar
¼ cup (½ dL) plain yogurt
1 teaspoon vanilla extract
1 cup (4 oz./115 g) whole shelled pecans

1. Adjust oven rack to middle position. Heat oven to 300° F (150° C). Oil a 7-cup (1¾-L) loaf pan; set aside.

2. Insert the *metal knife blade* in container. Add unbleached flour, cake flour, baking powder, baking soda, cinnamon, and salt; process to rapid-sift with 2 five-second pulses; transfer to waxed paper.

3. Change to the *medium shredding disk*. Set blade aside. Shred zucchini with a firm push; transfer to waxed paper; replace blade.

4. Place eggs in container. With machine running, add oil through food chute within 15 seconds; process 15 seconds. With machine still running, pour 1 cup (190 g) of the sugar through food chute within 15 seconds; process 20 seconds and scrape down sides of container.

5. Add zucchini, yogurt, and vanilla. Process to mix with 2 one-second pulses. Add half the flour mixture and the pecans. Process with 5 half-second pulses. Add remaining flour mixture; process with 5 or 6 half-second pulses, or just until flour is mixed into batter.

6. Pour batter into loaf pan; sprinkle with remaining sugar. Bake until a cake tester inserted into center of loaf is withdrawn clean, about 1 hour 25 minutes. Cool on cake rack 30 minutes. Remove bread from pan; cool to room temperature. Wrap and refrigerate overnight before serving. Bread may be stored, well wrapped, in refrigerator up to 1 week or in freezer up to 2 weeks.

APRICOT AND THREE-GRAIN BREAD
Makes 1 loaf, 10 to 12 servings

Unprocessed or miller's bran is available in the cereal section of the supermarket or at health-food stores.

1 cup (120 g) cake flour
¾ cup (117 g) whole wheat flour (not stone ground)
¼ cup (20 g) unprocessed (miller's) bran
¼ cup (25 g) rolled oats
1½ tablespoons baking powder
½ teaspoon each: baking soda, salt, ground cinnamon
¼ teaspoon ground nutmeg
½ cup (2 oz./60 g) dried apricots, firmly packed
½ cup (2 oz./60 g) shelled whole walnuts
2 eggs, room temperature
1 teaspoon vanilla extract
⅔ cup (1½ dL) safflower or vegetable oil
½ cup (1 dL) honey

1 ripe medium banana, peeled, cut into 1-inch chunks
½ cup (1 dL) plain or lemon yogurt

1. Adjust oven rack to middle position. Heat oven to 300° F (150° C). Lightly oil a 7-cup (1¾-L) loaf pan. Insert the *metal knife blade.* Process to rapid-sift cake flour, whole wheat flour, bran, oats, baking powder, baking soda, salt, cinnamon, and nutmeg with 2 five-second pulses; transfer to waxed paper.

2. Return ¼ cup (30 g) of the flour mixture to container. Add apricots and walnuts. Process to chop with 7 one-second pulses; transfer to waxed paper.

3. Process eggs with vanilla 15 seconds. With machine running, add oil through food chute within 25 seconds. Process 15 seconds; then add honey through food chute within 20 seconds. Process 15 seconds longer; scrape down sides of container.

4. Add banana and yogurt; process 1 minute, until smooth. Mix in half the sifted flour mixture, processing with 5 half-second pulses; scrape down sides of container. Add remaining flour mixture, apricot-walnut mixture and process with 5 or 6 half-second on/off turns or pulses, until flour is mixed into batter.

5. Pour batter into prepared pan. Bake until a cake tester inserted into center is withdrawn clean, about 1 hour 20 minutes. Cool bread in pan on cake rack 20 minutes. Remove from pan and cool on cake rack to room temperature. Wrap and refrigerate overnight before serving.

CHRISTMAS PUDDING BREAD
Makes 1 loaf, 10 to 12 servings

The combination of oil and butter gives this bread an extra moistness; puréed plums add that rich "Christmas pudding" flavor.

½ lb. (225 g) mixed chopped candied fruits
2 oz. (60 g) natural candied pineapple slices, cut in eighths
½ cup (3 oz./85 g) white sultana raisins
½ cup (3 oz./85 g) dark seedless raisins
¼ cup (½ dL) port
¼ cup (½ dL) brandy
2¼ cups (265 g) cake flour
¾ teaspoon baking soda
¼ teaspoon each: ground cinnamon, ground allspice, ground nutmeg, salt
1 medium lemon
1 small orange
¼ cup (50 g) sugar
3 eggs, room temperature
¼ cup (60 g) hot melted butter (160 to 180° F/71 to 82° C)
⅓ cup (¾ dL) vegetable oil
¾ cup (150 g) packed dark brown sugar
¼ cup (½ dL) dark molasses
½ cup (1 dL) pitted drained purple plums
Red and green candied pineapple slices, for garnish

1. Mix candied fruits, pineapple slices, raisins, port, and brandy in a small bowl; let stand 2 hours. Adjust oven rack to middle position. Heat oven to 300° F (150° C). Streak an 8-cup (2-L) loaf pan with butter; line with baking parchment paper; set aside.

2. Insert *metal knife blade.* Place flour, baking soda, cinnamon, allspice, nutmeg, and salt in container. Process to rapid-sift with 2 five-second pulses; remove to waxed paper.

3. Strip off lemon and orange rinds with a vegetable peeler; reserve fruit for another use. Process lemon and orange rind with sugar until finely ground, about 1 minute.

4. Add eggs to sugar mixture. With machine running, pour hot melted butter in a thin stream through food chute within 10 seconds. Continue processing, adding oil in a thin stream within 10 seconds; scrape down sides of container. With machine running, add brown sugar and molasses through food chute within 15 seconds; process 30 seconds. Add plums; process 20 seconds; scrape down sides of container.

5. Add half the flour mixture and half the candied fruit mixture. Process with 4 half-second pulses; scrape down sides of container. Add remaining flour and candied fruit and process with 6 half-second pulses; or until flour is mixed into batter; scrape down sides of container.

6. Pour batter into prepared loaf pan. Bake until a cake tester inserted into center of loaf is withdrawn clean, about 1 hour 20 minutes. Cool on cake rack 30 minutes. Remove loaf from pan leaving it in parchment paper; cool to room temperature. Refrigerate in parchment wrapped in aluminum foil for 2 days before serving. Garnish with additional pineapple slices. Bread will keep up to 2 weeks in refrigerator.

BANANA-WALNUT BREAD

Makes 1 loaf, 10 to 12 servings

The rich flavors of bananas and walnuts make this quick bread an old-fashioned favorite.

1½ cups (225 g) unbleached all-purpose flour
¾ cup (85 g) cake flour
1½ teaspoons baking powder
½ teaspoon ground cinnamon
¼ teaspoon baking soda
¼ teaspoon salt
Pinch nutmeg
2 eggs, room temperature
½ cup (1 dL) vegetable oil
½ cup (100 g) sugar
½ cup (100 g) packed dark brown sugar
¾ lb. (340 g) ripe bananas, peeled, cut into 1-inch chunks
¼ cup (½ dL) orange juice
1 teaspoon vanilla extract
1 cup (4 oz./115 g) whole shelled walnuts

1. Adjust oven rack to middle position. Heat oven to 325° F (165° C). Lightly oil a 7-cup (1¾-L) loaf pan; set aside.

2. Insert *metal knife blade.* Combine unbleached flour, cake flour, baking powder, cinnamon, baking soda, salt, and nutmeg in container. Process to rapid-sift with 2 five-second pulses; transfer to waxed paper.

3. Process eggs, adding oil in a thin stream within 15 seconds; process 15 seconds longer. With machine running, gradually add sugar and brown sugar through food chute within 15 seconds; process 20 seconds longer; scrape down sides of container.

4. Add bananas, orange juice, and vanilla to container. Process 1 minute. Add half the dry ingredients and walnuts. Process to mix with 4 half-second pulses; scrape down sides of container. Add remaining flour mixture and process with 4 or 5 half-second pulses, or just until flour is mixed into batter.

5. Pour batter into loaf pan. Bake until a cake tester inserted into the center of the loaf is withdrawn clean, about 1 hour 10 minutes. Cool in pan on cake rack 30 minutes. Remove bread from pan; cool to room temperature. Wrap and refrigerate overnight before serving. Store in refrigerator, well wrapped, up to 1 week or up to 2 weeks in freezer.

PLAIN POUND CAKE

Makes 10 to 12 servings

This dense, moist pound cake has a fine crumb and a pure butter taste. Unsalted or sweet butter is a must here.

2 cups (240 g) cake flour
1½ teaspoons baking powder
¼ teaspoon salt
¼ lb. (115 g) unsalted butter, slightly softened
4 eggs, room temperature
2 teaspoons fresh lemon juice
1½ teaspoons vanilla extract
½ cup (115 g) hot melted unsalted butter (160 to 180° F/71 to 82° C)
1¼ cups (240 g) sugar

1. Line an 8-cup (2-L) loaf pan with brown paper as described in Marble Pound Cake recipe on page 137; set pan aside. Adjust oven rack to middle position. Heat oven to 325° F (165° C).

2. Insert the *metal knife blade.* Process cake flour, baking powder, and salt with 2 five-second pulses to rapid-sift; remove to waxed paper.

3. Place softened butter in container and process 30 seconds; scrape down container sides. Add to container eggs, lemon juice, and vanilla; process 30 seconds. With machine running,

add hot melted butter through food chute in a thin stream within 20 seconds; process 15 seconds.

4. Attach funnel if desired. With machine running, add sugar through food chute within 15 seconds; process 20 seconds and scrape down sides of container.

5. Add half the flour mixture; process with 4 or 5 half-second pulses and scrape down sides of container. Add remaining flour mixture and process with 4 or 5 half-second pulses, or until flour is mixed into batter; scrape down sides of container.

6. Pour batter into prepared liner. Bake until a cake tester inserted into the center of the loaf is withdrawn clean, about 1 to 1¼ hours. Cool on cake rack 30 minutes. Remove loaf from pan and cool to room temperature. Cake is best if wrapped in plastic and set aside at room temperature overnight before serving.

CHOCOLATE POUND CAKE
Makes 10 to 12 servings

If you have never before ground chocolate in the food processor, test your machine with half the amount specified here. The large-capacity machines will normally handle up to ½ pound (225 g) of chocolate in one batch.

2 cups (240 g) cake flour
1½ teaspoons baking powder
¼ teaspoon salt
6 oz. (180 g) semisweet chocolate, broken into ½-inch pieces
4 eggs, room temperature
½ cup (115 g) hot melted unsalted butter (160 to 180° F/71 to 82° C)
1¼ cups (240 g) sugar
½ cup (1 dL) sour cream
½ teaspoon vanilla extract

1. Adjust oven rack to middle position. Heat oven to 325° F (165° C). Make liner for 8-cup (2-L) loaf pan from lightweight brown paper bag as described in Step 1 of Marble Pound Cake (following); place in loaf pan and set aside.

2. Insert the *metal knife blade.* Combine flour, baking powder, and salt in container. Process to rapid-sift with 2 five-second pulses; transfer to waxed paper.

3. Process chocolate until beads form. Add eggs; process 15 seconds. With machine running, add hot melted butter in a thin stream within 15 seconds; process 20 seconds longer; scrape down sides of container. With machine running, gradually add sugar within 15 seconds; process 20 seconds longer. Add sour cream and vanilla extract; process with 5 half-second pulses; scrape down sides of container.

4. Add half the flour mixture to batter; process with 4 half-second pulses and scrape down sides of container. Add remaining flour mixture; process with 5 or 6 half-second pulses, or just until flour is mixed into batter.

5. Pour batter into prepared liner. Bake until cake tester inserted into center of loaf is withdrawn clean, about 1 hour 25 minutes. Cool cake in pan on cake rack 15 minutes. Remove cake from pan; cool in paper liner to room temperature. Refrigerate in liner, well wrapped in plastic, overnight before serving. Store up to 3 days in refrigerator or up to 1 week in freezer.

MARBLE POUND CAKE
Makes 10 to 12 servings

Do not be alarmed if chocolate batter, which is heavy, begins to sink as it is added to the loaf pan. The liner permits the cake to be unmolded easily.

2 cups (240 g) cake flour
1½ teaspoons baking powder
¼ teaspoon salt
4 large eggs, room temperature
2 teaspoons fresh lemon juice
1½ teaspoons vanilla extract
¾ cup (180 g) hot melted unsalted butter (160 to 180° F/71 to 82° C)
1¼ cups (240 g) sugar
½ cup (115 g) sour cream
¼ lb. (115 g) semisweet chocolate, broken into ½-inch pieces

1. Adjust oven rack to middle position. Heat oven to 325° F (165° C). Make liner from lightweight brown paper bag for an 8-cup (2-L) loaf pan by cutting out and folding the largest side of the bag over the back of the pan. Slip off folded liner and place it inside pan, smoothing as necessary. Trim so liner fits pan neatly; set pan aside.

2. Insert the *metal knife blade.* Place cake flour, baking powder, and salt in container. Process to rapid-sift with 2 five-second pulses; transfer to waxed paper.

3. Place eggs, lemon juice, and vanilla extract in container. With machine running, pour all but ¼ cup (½ dL) of the hot melted butter through food chute in a thin stream within 15 seconds; process 20 seconds. Process, gradually adding sugar within 15 seconds; then process 20 seconds longer. Mix in sour cream with 5 half-second pulses.

4. Add half the flour mixture and process with 4 to 6 half-second pulses; scrape down sides of container. Add remaining flour mixture with 6 to 8 half-second pulses.

5. Pour 1¼ cups (3 dL) batter into a measuring cup. Pour remaining batter into paper liner. Return container and blade to processor base without washing. Add chocolate to container and process until chocolate forms coarse beads about the size of peas or larger; scrape down container sides.

6. Reheat remaining ¼ cup of butter. Process, pouring hot melted butter through food chute within 5 seconds. Scrape down sides of container and add reserved plain batter. Process to mix with 3 two-second pulses.

7. Pour chocolate batter into paper liner on top of plain batter. With a tablespoon, marbleize batters by folding them together down the center using no more than 5 or 6 strokes. Bake cake until a cake tester inserted into the center of the loaf is withdrawn clean, about 1 hour 10 minutes to 1 hour 15 minutes. Cool in pan on cake rack 20 minutes. Remove and cool cake in paper liner to room temperature. Cake is best if wrapped in plastic and set aside overnight before serving; it may be stored in plastic wrap in refrigerator up to 3 days or in freezer up to 1 week.

CARROT CAKE
Makes 10 to 12 servings

A sweet fragrant carrot cake that disappears very quickly. If small walnut pieces are used, omit the chopping in Step 3.

3 medium carrots, peeled, ends trimmed
½ cup (2 oz./60 g) whole shelled walnuts
1½ cups (225 g) unbleached all-purpose flour
1 teaspoon baking soda
¼ teaspoon salt
¼ teaspoon each: ground cinnamon, ground nutmeg, ground allspice, ground cloves
6 tablespoons (85 g) softened butter, cut into 1-inch chunks
2 eggs, room temperature
1 teaspoon vanilla extract
⅓ cup (85 g) hot melted butter (160 to 180° F/71 to 82° C)
1¼ cups (240 g) sugar
½ cup (4 oz./115 g) drained crushed pineapple

1. Adjust oven rack to middle position. Heat oven to 350° F (175° C). Coat an 8-inch (20-cm)-square baking pan with butter; set aside.

2. Insert the *medium shredding disk.* Place carrots upright in food chute and shred with a firm push; transfer to waxed paper. Change to the *metal knife blade* and wipe container and lid dry with paper toweling.

3. Process to chop walnuts with 6 to 8 half-second pulses; transfer to waxed paper. Process to rapid-sift flour, baking soda, salt, cinnamon, nutmeg, allspice, and cloves with 2 five-second pulses; transfer to waxed paper.

4. Place softened butter in container and process 30 seconds. Add eggs and vanilla. With machine running, pour hot melted butter through food chute within 15 seconds; process 20 seconds. Gradually add sugar through food chute within 20 seconds; process 20 seconds longer and scrape down sides of container.

5. Mix in half the dry ingredients with 5 half-second pulses; scrape down sides of container. Add carrots, walnuts, pineapple, and remaining dry ingredients to container. Process with 6 to 8 half-second pulses, or until ingredients are mixed into batter (which will be very thick and heavy).

6. Immediately spoon batter into baking pan. Bake until a cake tester inserted in the center is withdrawn clean, about 45 to 50 minutes. Cool in baking dish on cake rack to room temperature. Cut cake into 2-inch (5-cm) squares. Store in refrigerator up to 1 week or in freezer up to 3 weeks.

APPLE-SPICE CAKE
Makes 8 to 12 servings

Firm green Granny Smith apples, grated lemon rind, and a touch of spice flavor this easy coffee cake baked in a springform pan.

1¾ cups (205 g) cake flour
¼ cup (30 g) unbleached all-purpose flour
½ cup (2 oz./60 g) whole shelled walnuts
1½ teaspoons baking soda
¼ teaspoon salt
¼ teaspoon each: ground cinnamon, ground cardamom
¾ lb. (340 g) Granny Smith apples (2 large), pared, cored, quartered
1 small lemon, rind stripped off with a vegetable peeler
1 cup (190 g) sugar
2 eggs, room temperature
½ cup (115 g) hot melted butter (160 to 180° F/71 to 82° C)
½ teaspoon vanilla extract
Powdered sugar, for garnish

1. Adjust oven rack to middle position. Heat oven to 350° F (175° C). Butter an 8-inch (20-cm) springform pan; set aside.

2. Insert the *metal knife blade*. Place cake flour, unbleached flour, walnuts, baking soda, salt, cinnamon, and cardamom in container. Process until nuts are finely ground, about 40 seconds; transfer to waxed paper; set blade aside.

3. Change to the *medium shredding disk*. Shred apples with a moderate push, emptying container into a bowl as necessary. Return *metal knife blade* to container. Process rind strips with ¼ cup (50 g) sugar to a fine consistency. Add eggs to container. With machine running, add hot butter in a thin stream within

15 seconds; process 15 seconds. Process adding remaining ¾ cup (140 g) sugar through food chute; process 20 seconds longer; scrape down sides of container.

4. Add apples and vanilla to container. Process to mix with 2 one-second pulses. Add flour mixture; process with 6 or 7 half-second pulses, or just until flour is mixed into batter; scrape down sides of container.

5. Pour batter into springform pan. Bake until a cake tester inserted into center of cake is withdrawn clean, about 50 to 60 minutes. Cool on cake rack to room temperature. Remove pan side. Decorate with powdered sugar before serving.

WHOLE WHEAT BLACK FOREST RING
Makes 12 to 14 servings

Semisweet chocolate ground to medium-fine consistency becomes tiny chocolate nuggets in the finished cake. Both cherries and walnuts are chopped and mixed into the batter simultaneously.

1 cup (120 g) cake flour
1 cup (155 g) whole wheat flour
1½ tablespoons baking powder
¼ teaspoon baking soda
¼ teaspoon each: ground cinnamon, ground nutmeg, salt
3 oz. (85 g) semisweet chocolate, broken into ½-inch pieces
3 eggs, room temperature
½ cup (115 g) hot melted butter
½ cup (100 g) sugar
½ cup (100 g) packed dark brown sugar
½ cup (1 dL) orange juice
½ teaspoon vanilla extract
1 cup (4 oz./115 g) whole shelled walnuts
1 cup (¼ L) drained pitted dark sweet cherries
Powdered sugar, for garnish

1. Adjust oven rack to middle position. Heat oven to 325° F (165° C). Butter an 8-cup (2-L) ring mold; set aside.

2. Insert the *metal knife blade*. Process cake flour, whole wheat flour, baking powder, baking soda, cinnamon, nutmeg, and salt with 2 five-second pulses to rapid-sift; remove to waxed paper.

3. Process chocolate to medium-fine consistency, about 15 seconds; remove to waxed paper.

4. Process eggs, adding hot melted butter in a thin stream within 10 seconds; process 15 seconds. With machine running, add sugar and brown sugar through food chute within 15 seconds; process 20 seconds longer and scrape down sides of container. Add orange juice and vanilla; process 5 seconds.

5. Add half the flour mixture and the walnuts to container. Process to mix with 5 half-second pulses; scrape down sides of container. Add remaining dry ingredients, the grated chocolate and cherries; process with 7 or 8 half-second pulses, or just until flour is mixed into batter.

6. Pour batter into ring mold. Bake until cake tester inserted into center of cake is withdrawn clean, about 45 minutes. Cool on cake rack 1 hour before removing ring from pan. Cool to room temperature; garnish with powdered sugar. Wrap and store in refrigerator up to 2 weeks or in freezer up to 3 weeks.

ALMOND-STREUSEL COFFEE CAKE
Makes 10 to 12 servings

Be sure that the top of the cake is fully rounded and set before adding the streusel. This cake should be served warm; cover and heat at 325° F (165° C) for 7 minutes before serving.

¾ cup (4 oz./115 g) unblanched almonds
½ cup (75 g) unbleached all-purpose flour
1 cup (120 g) cake flour
1 teaspoon baking powder
¼ teaspoon baking soda
¼ teaspoon salt
2 eggs, room temperature

½ cup (115 g) hot melted butter
1 cup (190 g) sugar
½ cup (1 dL) buttermilk
1½ teaspoons vanilla extract

Streusel Topping:

½ cup (75 g) unbleached all-purpose flour
¼ cup (1 oz./30 g) unblanched almonds
3 tablespoons (36 g) sugar
3 tablespoons packed dark brown sugar
Pinch each: ground ginger, ground nutmeg, ground cinnamon
4 tablespoons (60 g) chilled butter, cut into 4 pieces

1. Insert *metal knife blade* in dry container. Process almonds and unbleached flour until almonds are finely ground. Add cake flour, baking powder, baking soda, and salt; process to rapid-sift with 2 five-second pulses; transfer dry ingredients to waxed paper.

2. Adjust oven rack to middle position. Heat oven to 350° F (175° C). Butter an 8-inch (20-cm)-square baking dish; set aside.

3. Place eggs in container. Process, adding melted butter in thin stream within 15 seconds; process 15 seconds. With machine running, add sugar within 15 seconds; process 20 seconds longer; scrape down sides of container. Add buttermilk and vanilla; process 5 seconds. Add flour mixture and process with 6 or 7 half-second pulses, or just until flour is mixed into batter; scrape down sides of container.

4. Pour batter into baking pan. Bake until a cake tester inserted into the center of cake is withdrawn barely clean, about 30 to 35 minutes. Clean and return container and blade to base.

5. Meanwhile, prepare Streusel Topping. Place unbleached flour, almonds, sugar, dark brown sugar, ginger, nutmeg, and cinnamon in container. Process until almonds are finely ground. Add cold butter and process with 4 to 6 one-second pulses, or until mixture forms coarse crumbs.

6. Remove cake from oven. Sprinkle with Streusel Topping. Bake until a crust forms, about 15 to 20 minutes. Cool slightly on cake rack; serve warm.

GREEK ALMOND COOKIES
Makes about 4 dozen

Called *kourabiethes* in Greek, these fragile cookies will crumble in your mouth at the first bite. Keep them covered with powdered sugar in an airtight tin and they will stay fresh for 2 weeks.

½ cup (3 oz./85 g) whole, shelled, unblanched almonds
2 cups (240 g) cake flour
½ teaspoon baking powder
6 oz. (180 g) butter, slightly softened
1½ cups (120 g) powdered sugar
2 egg yolks
1½ teaspoons vanilla extract

1. Insert the *metal knife blade*. Process to grind almonds with 3 tablespoons cake flour until powdery. Add remaining cake flour and baking powder. Process to rapid-sift with 5 two-second pulses; transfer to waxed paper.

2. Cut butter into 1-inch (2½-cm) chunks. Process 30 seconds; scrape down sides of container. Add ½ cup (40 g) of the powdered sugar. Process 20 seconds. Add egg yolks and vanilla; process 20 seconds. Add flour mixture; process until dough begins to form a ball, about 7 seconds. Wrap and refrigerate 10 minutes.

3. Adjust oven rack to middle position. Heat oven to 350° F (175° C). Pinch off pieces of dough and roll into 1-inch balls. Place 1½ inches (4 cm) apart on ungreased baking sheets. Bake 20 to 25 minutes. Center a large cake rack over waxed paper. Place warm cookies on rack and immediately sift powdered sugar over. Repeat until all cookies are baked and heavily coated with powdered sugar. Cool to room temperature. Store with all excess sugar in a foil-lined, airtight tin.

CHOCOLATE BAR COOKIES
Makes about 3 dozen

The egg yolk is processed with warm water until fluffy (a sauce-making technique) to ensure that it will be evenly distributed through the bottom dough layer. If desired, coarsely ground semisweet chocolate may be substituted for chocolate chips.

1 tablespoon (15 g) butter
1¼ cups (180 g) unbleached all-purpose flour
1 teaspoon sugar
1 teaspoon baking powder
1 cup (4 oz./115 g) whole shelled walnuts
1 egg yolk
2 tablespoons warm water
¼ lb. (115 g) slightly softened butter, cut into 1-inch chunks
1 package (12 oz./360 g) semisweet chocolate chips
2 eggs
2 teaspoons vanilla extract
⅓ cup (85 g) hot melted butter (160 to 180° F/71 to 82° C)
¾ cup (145 g) sugar

1. Adjust oven rack to lower position. Heat oven to 350° F (175° C). Generously coat an 11¾- × 7½- × 1½-inch (30- × 18- × 4-cm) baking dish with 1 tablespoon butter; set dish aside. Insert the *metal knife blade*. Place flour, sugar, and baking powder in container; process to rapid-sift with 2 five-second pulses; remove ingredients to waxed paper. Add nuts to container; chop to medium-fine consistency with 6 to 8 half-second pulses; set nuts aside.

2. Place egg yolk and water in container; process 10 seconds. Add butter and flour mixture. Process with 6 one-second pulses, or until mixed to small pebble consistency. Empty contents of container into baking dish and spread over bottom. Press into an even layer with fingers. Bake 10 minutes.

3. Remove baking dish from oven. Sprinkle chocolate chips over baked crust as evenly as possible. Return to oven and bake 1 minute; remove and set aside.

4. Wipe out food processor container, rinse blade and return both to processor base. Place eggs and vanilla extract in container. With machine running, add hot melted butter in a thin stream within 15 seconds; process 20 seconds longer. Process, adding sugar through food chute within 15 seconds; process 30 seconds longer and scrape down the sides of the container.

5. Sprinkle nuts evenly over chocolate chips. Pour contents of container over nuts. Return dish to oven and bake until a light brown crust forms on top, about 30 to 35 minutes. Place dish on cake rack to cool for 45 minutes, until just warm. Cut cookies into 1¼-inch (3-cm) squares while still warm. Remove from pan and store in an airtight tin.

SWEDISH BUTTER COOKIES
Makes 4 to 5 dozen

My friend Helen Jonsson, a cookie baker *extraordinaire,* has made these by hand for about 20 years. Here is an updated method. If desired, these cookies may be shaped with a "spritz" gun.

½ lb. (225 g) butter, softened to room temperature, cut into 1-inch chunks
¾ cup (145 g) sugar
¼ teaspoon salt
Scant ¼ teaspoon almond extract
2 egg yolks
2 cups (300 g) unbleached all-purpose flour
Nuts, colored sugar, or candied fruit, for garnish

1. Insert the *metal knife blade.* Process the softened butter just long enough to break up the pieces, about 20 seconds. Add sugar, salt, and almond extract; process to mix about 10 seconds longer; add egg yolks and process 5 seconds, until mixed. Add flour to container and process with 6 one-second pulses, or until dough begins to clump.

2. Cut a 24-inch (60-cm)-long sheet of plastic wrap and spoon dough down the center to form a log about 18 inches (45 cm) long. Roll up so dough is rounded and pressed together; refrigerate 1 hour or until firm enough to slice, as long as overnight if desired. Or, if using a "spritz" gun, simply spoon the dough from the processor container into the gun.

3. Adjust the oven rack to middle position. Heat oven to 400° F (205° C). Slice chilled dough into ⅛-inch (½-cm)-thick coins and

place on ungreased baking sheets. Garnish as desired with nuts, colored sugar, or candied fruit. Bake 1 sheet at a time until cookies are pale and a light brown ring forms around the bottom edge, about 7 to 8 minutes; cool on cake rack 5 minutes; remove from baking sheet and cool to room temperature. Repeat to bake remaining cookies. Store in an airtight tin.

WHOLE WHEAT AND YOGURT PANCAKES
Makes 4 to 6 servings

The batter for these healthy and absolutely delicious pancakes takes only seconds to make from scratch.

¾ cup (117 g) whole wheat flour (not stone ground)
½ cup (60 g) cake flour
1 teaspoon baking powder
½ teaspoon baking soda
½ teaspoon salt
⅓ cup (¾ dL) plain yogurt
1 egg
2 tablespoons melted butter
¾ cup (1¾ dL) milk
Vegetable oil
Maple syrup
Butter

1. Insert the *metal knife blade.* Process to rapid-sift whole wheat flour, cake flour, baking powder, soda, and salt with 2 five-second pulses. Add yogurt, egg, and butter to container. With machine running, pour milk through food chute within 8 seconds; process 5 seconds; scrape down sides of container. Process 10 seconds.

2. Heat a pancake griddle or skillet and brush with vegetable oil. Spoon a generous tablespoon or more of batter onto griddle for each pancake, placing them 1½ inches (4 cm) apart. Cook over medium heat until pancakes bubble, about 2 minutes. Flip over and cook until lightly browned, about 2 minutes longer. Repeat to use all batter. Serve immediately with maple syrup and additional butter, if desired.

17

Pies and Pastries

Tarts and pies, like Motherhood and Old Glory, are dessert institutions that strike a chord deep in our gastronomic heritage. Even those of us who are fat phobic to a fault, still succumb to the irresistible urge to make these luscious pastries and serve them proudly.

The making of fine pastry is an art, and light flaky crusts have always been considered the most severe test of a good cook. Recipes and techniques for pastry making were often well-guarded family secrets. Many a reputation rose or fell on the excellence of a pie or the delicacy of a tart.

Yet there really are no special secrets to good pastry. Confidence and a light hand are the main ingredients, but patience, an uncluttered workspace, and good equipment will help tremendously.

This chapter is based on five doughs, each used for a different purpose. Beginners should start with the Fast Pie Crust and work their way through to the Quick Puff Pastry. Using the processor, doughs take only a few seconds to prepare and fillings are also mixed, sliced, or chopped in a fraction of the usual time.

THE "PULSE-AND-CLUMP" METHOD FOR PASTRY DOUGHS

Measure flour in dry-measure cups, sweeping them level with a spatula or the back of a knife. No sifting is required. Be sure that butter is chilled (not frozen), and other ingredients are on hand.

Most of the doughs are processed by what I call the "pulse-and-clump" method. This method, only for dough that does not contain egg, uses half-second pulses to cut the shortening thoroughly into the flour until it disappears. The pulses duplicate the action of a pastry blender or two knives. Processing is finished when dough begins to clump or hold together in pieces about the size of walnuts—at this point, remove blade and dump contents of the container onto plastic wrap. Press dough together and chill thoroughly before rolling.

The advantage of using the pulse-and-clump method is that doughs stay cool, chill quickly, and tend not to become overworked, thus minimizing toughness. Pulse-and-clump combines dough more evenly than straight processing because stopping the motor allows the ingredients to fall down off the sides of container and back onto the blades.

Flour varies from place to place and season to season and will affect the texture of the doughs. As a rule, it is better to have a dough too wet than too dry, because additional flour can be worked in during rolling. Use smallest amount of liquid specified in recipes, processing as directed. If dough does not "clump" properly, add remaining liquid and process with 3 to 5 half-second pulses or until dough clumps. Do not add additional flour to container unless dough is so wet that it resembles putty.

TIPS FOR ROLLING OUT DOUGH

Before rolling dough, clean off an ample work space. Any clean dry surface—wood, formica, or a kitchen tabletop—will suffice. A table is always preferable to a kitchen counter since it is lower and good leverage is needed to roll dough easily.

Because these doughs tend to be softer and wetter than normal, they should be easier to roll. However, they will require slightly more flour than usual: begin with at least 2 tablespoons flour under dough and 1 to 2 tablespoons over dough. Because too much flour toughens dough, use a soft, dry pastry brush to completely brush off excess flour after rolling. Do not use a brush that previously has been dipped in oil or barbecue sauce, however.

If dough cracks apart—this is a common syndrome in centrally air-conditioned kitchens—simply moisten your hands with cold water and work it quickly into the dough. Chill 10 minutes; reroll.

Begin in the center of the dough and roll outward, as quickly as possible. Many cooks forget to do this and end up with dough of varying thickness. Work quickly but without hurrying and begin in the center. Roll outward in each direction—away from and towards your body, right and left. Quickly run your palm over the surface of the dough to feel for "hills and valleys"; reroll as necessary to even dough. Above all, don't fuss over dough or work it so hard that it becomes warm.

SOME HELPFUL EQUIPMENT FOR PASTRY MAKING

Rolling pin: It is good to have a smooth, nontapering, heavy wooden rolling pin at least 19 inches (48 cm) long. I prefer the wooden cylinder type without ball bearings or handles because it gives me a better feel for the dough.

Ruler and pastry brushes: A ruler will help to eliminate guesswork. A small round brush is useful for applying egg and water glazes; a large one (2 inches [5 cm] wide is best) for removing excess flour.

Metal tart and pie pans: I prefer metal, especially aluminum, pans to glass because metal is a better heat conductor and as a result pastry is crisper. I have found that black-finish pans work especially well. The loose-bottom tart or quiche pan is inexpensive and can be found in specialty cookware stores.

Pie weights: Metal pie weights, uncooked rice or beans may be used to weight crusts which are baked blind (weights replace filling to preserve shape of dough). Save them in a jar for reuse.

Other useful equipment includes a sharp paring knife for trimming and a fluted ravioli cutter for crimping and sealing edges. A plastic pastry scraper also will be handy for cleaning work surfaces.

FAST PIE CRUST
Makes crust for one 9-inch (23-cm) pie

This very soft dough is especially easy to roll and shape. Use when recipe specifies a single pie crust. This may also be baked completely until golden brown, usually 25 to 30 minutes.

1¼ cups (180 g) unbleached all-purpose flour
½ cup (60 g) cake flour
2 tablespoons sugar
½ teaspoon salt
⅔ cup (1½ dL) vegetable shortening
¼ to ⅓ cup (½ to ¾ dL) cold milk

1. Insert the *metal knife blade.* Place unbleached flour, cake flour, sugar, salt, and shortening in container. Process with half-second pulses until shortening disappears. Add milk to container and process to mix dough thoroughly with half-second pulses, or until dough begins to clump. Gather dough together into a ball and wrap in plastic. Refrigerate 1 hour.

2. Adjust oven rack to middle position. Heat oven to 350° F (175° C). Generously flour work surface and dough, using 3 to 4 tablespoons (30 g) flour. Roll out dough to a 13-inch (32-cm) circle. Loosen from work surface and carefully roll up on rolling pin. Unroll over a 9-inch pie plate, working carefully as dough is brittle. If dough crumbles, add a tablespoon or two of milk, reroll and replace in pie plate.

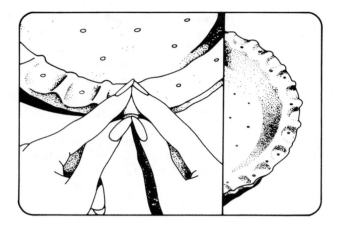

3. Trim dough to ¼ inch (¾ cm) beyond plate rim. Turn edges under, doubling dough along rim. Dough will crack: push together and flute rim of crust. Flatten bottom and sides gently against pie plate. With a skewer, pierce bottom and rim of crust at even intervals. Refrigerate 10 minutes to firm. Bake 15 minutes. Cool. Crust is partially baked and ready to fill.

CUSTARD PIE
Makes 6 to 8 servings

Custard Pie is an old-fashioned favorite. The coconut variation is best with freshly shredded coconut. Freeze remaining coconut for another use or extract and freeze coconut milk for Curry (see page 70).

Fast Pie Crust, page 144, partially baked
3 eggs
2 egg yolks
¼ cup (50 g) sugar
1 teaspoon vanilla extract
Dash cinnamon
1½ cups (3½ dL) whipping cream
Whipped cream, for garnish

1. Prepare pie crust. Adjust oven rack to middle position. Heat oven to 350° F (175° C). Insert the *metal knife blade.* Place eggs and egg yolks in the container. Process to mix 5 seconds. With machine running, pour sugar through food chute within 15 seconds; scrape down sides of container. Process 10 seconds longer; add vanilla and cinnamon. With machine, pour cream through food chute within 40 seconds.

2. Pour contents of container into pie crust. Bake 35 to 40 minutes, until top is browned and filling is set in the center. Cool thoroughly. Serve chilled or at room temperature, garnished with whipped cream.

Variation:

Coconut Custard Pie
Prepare ¾ cup (1¾ dL) fresh shredded coconut (consult food chart, page 164). Before pouring custard mixture into pie crust in Step 2, sprinkle ½ cup (1 dL) coconut on bottom of crust. Add filling and top with remaining coconut. Continue as recipe directs.

PUMPKIN-PECAN PIE
Makes 6 to 8 servings

Recycle your Halloween pumpkin by cooking, puréeing, and freezing it for this pie or for Pumpkin-Yogurt Mousse, page 161.

Fast Pie Crust, page 144, partially baked

Topping:

¾ cup (3 oz./85 g) whole shelled pecans
3 tablespoons (45 g) butter, slightly softened
2 tablespoons dark brown sugar

Filling:

2 cups (½ L) pureed cooked pumpkin
⅔ cup (126 g) packed dark brown sugar
⅓ cup (65 g) granulated sugar
2 teaspoons ground cinnamon
1 teaspoon ground ginger
½ teaspoon ground nutmeg
¼ teaspoon ground cloves
¼ teaspoon ground mace
3 eggs
1 cup (¼ L) whipping cream
¼ cup (½ dL) milk
¼ cup (½ dL) bourbon or rum

1. Prepare pie crust. Adjust oven rack to middle position. Heat oven to to 350° F (175° C).

2. To prepare topping, insert the *metal knife blade.* Process to chop pecans with 4 one-sec-

ond pulses; set aside. Cut butter in 3 pieces and add to container with brown sugar. Process to mix 10 seconds; scrape down container sides. Add chopped pecans and mix with 2 one-second pulses; refrigerate until ready to use.

3. To prepare filling, return *metal knife blade* to container. Place pumpkin, brown sugar, granulated sugar, cinnamon, ginger, nutmeg, cloves, and mace in container. Process to mix 5 seconds; scrape down container sides. Add eggs, cream, milk, and bourbon. Process to mix 10 seconds; scrape down container sides; process 5 seconds.

4. Pour filling into partially baked crust. Bake 35 minutes. Remove pie from oven and spoon topping around rim. Return pie to oven and bake 25 minutes longer, until a knife inserted in the center of the custard is withdrawn clean. Cool. Serve chilled or at room temperature.

DOUBLE-CRUST PIE DOUGH

Makes top and bottom crusts for one 9-inch (23-cm) pie

Here is a perfect example of the pulse-and-clump method to be used for flaky pastry (and *pâte brisée*). Use this dough for any 9-inch double-crust pie.

¼ lb. plus 2 tablespoons (5 oz./145 g) chilled unsalted butter
2 cups (285 g) unbleached all-purpose flour
¼ teaspoon salt
⅓ to ½ cup (¾ to 1 dL) ice cold water

1. Cut the stick of butter in half and insert the pieces upright from underneath food chute. Attach the *medium slicing disk.* Slice with a moderate push; repeat to slice remaining butter. Move butter pieces to 1 side of container and insert the *metal knife blade.* Add flour and salt to container. Process with half-second pulses until butter disappears. Add water and process with half-second pulses, or until water is absorbed and dough begins to clump.

2. Press dough together, wrap in plastic and refrigerate until firm, about 45 minutes to 1 hour.

3. To roll out the bottom crust, generously flour a work surface and half the dough. Roll out this half to a 13-inch (32-cm) circle. Loosen dough carefully from work surface and roll up on the rolling pin. Unroll over a 9-inch pie plate. Fill as desired.

4. To roll out the top crust, generously flour work surface and remaining half of dough. Roll out dough to a 13-inch circle. Carefully loosen dough from work surface and brush off excess flour. Roll up on rolling pin. Unroll over pie.

5. To prepare pie for baking, trim both crusts to ¼ inch (¾ cm) beyond pie plate rim. To seal, dip a fork into flour and press around rim. Trim crust to slightly beyond pie plate rim (it will shrink slightly as it bakes). Glaze and bake as directed in pie recipe.

OLD-FASHIONED APPLE PIE

Makes 8 to 10 servings

Dry bread crumbs do a marvelous job of absorbing fruit juices so that the bottom crust stays crisp and dry.

Double-Crust Pie Dough (preceeding)
3 lbs. (1,350 g) Granny Smith or other tart green apples, peeled, quartered, cored
¾ cup (145 g) sugar
½ teaspoon cinnamon
⅛ teaspoon nutmeg
1 tablespoon brandy or dark rum
1 tablespoon fresh lemon juice
¼ cup (½ dL) dry bread crumbs
2 tablespoons (30 g) chilled butter, cut into ½-inch dice
Cold water
Egg Glaze, page 5

1. Follow pie dough recipe through Step 3.

2. Insert the *medium slicing disk.* Place apple quarters sideways in food chute and slice with a moderate push. Repeat until all apples are sliced, emptying container into a bowl as necessary.

3. Change to the *metal knife blade.* Mix sugar, cinnamon, nutmeg, brandy, and lemon juice with 4 two-second on/off turns or pulses. Add

sugar mixture to apple slices in bowl. Toss well.

4. Adjust oven rack to middle position. Heat oven to 350° F (175° C). Spread bread crumbs over bottom pie crust. Add apples and arrange in a high mound, using all apples. Place butter cubes over apples. Brush edge of crust lightly with cold water. Roll out top crust and seal as directed in Steps 4 and 5 of pie dough recipe.

5. Cut an X in center of top crust to form a vent. Prepare Egg Glaze and brush over top of crust. Bake until golden brown, about 1 hour 10 minutes. Cool to room temperature before serving.

PASTRY SCALLOP SHELLS
Makes 8 servings

A flaky pie dough works surprisingly well for these lovely pastry shells, which may be prepared several hours in advance and set aside at room temperature.

Use for Coquilles St. Jacques Nouvelles, page 55, or fill with fresh fruit, such as strawberries, and top with Raspberry Sauce, page 162. For a sublime *Pêche Melba,* brush shells with strained apricot jam, fill with a fresh poached peach, vanilla ice cream, and top with raspberry sauce.

Double-Crust Pie Dough (preceding page)

1. Prepare dough recipe through Step 2.

2. Divide dough in half. On a generously floured work surface, roll out half the dough to a 15-inch (38½-cm) circle. Cut circle into quarters. Loosen each piece from work surface and place over the rounded back of a natural scallop shell. Press dough gently onto shell. Place a second shell over dough and press gently to mold. Trim off excess dough even with bottom shell. Place shells on a baking sheet, rounded sides up. Cover and refrigerate 15 minutes. Repeat to roll out and mold remaining dough.

3. Adjust oven rack to middle position. Heat oven to 350° F (175° C). Uncover and bake 1 baking sheet of shells at a time for 35 minutes. Cool 15 minutes; remove top shells. Cool pas-

try shells to lukewarm and invert carefully to unmold; set aside until ready to use. Repeat to bake remaining dough.

LATTICE PIE CRUST DOUGH
Makes top and bottom for one 9-inch (23-cm) pie

Butter and shortening are combined here to produce a sturdy dough that is especially easy to handle. Cutting and weaving the lattice strips is fortunately more difficult to explain than to execute.

Fruits such as peaches, nectarines, and cherries also make good lattice-top pies.

2¼ cups (330 g) unbleached all-purpose flour
¼ teaspoon salt
¼ cup (½ dL) vegetable shortening
¼ lb. (115 g) chilled unsalted butter, cut into ½-inch chunks
⅓ to ½ cup (¾ to 1 dL) ice cold water
Additional cold water

1. Insert the *metal knife blade.* Place flour, salt, shortening, and butter in container. Process with half-second pulses until butter and shortening disappear. Add water to container and repeat processing with half-second pulses until dough begins to clump. Gather dough together and wrap in plastic. Refrigerate 1 hour.

2. To roll bottom crust, generously flour work surface and dough. Roll out two-thirds of the dough to a 13-inch (32-cm) circle. Loosen from work surface and carefully roll up on rolling pin. Unroll over a 9-inch pie plate. Trim to 1 inch (2½ cm) beyond pie plate rim.

3. Add pie filling and refrigerate until ready to place lattice top on pie.

4. To roll and cut lattice strips, generously flour work surface. Roll out remaining third of dough to a 14- × 7-inch (35- × 18-cm) rectangle. Trim to 12 × 6 inches (30 × 15 cm). Mark top and bottom of shorter edge every ½ inch (1½ cm). With a fluted ravioli cutter or sharp knife guided by a ruler, cut twelve 12- × ½-inch strips for lattice top. You have 2 extra strips for repairs. Loosen strips from work surface with a metal spatula. (Illustration follows)

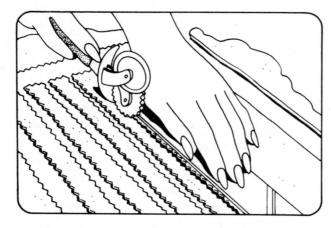

Lattice Pie Crust Dough, page 147
2 pints (1 L) fresh blueberries, rinsed, drained
¾ cup (145 g) sugar
¼ cup (½ dL) water
2 tablespoons instant tapioca
1 tablespoon fresh lemon juice
1 tablespoon vodka
¼ cup (½ dL) dry bread crumbs
Egg Glaze, page 5

1. Prepare dough through Step 2.

2. Insert the *metal knife blade.* Purée 1 cup (¼ L) blueberries by processing 10 to 15 seconds; set aside. Combine sugar, water, and tapioca in a medium saucepan. Stir over low heat until thickened and reduced to ½ cup (1 dL). Stir in lemon juice, vodka, and blueberry purée. Cover and set aside off heat.

3. Adjust oven rack to middle position. Heat oven to 350° F (175° C). Spread bread crumbs in bottom of pie crust. Mix blueberry mixture with remaining whole berries; add to crust.

4. Proceed with Steps 4 and 5 of dough recipe to cut out and weave lattice strips. Brush strips with glaze. Bake 1 hour 10 minutes, until golden brown. Cool to room temperature before slicing.

5. Place filled bottom crust on work surface; brush rim lightly with cold water. Space 5 strips evenly across the pie. Working left to right, secure each strip by pinching it onto the rim of the crust, but only on one end. Repeat with 5 more strips, placed at right angles to form a grid. Weave each horizontal strip alternately over and under vertical strips. Press down all loose ends to attach them to bottom crust. Press all around to thin rim slightly. Trim to ½ inch beyond edge of pie plate. Brush again lightly with cold water; then turn up overhanging dough. To seal, dip a fork into flour and press around rim. Bake according to instructions for pie filling.

BLUEBERRY LATTICE PIE
Makes 6 to 8 servings

Instant tapioca provides just enough thickening to give this filling a great consistency; the vodka (which is optional) adds punch.

PINEAPPLE LATTICE PIE
Makes 6 to 8 servings

This pie is surprisingly creamy with a sweet taste totally unlike a pineapple pie made with canned fruit.

The core is removed from the pineapple by cutting it apart, using the method for decorative slices on page 14 (upper left illustration). The short french-fry segments are perfect for pie filling, but pineapple may be sliced with the *medium* or *thick slicing disk,* then cut crosswise into slivers with a cleaver or chef's knife.

Lattice Pie Crust Dough, page 147
1 slice (1 oz./30 g) dry white bread, crusts removed or ⅓ cup (¾ dL) dry bread crumbs
3 tablespoons sugar
1 fresh ripe pineapple (3½ to 4 lbs./1½ kg), peeled, cored

1 tablespoon fresh lemon juice
1 cup (200 g) packed dark brown sugar
2 tablespoons vodka
3 tablespoons (45 g) butter
Egg Glaze, page 5

1. Prepare pie crust dough through Step 2.

2. Insert the *metal knife blade.* Process bread with sugar until fine crumbs form; remove to waxed paper. Change to the *french-fry disk.* Cut pineapple to fit food chute and process each piece with a firm push; reserve all juice. Measure 4 cups (1 L) pineapple chunks and transfer them to a large strainer or colander set over a bowl. Press gently to extract juice. There should be almost 1 cup (¼ L).

3. Place the juice in a medium nonaluminum saucepan. Add lemon juice, ½ cup (100 g) of the brown sugar, and the vodka. Heat to simmering, taking care mixture does not boil over. Simmer, stirring occasionally, until liquid reduces to ½ cup (1 dL). Add additional juice from draining pineapple to saucepan from time to time. Stir the butter into the hot reduced liquid and set aside for butter to melt.

4. Adjust oven rack to middle position. Heat oven to 375° F (190° C). Spread bread crumb mixture in bottom of pie crust. In a bowl, mix pineapple chunks with remaining brown sugar; then add the juice mixture to the pineapple and toss quickly. Spread pineapple mixture evenly in bottom of pie crust; pack gently.

5. Proceed with Steps 4 and 5 of dough recipe to cut out and weave lattice strips. Brush strips with glaze. Bake until golden brown, about 1 hour 10 minutes. Cool to room temperature before slicing.

WHOLE WHEAT TART CRUST
Dough for one 10-inch (25-cm) tart

The beauty of this dough lies in the nutlike taste of whole wheat and the extra nutrition it offers. The hard-boiled egg yolk adds tenderness and helps to create the consistency of a butter cookie when baked; in fact leftover dough makes nice cookies. Cooks who are not particularly adept with doughs will find this one (as well as the plain variation) easy to handle and patch. Without the lemon rind, sugar and cinnamon, this dough may be used for quiches.

Rind of 1 medium lemon
4 tablespoons (50 g) sugar
Pinch cinnamon
¼ cup (25 g) cake flour
1¼ cups (194 g) whole wheat flour
1 hard-boiled egg yolk
¼ lb. (115 g) chilled unsalted butter, cut into ½-inch chunks
1 raw egg yolk

1. Insert the *metal knife blade* in the processor container. Strip off the rind of the lemon with a vegetable peeler, allowing the strips to fall into the container. Add sugar and cinnamon and process until rind is ground very fine, about 45 seconds. Add cake flour, whole wheat flour, and hard-boiled egg yolk. Process to mix with 4 one-second pulses. Add butter and raw egg yolk. Process until dough begins to clump, usually about 20 seconds. Wrap and refrigerate dough 1 hour.

2. Place 2 overlapping sheets of waxed paper on work surface. Unwrap and place dough in center; cover with 2 additional overlapping waxed paper sheets. Roll out dough to a 14-inch (35-cm) circle. Remove top layer of waxed paper.

3. Place a 10-inch, fluted, loose-bottom, quiche or tart pan nearby on work surface. Grasping bottom waxed paper, lift and carefully invert dough over pan. Peel off waxed paper; carefully press dough into pan. Trim so that top edge of dough is even with pan rim. Dough sometimes can be troublesome to roll as flour varies from season to season. If it sticks to waxed paper it is too warm; refrigerate 10 minutes. If very crumbly, break apart and return dough to processor container fitted with *metal knife blade.* Cut 2 tablespoons butter into small dice; add to dough and use half-second pulses until dough begins to clump. Wrap and refrigerate 30 minutes; reroll as directed. Patch crust as necessary with excess dough; discard remainder or keep for cookies.

4. Wrap tart pan loosely and refrigerate 2 hours or freeze 30 minutes to harden dough. Adjust

oven rack to middle position. Heat oven to 375° F (190° C). Line hardened dough with a sheet of lightweight aluminum foil, shiny side down. Press foil smoothly onto dough and mold to fit contours of crust. Fill to brim with rice, beans, or metal pie weights. Bake 15 minutes. Cool 5 minutes. Remove weighting material and foil. Return crust to oven and bake 5 minutes longer; cool. Crust is partially baked and ready to fill.

Variation:

All-Purpose Tart and Quiche Crust
Omit lemon rind, sugar, and cinnamon. Substitute 1½ cups (185 g) unbleached all-purpose flour for whole wheat flour and 1 large raw whole egg for the raw egg yolk.

LEMON AND WHOLE WHEAT TART
Makes 8 servings

A tart in which the filling and the pastry play equally important roles may come as a surprise to those familiar with French fruit tarts. It is an exciting new idea (promulgated by many of the younger French chefs) because it places increased emphasis on the pastry—the most challenging part of the preparation.

Take special care to roll the dough evenly and to the specified size. When liquid, the filling will completely fill the partially baked tart shell; it will shrink significantly when baked.

Whole Wheat Tart Crust (preceding page),
   partially baked
¼ cup (½ dL) apricot preserves
2 small lemons
½ cup (110 g) sugar
3 eggs
Powdered sugar, for garnish
Whipped cream, for garnish

1. Set tart crust aside to cool. Stir preserves in a small saucepan over low heat until melted; strain. Brush 2 tablespoons strained preserves over bottom and sides of crust; set aside.

2. Insert the *metal knife blade*. Using a vegetable peeler, strip off the rind of 1 lemon, letting the strips fall into the processor container. Add 3 tablespoons sugar and process until rind is very fine; set aside. Completely peel both lemons, removing and discarding bitter white pith and remaining peel. Quarter and place lemons in container. Process about 40 seconds until completely puréed. Strain and reserve ⅓ cup (¾ dL) lemon juice; use remainder for another purpose.

3. Adjust oven rack to middle position. Heat oven to 375° F (190° C). Wipe out container. Process eggs with ⅓ cup (¾ dL) lemon juice until pale. Add rind-sugar mixture to container. With machine running, add remaining sugar through food chute within 20 seconds; scrape down container sides and process 2 minutes.

4. Pour contents of container into crust. Bake 20 to 25 minutes, until puffed and brown. Cool; remove pan ring before serving. Garnish with powdered sugar and pass whipped cream, if desired.

ALSATIAN APRICOT TART
Makes 8 servings

Made in the style of fruit tarts popular in the French province of Alsace, this pastry contains a light cream cheese custard with which lightly cooked fruit, such as apricots, cherries, plums, or peaches, may be baked; and in that sense it is the sweet counterpart of a quiche. Sugar has not been overlooked in the custard ingredients but purposely omitted—the sweetness of the jam glaze suffices.

Whole Wheat Tart Crust (preceding page),
   partially baked
1½ lbs. (675 g) fresh Poached Apricots, recipe
   follows, or 1 can (1 lb. 12 oz./790 g) apricots,
   drained
1 cup (¼ L) apricot preserves
2 teaspoons Grand Marnier
2 oz. (60 g) cream cheese, room temperature
Pinch cinnamon
Dash nutmeg
¾ cup (1¾ dL) whipping cream
1 egg
1 egg yolk

1. Cool tart crust. Halve and pit apricots; drain well on paper toweling. Place preserves and 1 teaspoon Grand Marnier in a small saucepan. Stir over low heat until preserves melt; strain into a bowl. Brush 2 tablespoons strained preserves over the crust to glaze, and set remainder aside.

2. Insert *metal knife blade.* Process cream cheese, cinnamon, and nutmeg until smooth; scrape down sides of container. Add cream, egg, and egg yolk and remaining Grand Marnier. Process to mix with 3 half-second pulses; do not process longer.

3. Adjust oven rack to middle position. Heat oven to 375° F (190° C). Slowly pour half the cream mixture into the glazed crust. Place apricot halves neatly into crust with rounded sides up. Carefully add remaining cream mixture around apricots so that the tops of apricots show after cream is added. Bake 35 minutes, until puffed and lightly browned. Cool to room temperature.

4. Reheat remaining strained preserves and brush or spread with back of spoon evenly over top of tart. Chill. To remove baked tart from pan, center bottom on a wide-mouth jar or bowl and let ring fall away.

Poached Apricots:

3 qts. (3 L) cold water
1 cup (190 g) sugar
1 teaspoon vanilla extract
1½ lbs. (675 g) fresh apricots

Combine water, sugar and vanilla in a 6-quart (6-L) soup kettle. Stir well. Add apricots. Set cover ajar and poach until apricots are tender when pierced with a knife. Do not allow liquid to simmer. In season, apricots will be poached in 5 to 6 minutes. Peel if skins are very thick. Cool and refrigerate apricots in their poaching liquid; drain before using.

Variation:

Alsatian Cherry Tart
Substitute 1 pound (450 g) fresh poached pitted Bing cherries for apricots. Use 2 teaspoons kirsch or brandy for Grand Marnier and 1 cup (¼ L) red currant jelly for apricot preserves.

QUICK PUFF PASTRY
Makes 1 to 1¼ pounds (500 g)

Puff pastry, that gorgeous dough layered, leavened, and bronzed by butter, is one of the pillars of the French pastry repertory. Traditionally, it has been difficult and time consuming to execute, and, until recently, it remained the province of advanced cooks.

Quick Puff Pastry takes about 2 hours to prepare. It is a small quantity designed for limited use with my fruit tart and *chaussons* (turnovers) because the dough is only turned 4 times. (Most recipes require the dough to be turned 6 to 8 times.) However, it is the easiest and one of the tidiest recipes I know—the dough (called the *détrempe*) is mixed in the processor and the butter for the filling is processor sliced and assembled directly on the rolled-out dough. While this is a traditional "quick" approach, using the processor to slice chilled (but *not* frozen) butter for puff pastry is especially convenient.

Both the flour and butter used in puff pastry are extremely important. I use unbleached all-purpose flour (substitute bread flour if unbleached is not available) cut with a small amount of cake flour for tenderness and easy handling. The finest quality unsalted butter (I use Land O'Lakes) with the least amount of moisture is best for puff pastry. In France, pastry chefs buy a special butter that is so hard (low in moisture) that when chilled it is difficult to pierce with a knife! A good "moisture test" for a stick of chilled butter is to snap it in half with your hands—good, firm butter will be very resistant; softer butter will snap in half easily and have a grainy, rather than a dense and smooth, interior texture.

I hope that everyone will try this puff pastry and go on to use it (increasing the turns to 6 or 8) for other recipes as well.

1¼ cups (180 g) unbleached all-purpose flour
(see page 5) or bread flour
½ cup (60 g) cake flour
¼ teaspoon salt
½ lb. (225 g) unsalted butter, chilled
⅓ to ½ cup (¾ to 1 dL) ice cold water

1. Insert the *metal knife blade.* Process to rapid-sift unbleached flour, cake flour, and salt with 2 five-second pulses. Add to container 4 tablespoons butter, first cut into 4 pieces. Pro-

cess with half-second pulses until butter disappears. Add water to container and process with half-second pulses until dough begins to clump. Gather dough together and wrap in plastic. Refrigerate 40 minutes.

2. Halve the remaining stick of butter crosswise. Turn lid over and insert pieces side by side from underneath food chute. Change to the *medium slicing disk*. Replace lid and add remaining butter to food chute from top. Slice with a moderate push; refrigerate.

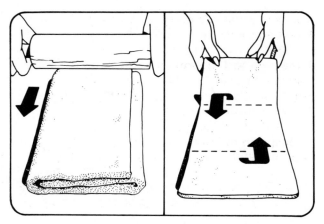

3. Generously flour work surface. Roll out dough to a 16- × 10-inch (40- × 25-cm) rectangle, adding only enough flour to keep dough from sticking. Remove any excess flour from dough with a dry pastry brush. With 1 short end of dough facing you, place butter slices over upper two-thirds of dough in close rows with edges touching. Begin 1½ inches (4 cm) from top and leave a 1½-inch border on each side. Do not place butter on bottom third of dough and work as quickly as possible. Fold up bottom third of dough over center portion. Brush off excess flour. Fold top third down like a business letter. Brush off excess flour. Wrap and refrigerate dough 20 minutes.

4. Working on same lightly floured work surface, place dough seam side up with one short end facing you. Roll out dough to a 16- × 10-inch rectangle, keeping edges as straight and even as possible. If butter oozes through, patch with flour and refrigerate 10 minutes. Brush off excess flour. Fold in thirds like a business letter. Wrap and refrigerate; first turn is completed.

5. After 20 minutes, repeat Step 4 to make 2

consecutive turns without refrigerating dough in between unless it becomes soft and butter oozes through. Rewrap and refrigerate 20 minutes.

6. Repeat Step 4 to make final (fourth) turn. Refrigerate dough 20 minutes. It may then be shaped, refrigerated overnight to shape the following day, or frozen. If refrigerated longer than 1 hour, bring to a workable texture by placing it at room temperature 20 to 30 minutes.

FRENCH APPLE TART
Makes 8 to 10 servings

There is a professional look to this long, rectangular tart, which is adapted from the type French pastry shops cut apart and sell by the piece. The difference is in the placement of the fruit slices, which here are set overlapping along the length of the dough rather than crosswise to yield a larger number of servings than would otherwise be possible.

The tart is not as difficult as it might seem, and the preparation may be done in several stages, as indicated in the recipe.

Quick Puff Pastry (preceding page)

Walnut Filling:

¼ **cup (1 oz./30 g) whole shelled walnuts**
1½ **tablespoons unbleached flour**
1½ **tablespoons butter, slightly softened**
2 **tablespoons sugar**
½ **teaspoon brandy**

¼ **teaspoon vanilla extract**
1 **raw egg yolk**

3 **medium tart green apples or small firm ripe**
    pears, peeled
Egg Glaze, page 5
2 **to 3 tablespoons sugar**
½ **cup (1 dL) apricot preserves**
1 **teaspoon brandy**

1. Prepare puff pastry. Line a baking sheet with waxed paper; set aside. Generously flour work surface and dough. Place dough seam side up with short end facing you. Roll out dough to a 16- × 9-inch (40- × 23-cm) rectangle. With a sharp knife or plain ravioli wheel guided by a ruler, trim to 14 × 8 inches (35 × 20 cm). Remove excess flour with a dry pastry brush. Place trimmed dough rectangle on waxed paper; refrigerate 10 minutes. Save scraps for Palmiers (page 155), if desired.

2. Place baking sheet on work surface. With a knife or ravioli wheel guided by a ruler, cut off a 1-inch-wide (2½-cm) strip from each long side of dough rectangle, cutting through waxed paper. Do not remove from baking sheet. Cover and refrigerate 30 minutes.

3. Slide waxed paper with dough onto work surface. Rinse baking sheet with cold water. Turn largest piece of dough over and onto center of wet baking sheet. Peel off and discard wax paper; brush off excess flour. This piece is the base of the tart. The dough strips will form raised borders.

4. To set borders in place on the base, use a wet pastry brush or your finger dipped in cold water to slightly moisten a 1½-inch (4-cm)-wide margin on each long edge of dough base. Remove dough strips from waxed paper. Turn strips over and place 1 on each side of base, matching outside edges perfectly. Brush off excess flour. Refrigerate 10 minutes.

5. To be sure raised borders bake evenly, use the tip of a sharp knife to cut into the base along the inside of each raised border, being careful to cut no more than halfway through the base. Lightly crisscross the center of the base between the two incisions, leaving 1 inch between each crisscross mark.

6. With the knife tip, make shallow straight

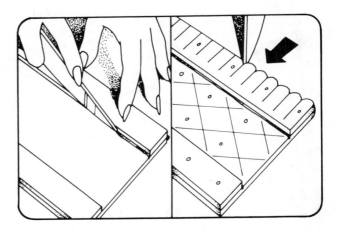

lines ¼ inch (¾ cm) apart across each border. Use a trussing needle or sharp toothpick to pierce the surface of the tart, including borders, every 2 inches (5 cm). To seal borders to base and scallop edges of tart, push the back of a paring knife into outside edge of borders every ¼ inch where top of border is marked with shallow lines. Cover with plastic wrap and refrigerate 20 minutes or up to 5 hours. Tart is now shaped and ready to be filled.

7. To prepare walnut filling, insert the *metal knife blade*. Process walnuts with flour until finely ground; remove to waxed paper. Process butter and sugar 10 seconds; scrape down sides of container. Add brandy, vanilla, egg yolk, and walnut mixture. Process with 5 half-second pulses to mix thoroughly. Refrigerate or freeze until ready to use.

8. Change to the *medium slicing disk* and clean the container. Make decorative slices (page 14, upper left illustration), processing apple pieces with a moderate push; they may discolor slightly.

9. Adjust oven rack to middle position. Heat oven to 425° F (220° C). To fill the tart shell, carefully brush Egg Glaze over the tops of the borders and over crisscrossed section of base. Take special care *not* to coat scalloped outside edges or incisions in base along insides or borders with egg mixture or pastry will not rise properly. Spoon walnut filling mixture down the center of the tart, leaving a 1-inch space between filling and border strips and a 1-inch margin at each end of base. Completely fill base with apples by placing slices, neatly overlapping, on top of walnut filling. Fill with fruit to ends of base. Sprinkle sugar over fruit. Refrigerate 15 minutes. (Illustration follows)

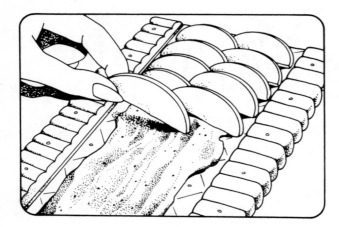

10. Just before baking, brush Egg Glaze again over tops of marked borders. Bake 15 minutes. Reduce heat to 350° F (175° C). Bake 15 minutes longer, until golden brown. Cool 10 minutes on baking sheet. Remove and cool to room temperature on a cake rack. Tart may then be left at room temperature for an hour or two before glazing.

11. Stir preserves with brandy in a small saucepan over low heat until melted; strain. Brush hot strained preserves over fruit slices. Set tart aside at room temperature until ready to serve, as long as 8 hours if desired.

CHEESE AND RAISIN CHAUSSONS
Makes 9 turnovers

Turnovers or *chaussons* filled with a luscious white cheese and raisin filling make a spectacular finale for a festive brunch. If filled with fruit, such as thinly sliced apples (first cooked in butter with a pinch of cinnamon and a dash of Calvados or brandy), lightly poached peaches, cherries, prunes, or plums, they work well for a lunch or an informal dinner. If prepared in advance, store in an airtight tin first lined with aluminum foil, and warm before serving.

Quick Puff Pastry, page 151

Filling:

5 oz. (145 g) cream cheese, room temperature, cut into 1-inch chunks

¼ cup (50 g) sugar
⅔ cup (6 oz./180 g) ricotta cheese, kneaded gently in cloth towel
Pinch powdered ginger
1 raw egg yolk
⅓ cup (2 oz./60 g) seedless raisins

Cold water
Egg Glaze, page 5

1. Prepare Quick Puff Pastry.

2. Cut out a cardboard circle 5 inches (13 cm) in diameter for a pattern; set aside. Generously flour work surface. Roll out dough to a 16-inch (40-cm) square. Using the cardboard circle, cut out 9 dough circles with a sharp knife. Remove excess flour from circles with a pastry brush. Turn circles over and brush off any excess flour. Place circles on baking sheet, bottoms up. Cover and refrigerate 20 minutes. Save scraps for Palmiers (recipe follows).

3. To prepare filling, insert the *metal knife blade*. Process cream cheese 5 seconds. With machine running, add sugar through food chute within 10 seconds. Process 5 seconds longer; scrape down the sides of container. Add ricotta cheese, ginger, and egg yolk to container. Process 15 seconds; scrape down container sides. Mix in raisins with 2 half-second pulses.

4. On lightly floured work surface, roll out each dough circle to 6 inches (15 cm) in diameter. Brush lightly with cold water. Place 2 (heaping) tablespoons filling in center. Fold circles in half over filling, matching edges evenly; press firmly. To seal, dip a fork in flour and press around edges. Pierce top of each turnover twice with a skewer or toothpick. Place turnovers on 2 baking sheets. Refrigerate uncovered 10 minutes. At this point, turnovers may be covered with plastic and refrigerated as long as overnight, or they may be individually wrapped in plastic and then double-wrapped in foil and frozen for as long as two weeks. If frozen, thaw in refrigerator before baking.

5. Adjust oven rack to middle position. Heat oven to 425° F (220° C). Just before baking, brush each turnover with glaze. Bake 1 sheet at a time, 25 to 30 minutes, until turnovers are puffy and browned. Cool 1 hour before serving.

PALMIERS
Makes 2 to 3 dozen

Crisp and sugary, these cookies make a lovely garnish for ice cream. Store in aluminum foil rather than plastic to prevent them from becoming sticky.

3 tablespoons (36 g) sugar
Scraps from Quick Puff Pastry (page 151), about 5 oz. (145 g)

1. Cover puff pastry scraps and refrigerate until ready to make cookies.

2. Sprinkle work surface with 1 tablespoon sugar. Lay scraps side by side over sugar with edges touching; gently press together to form 1 piece of dough. Sprinkle 1 tablespoon sugar over dough. Roll to a 16- × 5-inch (40- × 13-cm) rectangle. Place rolled dough with short end facing you and make a turn, folding dough in thirds like a business letter. Cover and refrigerate 15 minutes.

3. Sprinkle work surface with 1 tablespoon sugar. Place dough seam side up with short end facing you. Roll out dough to a 12- × 8-inch (25- × 20-cm) rectangle. Fold long sides of rectangle lengthwise, so edges meet in center. Fold dough in half lengthwise. Cover and refrigerate 15 minutes.

4. Place folded dough on work surface with long side facing you. Cut crosswise into ¼-inch (¾-cm) pieces. Refrigerate unwrapped for 20 minutes, or wrap and refrigerate overnight. Adjust oven rack to middle position. Heat oven to 400° F (205° C). Place dough pieces flat, 3 inches (8 cm) apart on baking sheets. Bake 1 sheet at a time 6 to 7 minutes; turn cookies over and bake 5 to 6 minutes longer, until golden brown. Immediately remove from baking sheet to cake rack and cool.

18

Cakes and Desserts

When I need a dessert for a special occasion, I want something memorable or unexpected that doesn't take all day to prepare. This chapter is a collection of exactly that kind of recipe.

Soufflés without flour, mousses, sorbets, and tortes are elegant without being terribly difficult to make. Layer cake and cheesecake are rich, but practical, since they serve a large number of persons.

The food processor dispatches all the little chores like grating citrus rind, grinding nuts, puréeing fruit, and whipping cream for mousses and fillings, as well as easily mixing batters for layer and cheesecakes.

ABOUT EGG WHITES

Egg whites are needed for many of these desserts and should not be beaten in the food processor—an electric mixer or whisk is required. When beating egg whites, here are some points to remember:

- Begin with a clean, dry, grease-free beating bowl of unlined copper, stainless steel, or glass. It is best to rinse bowl and whisk or beaters with lemon water to be sure all grease is removed. Clean unlined copper bowls with lemon juice or vinegar and salt,

scrubbing until bowl is shiny; rinse and thoroughly dry.

- Bring egg whites to room temperature before beating. If any whites are left over, refrigerate in a jar with a pinch or two of cream of tartar added to keep them fresh.

- Cream of tartar or salt may be added to whites which are not beaten in a copper bowl to increase acidity and help whites to beat to greater volume.

- Soft peaks are reached when whites are creamy, opaque, and lean over lazily as they are lifted on a spatula or whisk. If recipe calls for sugar (granulated or powdered), add it to beaten egg whites only after they have reached soft peaks.

- Firm peaks are reached when beaten whites stand firmly and do not lean over when lifted on a spatula or whisk. Do not overbeat, however, or whites can become dry (dry whites have a cotton-candy–like consistency); perfectly firm egg whites still remain creamy.

Before beginning any of the chocolate desserts, it is best to consult the notes on "quick-melting" chocolate techniques to be found on page 133.

CHOCOLATE CAKE LAYERS

Makes two 9-inch (23-cm) cake layers, one 14- × 10- × 1½-inch (35- × 25- × 4-cm) sheet cake, or one dozen cupcakes

Versatile is the word for this batter which, when baked, has a fine rich chocolate taste and rises surprisingly high.

2 cups (240 g) cake flour
½ cup (50 g) unsweetened powdered cocoa
1 tablespoon baking powder
1 teaspoon baking soda
½ teaspoon salt
1 oz. (30 g) semisweet chocolate, broken into ½-inch pieces
2 eggs, room temperature
1 egg yolk, room temperature
½ cup (115 g) hot melted butter (160 to 180° F/71 to 82° C)
1¼ cups (240 g) sugar
¾ cup (1¾ dL) sour cream
¼ cup (½ dL) milk
1½ teaspoons vanilla extract

1. Adjust oven rack to middle position. Heat oven to 350° F (175° C). Cut out waxed paper to line two 9-inch (23-cm) round cake pans or a sheet-cake pan. Butter sides of cake pans and waxed paper; line pans placing paper buttered side up; set pans aside.

2. Insert the *metal knife blade.* Place cake flour, cocoa, baking powder, baking soda, and salt in container. Process to rapid-sift with 2 five-second pulses; remove to waxed paper.

3. Place semisweet chocolate in container and process until ground to consistency of small beads. Add eggs and egg yolk. With machine running, pour hot melted butter through food chute in a thin stream within 15 seconds; process 20 seconds longer. Attach funnel if desired. Process, adding sugar through food chute within 15 seconds; process 20 seconds longer and scrape down side of container.

4. Add sour cream, milk, and vanilla extract to container and process to mix with 5 half-seconds pulses. Add half the dry ingredients, processing to mix with 4 half-second pulses. Repeat processing with 4 to 6 half-second pulses, or just until dry ingredients are mixed into the batter.

5. Divide batter evenly between cake pans. Bake pans on same rack (place them diagonally in oven if necessary) 25 to 30 minutes, until a toothpick inserted into the center of each layer is withdrawn clean. Place pans on cake rack; cool 10 minutes. Invert pans to remove layers; peel off waxed paper. Place layers upright on cake rack and cool to room temperature before frosting.

CHOCOLATE FUDGE BUTTERCREAM

Frosts two 9-inch (23-cm) cake layers, one 14- × 10- × 1½-inch (35- × 25- × 4-cm) sheet cake, or one dozen cupcakes

Buttercream is not usually possible to make in the food processor but this recipe is an exception. It is fast, very rich, and rather expensive to produce because it requires a large quantity of sweet (unsalted) butter. However, it spreads and firms beautifully.

For best results, the melted butter must be bubbling hot, an exception to the usual chocolate-melting procedure. The extra heat is needed to dissolve the powdered sugar in addition to melting the chocolate.

6 oz. (180 g) semisweet chocolate, room temperature, broken into ½-inch pieces
1 teaspoon powdered instant coffee
3 tablespoons crème de cacao or brandy
¾ cup (115 g) powdered sugar
¾ cup (180 g) bubbling hot melted unsalted butter
6 oz. (180 g) slightly softened unsalted butter, cut into 1-inch chunks

1. Insert the *metal knife blade.* Place half the chocolate in the container and process until thoroughly pulverized; remove to waxed paper. Repeat to pulverize remaining chocolate and return all chocolate to container. Add powdered coffee, crème de cacao, and powdered sugar. With machine running, pour hot melted butter through food chute within 30 seconds; process 15 seconds longer and scrape down sides of container.

2. Process 30 seconds; scrape down container sides. With machine running, drop remaining

chunks of butter one at a time through food chute within 1 minute. Process until butter is completely smooth, liquid and no small bits remain, scraping down container sides as necessary.

3. Pour buttercream into a bowl. Cover and refrigerate until spreadable, checking after 30 minutes.

HAZELNUT TORTE

Makes 10 servings

Especially impressive because it has a professional pastry shop look, this torte is also convenient to serve because it can be assembled and garnished a day in advance and gains in flavor as it mellows.

1 cup (5 oz./145 g) shelled whole hazelnuts
¼ cup (25 g) cake flour
3 eggs, separated, room temperature
½ teaspoon vanilla extract
2 teaspoons fresh lemon juice
½ cup (100 g) sugar
¼ teaspoon cream of tartar
Chocolate Fudge Buttercream, page 157
Powdered sugar, for garnish

1. Adjust oven rack to middle position. Heat oven to 375° F (190° C). Place hazelnuts on a baking sheet and toast 8 minutes. Transfer to a cloth towel and rub vigorously to remove as much skin as possible; set aside to cool.

2. Butter sides and ends of a 15- × 10-inch (38½- × 25-cm) jelly-roll pan. Line with buttered waxed paper. Flour waxed paper and pan sides; tap out excess flour; set aside.

3. Insert the *metal knife blade*. Process hazelnuts with 7 or 8 one-second pulses to coarsely chop. Set aside ½ cup (1 dL) for garnish. Add cake flour to remaining nuts in container and process 25 seconds, until ground to a flourlike consistency; remove to waxed paper.

4. Place egg yolks, vanilla, and lemon juice in container. With machine running, pour sugar through food chute very slowly, within 30 seconds; scrape down sides of container. Process

until mixture is light and fluffy, about 3 minutes. Add flour mixture to container. Process 5 seconds, just until flour is absorbed.

5. Beat egg whites with cream of tartar in a clean dry bowl, using an electric mixer or whisk, until firm peaks form. Add about ½ cup (1 dL) of the beaten whites to nut mixture in container and process to mix in and lighten nut mixture with 2 or 3 one-second pulses. Fold lightened nut mixture into remaining egg whites until no streaks remain and spread the batter in the jelly-roll pan to make 1 thin layer; smooth top. Bake 15 minutes. Cool 5 minutes in pan and invert cake layer onto a clean, damp cloth towel. Remove pan and waxed paper. Place layer right side up on work surface. While still warm, cut into four 10- × 3¾-inch (25- × 9½-cm) strips. Trim each strip to 9 inches (23 cm). Cool.

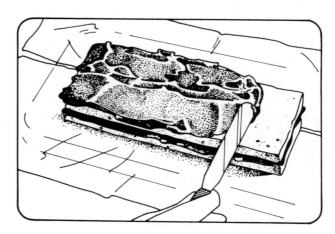

6. To assemble cake, place 1 cake strip on a sheet of waxed paper. Spread ⅓ cup (¾ dL) buttercream evenly over cake. Top with a second cake strip; press lightly. Repeat layering

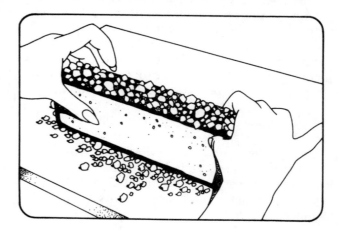

but do not frost top cake layer. Frost all 4 sides and refrigerate cake until buttercream firms.

7. Spread reserved hazelnuts on a sheet of waxed paper. Working carefully, dip each side of frosted cake into nuts and press gently so nuts adhere. Dust top of cake with powdered sugar. Fit a pastry bag with a #32 shell border tip or other decorative tip. Pipe a decorative border along each long edge of torte. Refrigerate until ready to serve. Reserve any leftover buttercream or nuts for another use.

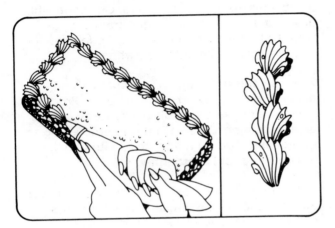

CHEESECAKE
Makes 10 servings

This New York–style cheesecake will be very rich and dense. The batter will fill up the processor container, but is so thick it does not, as a rule, leak out.

**Cookie Crumb Crust (following recipe), baked
    in springform pan**
**3 packages (8 oz./225 g each) cream cheese,
    room temperature, cut into 1-inch chunks**
1¼ cups (240 g) sugar
¾ cup (1¾ dL) whipping cream
½ cup (115 g) sour cream
2 teaspoons vanilla extract
3 tablespoons fresh lemon juice
4 eggs

1. Cool Cookie Crumb Crust. Adjust oven rack to lower position. Heat oven to 325° F (165° C).

2. Insert *metal knife blade.* Process cream cheese 30 seconds. Scrape down sides of con-tainer. Attach funnel. With machine running, pour sugar through food chute within 40 seconds. Scrape down container sides; process 10 seconds longer. With machine running, pour whipping cream through food chute within 20 seconds. Scrape down sides of container. Mix in sour cream, vanilla, and lemon juice with 3 two-second pulses. Add eggs. Process exactly 15 seconds. Scrape down sides of container. Process exactly 5 seconds longer.

3. Pour batter into prepared crust. Bake 1½ hours, until center of cake is just set. Cool in pan on cake rack to room temperature. Cover and refrigerate until thoroughly chilled, overnight is best. Top of cake may crack. Serve chilled.

Variation:

Chocolate Cheesecake
Use Cookie Crumb Crust (see below), using chocolate wafers. Omit lemon juice from batter. Follow Step 1. Before processing cream cheese in Step 2, break ½ pound (225 g) semisweet chocolate into ½-inch pieces. Process half the chocolate until small beads form; remove to waxed paper. Repeat. Return all chocolate to container. Heat ½ cup (1 dL) of the whipping cream to simmering. Attach funnel if desired. With machine running, immediately pour hot cream through food chute within 5 seconds. Process 5 seconds longer and scrape down sides of container. Add cream cheese and proceed with recipe. Add remainder of cream with sour cream.

COOKIE CRUMB CRUST
Crust for 8-inch (20-cm) springform pan

The crust may be assembled and baked up to two days in advance.

**6 oz. (180 g) graham crackers or chocolate
    wafer cookies, broken in pieces**
3 tablespoons (45 g) sugar
½ teaspoon cinnamon
3 tablespoons (45 g) warm melted butter

1. Adjust oven rack to middle position. Heat oven to 350° F (175° C). Lightly coat an 8-inch springform pan with butter; set aside. Insert the

metal knife blade. Process graham crackers 15 to 20 seconds. Add sugar and cinnamon and process 15 seconds to mix completely. With machine running, drizzle melted butter through food chute within 10 seconds. Stop and scrape down sides of container. Process 10 to 15 seconds longer to thoroughly mix.

2. Remove blade from container. Rake crumbs with your fingers, rubbing to dissolve any lumps that might remain. Pour crumbs into center of pan. Make a well in center and spread crumbs to side of pan. Move crumbs all the way up the sides and press into place. Work crumbs so that bottom and sides of pan are evenly coated and crust is slightly thicker along bottom edge. Gently press crust around top edge of pan to make a neat rim. Refrigerate 5 minutes. Bake 5 minutes. Cool to room temperature before filling.

Variation:

Crust for 9-inch (23-cm) Pie Plate
Substitute the following amounts for those listed above: 4 ounces (115 g) graham crackers or chocolate wafers, 1½ tablespoons (22 g) sugar, ¼ teaspoon cinnamon, 2 tablespoons (30 g) warm melted butter.

1. Insert the *metal knife blade.* Process half the chocolate until small beads form, about 1 minute. Repeat. Return all chocolate to container and scrape down sides. Add egg yolks. Process 10 seconds to mix. With machine running, pour hot melted butter and water through food chute within 15 seconds. Process 10 seconds longer, until chocolate is melted and smooth; scrape down container sides. Add crème de cacao and process 10 seconds longer to mix thoroughly.

2. In a clean dry bowl, whip the 5 egg whites with a pinch of cream of tartar to soft peaks, using whisk or electric beaters. Continue whipping, adding powdered sugar gradually, until whites just form firm peaks. Fold chocolate mixture thoroughly into egg whites.

3. Rinse and dry processor container and blade. Place in freezer for 5 minutes. Process whipping cream until soft peaks form; scrape down container sides. Continue processing to firm peaks. Add cream to bowl with chocolate mixture and fold thoroughly.

4. Spoon mousse into serving bowls. Refrigerate until thoroughly chilled, about 4 hours, overnight, or as long as 3 days in advance. Serve with Raspberry Sauce.

CHOCOLATE MOUSSE
Makes 6 servings

The total working time for this chocolate mousse is about 30 minutes and the recipe is especially easy to execute.

6 oz. (180 g) semisweet chocolate, cut into ½-inch pieces
2 eggs, room temperature, separated
¼ cup (60 g) hot melted butter (160 to 180° F/71 to 82° C)
¼ cup (½ dL) hot water
3 tablespoons crème de cacao
3 egg whites, room temperature
½ cup (75 g) powdered sugar
Pinch cream of tartar
1 cup (¼ L) chilled whipping cream
Raspberry Sauce, page 162, or whipped cream (optional)

BANANA YOGURT MOUSSE
Makes 6 to 8 servings

Lower in calories than most mousses and especially good with Raspberry Sauce.

3 ripe bananas, cut into 1-inch chunks
¼ cup (½ dL) cold water
1½ tablespoons (packages) unflavored gelatin
⅔ cup (125 g) sugar
1½ cups (3½ dL) plain yogurt
1 tablespoon banana liqueur or rum
3 large egg whites, room temperature
¼ teaspoon cream of tartar

1. Lightly oil a 4-cup (1-L) mold; set aside.

2. Insert the *metal knife blade* in a clean container. Purée bananas until no solid pieces remain. Mix cold water and gelatin in a 2-quart

(2-L) saucepan. Stir over low heat until gelatin dissolves. Stir in sugar and cook 2 to 3 minutes, until sugar is dissolved. Add banana purée and stir over low heat until mixture thickens slightly, 2 to 3 minutes. Set aside to cool to room temperature. Return blade and container to processor base without washing.

3. Place banana mixture, yogurt, and liqueur in container. Process to mix with 2 half-second pulses. Refrigerate in container with blade in place until thickened to the consistency of sour cream; stirring occasionally.

4. Return container to base. Process to remove lumps with 4 half-second pulses. Beat egg whites with cream of tartar with a whisk or mixer to firm peaks. Fold banana mixture into egg whites until no streaks remain.

5. Pour into prepared mold and refrigerate until firm, at least 6 hours or overnight. To unmold, loosen by running the tip of a sharp knife carefully around edge of mousse. Dip mold into warm water about 30 seconds. Center a serving dish over mold. Invert mold and dish; carefully lift off mold. Cover with plastic and refrigerate until ready to serve.

Variations:

Pumpkin Yogurt Mousse
Substitute 1 cup (¼ L) cooked, puréed pumpkin for bananas and 1 tablespoon bourbon for banana liqueur or rum. Add ¼ teaspoon cinnamon, ⅛ teaspoon ground cloves, and a dash of nutmeg to container with bourbon and yogurt.

Raspberry Yogurt Mousse
Substitute 1 pint fresh raspberries or 1 package (10 ounces/285 g) thawed frozen raspberries (well drained) for bananas. Strain puréed raspberries to remove seeds before adding to gelatin mixture. Substitute 1 tablespoon kirsch for banana liqueur or rum.

PINEAPPLE SORBET
Makes 1 quart (1 L)

The pineapple for this sorbet should be very ripe. The berries used in the variations should be just ripe. Sorbet is best when served within 6 hours, but if kept in an airtight freezer container it often holds well for 24 to 48 hours.

1 pineapple (2½ lbs./1¼ kg), cored, peeled
1 tablespoon fresh lemon juice
1 cup (190 g) sugar
1¼ cups (3 dL) water
1 tablespoon vodka

1. Cut pineapple into 1-inch (2½-cm) chunks. Insert the *metal knife blade*. Purée 2 cups (½ L) pineapple chunks until smooth, about 45 seconds; set aside. Repeat until all pineapple is puréed. Set a strainer over a bowl. Strain pineapple purée, pressing firmly to extract all juice. Discard fiber and pulp. Add lemon juice to pineapple purée.

2. Heat sugar and water to boiling in a nonreactive saucepan. Cover and simmer 5 minutes. Stir in pineapple purée and heat mixture quickly to simmering, stirring constantly. Immediately remove from heat and cool to room temperature. Add vodka.

3. Place cooled pineapple mixture in an ice-cream freezer and follow manufacturer's instructions for freezing. Or pour into ice-cube trays without cube dividers or 9-inch (23-cm) cake pans. Cover and freeze until partially frozen. Purée mixture 20 seconds. Return mixture to freezer and freeze until nearly frozen. Cut into 2-inch (5-cm) squares and purée 1 minute. Cover and freeze until firm and ready to serve.

Variations:

Blueberry or Strawberry Sorbet
Substitute 2 pints (1½ pounds/675 g) blueberries or strawberries for pineapple chunks. Substitute kirsch for vodka.

Cranberry Sorbet
Substitute 2 pints (1 pound/450 g) cranberries for pineapple and add ¼ cup (½ dL) orange juice to cooled cranberry mixture.

Kiwi Sorbet
Substitute 5 medium very ripe kiwis (about 1¼ pound/565 g) for pineapple. Peel kiwis with a small sharp knife (not a vegetable peeler) before puréeing.

FRESH BLUEBERRY SOUFFLE

Makes 2 to 4 servings

When puréed and cooked with sugar, blueberries thicken well enough to act as the base for this flourless soufflé. Flattening the top of the soufflé before baking eliminates the need for a collar and gives it a beautiful look.

½ lb. (1¾ cups/4 dL) fresh or thawed frozen
    blueberries, rinsed
½ cup (100 g) sugar
1 tablespoon butter
3 tablespoons sugar
4 egg whites
Pinch cream of tartar
Powdered sugar, for garnish

1. Insert the *metal knife blade*. Process to purée blueberries 20 seconds. With machine running, pour ¼ cup (50 g) of the sugar through the food chute within 10 seconds; process 5 seconds. Transfer mixture to a medium saucepan and stir over medium heat until mixture turns dark and shiny and is reduced to 1 cup (¼ L). Remove from heat and cool to lukewarm.

2. Use the butter to generously coat a 4-cup (1-L) soufflé dish. Add 3 tablespoons sugar; turn to coat dish; tap out excess. Adjust oven rack to lower position. Heat oven to 450° F (230° C). Fill a baking dish just large enough to contain soufflé dish with about 1 inch (2½ cm) cold water. Place baking dish in oven.

3. In a clean, dry bowl beat egg whites with cream of tartar to soft peaks. Continue beating, adding remaining ¼ cup (50 g) sugar gradually but do not beat whites to firm peaks—they should remain slightly creamy. Fold the blueberry mixture thoroughly into the egg whites. Pour into prepared soufflé dish and smooth top of mixture with a spatula to make it level with top of dish.

4. Place soufflé dish in water bath. Bake 20 to 25 minutes, until soufflé is puffed and browned. Remove dish from oven and sprinkle immediately with powdered sugar; serve immediately.

Note: To freeze fresh blueberries in season, pour them onto a baking sheet with sides. Freeze about 2 hours; then pack in airtight plastic bags. Keep frozen until ready to use. Thaw in refrigerator; drain off and use any juice.

GRAND MARNIER PAN SOUFFLE

Makes 4 to 6 servings

Bake this flourless soufflé in a handsome omelette or gratin pan and bring it right to the table.

1 tablespoon butter
½ medium orange
½ cup (100 g) sugar
3 tablespoons Grand Marnier or orange liqueur
1 teaspoon vanilla extract
6 eggs, separated, room temperature
¼ teaspoon cream of tartar
Powdered sugar

1. Melt butter in a 9-inch (23-cm) omelette or gratin pan and swirl to coat sides of pan; set aside. Adjust oven rack to lower position and heat oven to 375° F (190° C).

2. Strip off the orange rind with a vegetable peeler; reserve orange for another use. Insert the *metal knife blade*. Place rind strips and sugar in container. Process until rind is ground very fine. Add Grand Marnier and vanilla. With machine running, drop 1 egg yolk through food chute every 50 seconds, scraping down sides of container as necessary. After last yolk is added, process 1 minute.

3. Place egg whites and cream of tartar in a clean dry bowl. With an electric mixer or whisk, beat egg whites to firm peaks. Pour Grand Marnier mixture into egg whites and fold thoroughly, until no streaks remain.

4. Gently reheat butter in pan. Add batter; smooth top. Bake 13 to 15 minutes, until puffed and browned. Sprinkle with powdered sugar and serve immediately from pan.

RASPBERRY SAUCE

Makes about 1½ cups (3½ dL)

This dessert sauce goes well with fruit and chocolate desserts. It may be prepared and kept refrigerated up to three days in advance.

1 pint fresh raspberries or 2 packages (10 oz./285 g each) thawed frozen raspberries, well drained
2 tablespoons water
¼ cup (50 g) sugar, or more to taste
1 tablespoon kirsch, or more to taste

1. Insert the *metal knife blade.* Purée raspberries until smooth, about 45 seconds to 1 minute. Strain through drum sieve or close-mesh strainer, working purée with a plastic spatula or the back of a serving spoon until seeds clump together and all liquid has been removed.

2. Place water and ¼ cup (50 g) of the sugar in a medium nonreactive saucepan. Heat to boiling. Cover and slowly simmer 5 minutes. Add raspberry purée; return to a boil; then simmer 3 to 4 minutes until mixture is just slightly reduced and very shiny. Taste. If necessary, add additional sugar to taste and return mixture to a simmer, stirring. Add kirsch to taste. Refrigerate until ready to serve.

Conversion Chart for Commonly Processed Foods

This chart lists over 70 commonly processed foods in alphabetical order and is designed to shortcut processing and converting normal recipes to food processor use.

The chart specifies food (amount, size, or weight); the process (slice, shred, purée, chop); the blade or disk to use; the preparation required; time or pressure; and yield. All times and measurements are approximate and can vary slightly.

If a conventional recipe specifies ½ cup chopped onions, for example, the chart will tell you at a glance that 1 medium or 4-ounce onion chopped with 4 to 6 half-second on/off turns or pulses will yield ½ cup (1 dL). *In large capacity machines adjust timing as specified on page 10.*

ABOUT METRIC MEASUREMENTS

Metric measurements are used in recipes because it is so important for American cooks to become familiar and comfortable with them. When I lived in France, I found it surprisingly easy to remember and use metrics, provided they were adjusted slightly to correspond with familiar American measurements. Therefore, I have included approximate metrics, sometimes expressing measurements by volume rather than weight, except in baking where flour and sugar have been weighed exactly.

Liquid measurements are expressed in decilitres (dL) because they are easier to use than centilitres (hundredths of a litre) or mililitres (thousandths of a litre) and because decilitres (or tenths of a litre) are commonly used in metric system cookbooks.

For clarity, however, I have omitted metrics from the conversion chart. Here are some simple equivalents:

Weight—Ounces to Grams

1 oz.	30 g
1½ oz.	45 g
2 oz.	60 g
3 oz.	85 g
4 oz./¼ lb.	115 g
5 oz.	140 g
6 oz.	180 g
8 oz./½ lb.	225 g

Volume—Cups to Decilitres (1/10 L)

¼ cup	½ dL
⅓ cup	¾ dL
½ cup	1 dL
⅔ cup	1½ dL
¾ cup	1¾ dL
1 cup/½ pt.	¼ L
1½ cups	3½ dL
2 cups/1 pt.	½ L
3 cups	¾ L
4 cups/1 qt.	1 L

Chart Abbreviations

MKB	Metal Knife Blade
MSD	Medium Slicing Disk (4 mm)
MShD	Medium Shredding Disk
FFD	French-Fry Disk
fc	Food Chute
cube	1-inch (2½-cm) cubes or lengths

Food	Weight/ Size	Procedure	Blade/ Disk	Preparation	Processing Time/Push	Yield
Almonds (whole)	1 cup (4 oz.)	Chop	MKB		8 one-second pulses	1 cup
		Grind		Process with 3 tbsp. sugar/flour from recipe	30–60 seconds	1 cup
Anchovies	1 can (2 oz.)	Purée	MKB	Drain, rinse. Process dropping through fc	20 seconds	3 tbsp.
Apples	1 medium (4 oz.)	Chop	MKB	Peel, core, cube	3–4 one-second pulses	⅔ cup
		Slice	MSD	Core, quarter, load sideways	Moderate	¾ cup
		Shred	MShD	Core, quarter, peel		⅔ cup
Avocado	1 medium (8 oz.)	Purée	MKB	Peel, pit, cube	15–20 seconds	⅔ cup
Bacon (cooked, drained)	4 slices (4 oz.)	Chop	MKB	Break in chunks	5–8 seconds	2 tbsp.
Banana (very ripe)	1 medium (4 oz.)	Purée	MKB	Peel, cube	20 seconds	½ cup
		Slice	MSD	Peel, blunt ends, halve crosswise, insert upright in fc	Gentle	⅔ cup
Beef (raw)	½ lb.	Grind	MKB	1-inch cubes, remove gristle	4 two-second pulses	1¼ cups medium consistency
(partially frozen)	½ lb.	Slice	MSD	Rectangular chunk	Moderate	2 cups
Beets (cooked)	1 medium (5 oz.)	Shred	MShD	Peel, trim	Gentle	1 cup
		Slice	MSD			½ cup
Bleu Cheese or Roquefort	4-oz. wedge	Chop	MKB	1-inch chunks	5 one-second pulses	1 cup lightly packed
Bread Crumbs (fresh)	1 slice fresh white bread (1 oz.)	Crumb	MKB	Cube	60 seconds	½ cup
(dry)	1 (1-inch thick slice dry french bread—½ oz.)					⅓ cup
Cabbage (Savoy or curly)	1 medium (1 lb.)	Shred	MSD	Core, cut in wedges to fit upright in fc	Firm	7½ cups shredded
Red or Green						6 cups shredded
Cantaloupe	1 medium (3½ lbs.)	Slice	MSD	Peel, seed, cut in wedges, halve cross-wise to fit fc	Moderate	3½ cups

Food	Weight/Size	Procedure	Blade/Disk	Preparation	Processing Time/Push	Yield
Carrots (raw)	2 medium (4 oz.)	Chop	MKB	Peel, cube	4–6 one-second pulses	¾ cup
		Slice (rounds)	MSD	Peel, cut even lengths to fit upright in fc	Firm	1½ cups
		Shred (short & long)	MShD	Peel, insert upright or sideways		2 cups
Celery (leaves removed)	1 rib (2 oz.)	Chop	MKB	Peel, cube	4–6 half-second pulses	½ cup
	4 ribs (½ lb.)	Slice	MSD	Peel, cut in even lengths to fit upright in fc	Gentle	1½ cups
Cheese (Cheddar or Colby, chilled)	4-oz. chunk	Shred	MSD	Insert from underneath fc if necessary	Gentle	1½ cups
		Slice	MSD			1 cup (about 16 slices)
Chicken Breasts (cooked, boned, skinned, split)	1 medium (½ lb.)	Shred	MSD	Cut crosswise, blunt ends, insert upright in fc	Gentle	1½ cups
		Chop	MKB	1-inch chunks	5–6 one-second pulses	1 cup
Raw, boned, skinned, split, and partially frozen		Slice	MSD	Blunt ends, halve crosswise, insert from underneath fc	Moderate	1½ cups
Chocolate (semisweet, room temperature)	4 oz.	Bead (grind)	MKB	Break in ½-inch cubes	30 seconds	¾ cup
Clams, Littlenecks (fresh, whole, cooked, meat only)	3 dozen (4 oz. meat)	Chop	MKB	Chill	6 one-second pulses	⅔ cup
Coconut (whole)	1 small (1 lb.)	Shred	MShD	Poke out eyes; drain liquid. Bake at 500° F for 15 minutes; remove shell. Peel bark off meat; break meat in chunks to fit fc	Firm	3½ cups
Milk		Grind	MKB	Prepare and shred coconut. Process, adding 1½ cups hot water within 5 seconds. Let stand 15 minutes; strain and discard pulp.		1¼–1½ cups coconut milk

Food	Weight/ Size	Procedure	Blade/ Disk	Preparation	Processing Time/Push	Yield
Cookie Crumbs	6 oz. graham or chocolate wafers	Grind	MKB	Break in 1-inch pieces	15–20 seconds	1 ⅓ cups crumbs
Corned Beef (cooked, chilled)	½-lb. chunk	Slice	MSD	Trim off fat and fiber, blunt ends, cut to fit upright in fc	Firm	2 cups
Cucumbers (regular)	1 medium (8 oz.)	Slice	MSD	Peel and seed, if desired. Cut even lengths to fit upright in fc	Gentle	1¼ cups
		Purée	MKB	Peel, seed, cube	25 seconds	½ cup
Dates (whole, pitted)	½ cup (3 oz.)	Chop	MKB	Halve if large; add 3 tbsp. flour from recipe	8–9 half-second pulses	½ cup
Eggs (hard-boiled, peeled)	2 large	Chop	MKB	Quarter	6–8 half-second pulses	¾ cup
Garlic (fresh, peeled)	6 medium cloves (½ oz.)	Mince	MKB	Process by dropping through fc one at time		1 tbsp.
Gherkins (sweet)	1 medium (¾ oz.)	Chop	MKB	Halve, process by dropping through fc	5 seconds	1½ tsps.
Ginger (fresh, peeled)	1-inch length (1 oz.)	Mince	MKB	Halve, process by dropping through fc	5 seconds	1 tbsp.
		Slice	MSD	Blunt ends, stand on disk	Firm	4 slices
Ham (cooked, chilled)	¼-lb. chunk	Chop	MKB	Cube, remove rind	6–7 one-second pulses	¾ cup
		Slice	MSD	Fit upright in fc	Gentle	⅔ cup
	¼-lb. sliced	Julienne	MSD	Stack, roll, cut crosswise; insert from underneath fc	Gentle	1 cup
Hazelnuts or Filberts (shelled, toasted, skinned)	½ cup (2 oz.)	Grind	MKB	Add ¼ cup flour from recipe	15–20 seconds	½ cup
Leeks (fresh, trimmed)	1 medium (6 oz.)	Slice	MSD	Blunt ends, cut to fit upright in fc	Gentle	3¾ cups
	white part only (2 oz.)					1¼ cups
		Chop	MKB	Towel dry, cube	4–5 one-second pulses	1¼ cups
Lemons (fresh, peel on)	1 medium (4 oz.)	Slice	MSD	Blunt ends, insert from underneath fc	Moderate	10–15 slices
Peel removed		Juice	MKB	Peel completely, quarter, purée, strain	40 seconds	⅓ cup strained juice

Food	Weight/Size	Procedure	Blade/Disk	Preparation	Processing Time/Push	Yield
Lemon Rind or Zest	1 medium (4 oz.)	Grate	MKB	Remove zest or rind with vegetable peeler, add 3 tbsp. sugar or ½ tsp. salt from recipe	60–90 seconds	1 tbsp. grated zest or rind (¼ cup with sugar)
Lettuce (iceberg)	1 medium (12 oz.)	Shred	MSD	Core, cut in wedges, blunt ends	Gentle	4 cups
Limes (fresh, peel on)	1 medium (3 oz.)	Slice	MSD	Blunt ends, insert upright in fc	Firm	8–10 slices
Peel removed		Juice	MKB	Peel completely, quarter, purée, strain	30 seconds	2½–3 tbsp. strained juice
Lime Rind or Zest	1 medium (3 oz.)	Grate	MKB	Remove rind with vegetable peeler, add 3 tbsp. sugar from recipe	90 seconds	2 tsps. grated rind or zest (¼ cup with sugar)
Mozzarella Cheese (chilled)	4-oz. chunk	Shred	MShD	Cut to fit fc	Gentle	1 cup
Mushrooms (fresh, raw, clean)	1 cup (3 oz.)	Slice	MSD	Load with caps alternating	Gentle	1 cup
		Chop	MKB	Halve if large	8–10 half-second pulses	1 cup
		Shred	MShD		Gentle	1 cup
Cooked	¾ lb.	Purée	MKB		60 seconds	1 cup
Olives (jumbo/black, pitted, drained)	12 olives (2½ oz.)	Chop	MKB	Towel dry	4–5 one second pulses	¾ cup
	5 olives (1 oz.)	Slice	MSD	Stand on blade, pitted end down in area of fc	Gentle	⅓ cup
Onions, green, or **Scallions** (roots removed)	4 medium white only	Dangle Slice	MSD	Process holding onions against side of chute opposite direction of disk		¼ cup
	4 medium whole (2 oz.)	Chop	MKB	1½-inch lengths	4–6 one-second pulses	½ cup
Onions, yellow, red, white (peeled)	1 medium (4 oz.)	Chop	MKB	Cube	4–6 half-second pulses	½ cup
		Grate	MKB	Cube; add ¼ cup water	15 seconds	½ cup
		Slice	MSD	Blunt ends, halve lengthwise	Gentle	1 cup

Food	Weight/ Size	Procedure	Blade/ Disk	Preparation	Processing Time/Push	Yield
Oranges (peel on)	1 medium (5–6 oz.)	Slice	MSD	Halve lengthwise, blunt ends, insert from underneath fc	Firm	10–12 slices
Peel removed		Juice	MKB	Peel completely, cut in eighths, purée, strain	45 seconds	½ cup strained juice
Orange Rind or Zest	1 medium (5–6 oz.)	Grate	MKB	Remove rind in strips with vegetable peeler, add ¼ cup sugar from recipe	60–90 seconds	2–3 tbsp. rind or zest (⅓ cup with sugar)
Parsley Leaves	¼ cup firm- ly packed	Mince	MKB	Towel dry	30–60 seconds	3–4 tbsps.
Parmesan Cheese (room temperature)	2 oz.	Grate (grind)	MKB	Remove rind; cube. If less than 2 oz., process, dropping cubes through fc	30 seconds or longer	½ cup
Peaches (Freestone, fresh)	1½ lbs. medium	Slice	MSD	Peel, pit, quarter, load sideways in fc	Gentle	2¼ cups
		Chop	MKB	Peel, pit, quarter	2–4 half-second pulses	2¼ cups
		Chunk	FFD	Peel, pit, quarter, load upright in fc	Gentle	2 cups
Pecans (whole, shelled)	½ cup (2 oz.)	Chop	MKB	Dry bowl and blade, no sugar required	4–5 one-second pulses	½ cup
		Grind	MKB	Add 3 tbsp. sugar or flour from recipe	30 seconds	½ cup
Peppers, Bell (green, red, yellow)	1 medium (4 oz.)	Slice	MSD	Core, seed, blunt ends, halve crosswise	Gentle	¾ cup
		Chop	MKB	1-inch squares	3–4 half-second pulses	¾–1 cup
		Julienne	MSD	Core, seed; cut in 1½- inch or wider strips (width of strips deter- mines length); insert upright in fc	Gentle	¾ cup
Pineapple (fresh)	1 medium (3½ lbs.)	Slice	MSD	Remove top, peel, cut in rectangular chunks around core	Firm	6 cups
		Purée	MKB	Peel, core, 1-inch chunks	45 seconds	3¾ cups
Pork (raw, boneless)	½-lb. chunk	Slice	MSD	Partially freeze	Firm	2½ cups
		Grind	MKB	Trim well; cube	4 two-second pulses	1¼ cups medium consistency
Partially frozen		Slice	MSD	Cut to fit fc	Firm	2½ cups

Food	Weight/Size	Procedure	Blade/Disk	Preparation	Processing Time/Push	Yield
Potato russet (raw)	1 medium 6 ozs.	Slice	MSD	Peel, blunt ends, trim as necessary	Moderate	1 cup
		Shred	MShD		Firm	⅔ cup
Sweet Potato (cooked)	1 medium (8 oz.)	Purée	MKB	Cook in jacket, peel, cube	20 seconds	½ cup
Pumpkin (raw)	1 medium (3–4 lbs.)	Purée	MKB	Cook, scrape out meat; discard shell	2 minutes	3–4 cups
Radishes (red)	9 medium (4 oz.)	Slice	MSD	Blunt ends, stand on disk	Firm	1 cup
Raspberries (fresh)	½ pt. (6 oz.)	Purée	MKB	Rinse, towel dry	45 seconds	1¼ cups with seeds; 1 cup strained
Frozen, thawed, drained	1 pkg. (10 oz.)			Discard juice		1 cup with seeds; ¾ cup strained
Romano Cheese (room temperature)	2 oz.	Grate (Grind)	MKB	Remove rind; cube. If less than 2 oz., process dropping through fc	60 seconds	½ cup
Shallots (fresh, peeled)	4 medium (1 oz.)	Mince	MKB	Process, dropping through fc one at a time		1½ tbsps.
Spinach (fresh, raw)	¾ lb. (3 cups leaves)	Shred	MSD	Stem, rinse, and towel dry leaves; stack, roll, and insert from underneath fc	Gentle	2¾ cups
Chopped, frozen	1 pkg. (10 oz.)	Purée	MKB	Thaw, drain, squeeze dry in cloth towel	90 seconds	⅔ cup
Squash (acorn, cooked)	1 medium (1½ lbs.)	Purée	MKB	Scoop out, discard pulp	20 seconds	1 cup
Steak (partially frozen)	½ lb.	Slice	MSD	Trim off fat load from underneath fc	Moderate	2 cups
Strawberries (fresh)	1 pt. (14 oz.)	Slice	MSD	Hull. Stand on blade for round slices or load fc sideways	Very gentle	2 cups
		Purée	MKB	Rinse, hull, halve if large	15–20 seconds	1½ cups with seeds; 1 cup strained
Frozen, thawed	1 pkg. (10 oz.)			Drain		1¼ cups with seeds; ¾–1 cup strained

Food	Weight/ Size	Procedure	Blade/ Disk	Preparation	Processing Time/Push	Yield
Swiss Cheese or Gruyère (chilled)	¼-lb. chunk	Shred	MShD	Blunt ends	Gentle	1½ cups
		Slice	MSD	Place upright in fc		1 cup (about 16 slices)
		Match-sticks		Slice; then load slices from underneath fc		1 cup
Tomatoes (fresh, firm)	1 medium (4 oz.)	Chop	MKB	Core, quarter	3–4 half-second pulses	½ cup
		Purée	MKB	Peel, seed, core, quarter	15 seconds	½ cup
		Slice	MSD	Blunt ends, halve lengthwise, insert from underneath fc	Gentle	1 cup
Italian plum (canned, drained, seeded)	1 can (1 lb. 12 oz.)	Chop	MKB		4–5 half-second pulses	2 cups
		Rough dice	FFD	Insert stem ends down	Gentle	2 cups
		Purée			5 seconds	2 cups
Turkey (cooked, boneless)	12 oz. (2 cups)	Shred	MSD	Remove all skin and gristle	Moderate	1¾ cups
Walnuts (shelled, whole)	½ cup (2 oz.)	Chop	MKB	Add 3 tbsp. flour or sugar from recipe	6–8 half-second pulses	½ cup
		Grind			10 seconds	½ cup
Water Chestnuts (drained)	1 can (8 oz.)	Slice	MSD	Lay flat on disk and stack in area of fc	Moderate	1 cup
Watercress	1 medium bunch (4 oz.)	Purée	MKB	Remove stems	10–15 seconds	¾ cup
Whipping Cream (chilled)	½ pt. (1 cup)	Whip	MKB	Chill container and blade 5 minutes	15–60 seconds, depending on consistency desired	1⅔ cups
Zucchini (fresh, raw)	1 medium (4 oz.)	Shred	MShD	Blunt ends, cut to fit fc	Firm	1 cup
		Slice	MSD	Insert upright in fc for round slices; sideways for long slices	Firm	5 cups rounds

Index